IN

The Schnauzer Handbook

LINDA WHITWAM

ISBN-13: 978-1481111485

Table of Contents

Copyright

Chapter 1. The Miniature Schnauzer

Character

The Miniature Schnauzer is a dog with universal appeal and the most popular of the three Schnauzer breeds. Generally, these dogs are perky, playful and affectionate. Some owners would even say they have a sense of humor.

This is an extremely handsome breed with an almost square, boxy shape and unique beard. Incidentally, just as with humans, the length of beard varies from one Mini to another. Physically these dogs combine elegance with certain ruggedness and a jaunty gait.

The different faces of the Miniature Schnauzer

They have terrier-like instincts and many love to chase small animals or birds for fun, but they will rarely attack other animals or dogs. Others may live happily with cats and other small animals if introduced at an early age. They also make good watch dogs and, although they may be quiet as puppies, adults will usually bark when somebody knocks at the door.

Minis are not by nature 'laid back' dogs. Don't expect them to be happy to snooze in a corner all day. They want to be involved and demand your attention. If you have a garden, you'll have to fence them in to stop them running off, either in pursuit of small animals and birds, or simply to say hello to passers-by. These dogs want to be with humans, love being part of the family and form strong bonds with their owners.

As with all purebred dogs, the breed characteristics remain the same, but the individual temperament and character varies from one dog to another. Miniature Schnauzers are adaptable and they are at home both in town and country. They need a medium amount of exercise – the exact amount will vary depending on what they have got used to.

Some which are used to plenty exercise will enjoy a hike lasting several hours while others can be happy with a large garden and a short daily walk. Because they are playful dogs, Miniatures are often easily distracted by people, other dogs or interesting smells.

One very strong trait common to all three breeds of Schnauzers is that they certainly love to be with people and to take part in all aspects of family life. Being with people is perhaps their greatest desire, these are not dogs which will be happy left alone all day.

It is difficult not to form very strong emotional bonds with these little dogs that become a part of the family. It's sometimes easy to forget that they are canines and not humans. But it's important to remind them every now and again that you are in charge. Given a free rein, like a spoilt child, they can become selfish and stubborn.

Mini Schnauzers thrive on the attention of their owners and may even follow them around the house. They like to sleep on the bed or at least in the same room as their owners, when allowed. Minis make excellent companion dogs, but given too much attention, they can become demanding. They can also have a stubborn streak, so good training early on is recommended.

Well-bred and trained Miniature Schnauzers are a delightful addition to any dog-loving home. You will find that they are unlike any other dog; they will become a unique, irreplaceable friend for life.

Popular Breed

The Miniature – or Mini Schnauzer as they are often called – is now the 11th most popular dog breed in America and number 8 in Canada. The breed is, however, probably even more popular that the official figures state.

White and colored Minis are becoming ever more popular in North America, but the only colors recognized by the Kennel Clubs are **salt and pepper**, **black** and **black and silver.**

White, parti (another color with white), liver and chocolate colored schnauzers are not officially registered by the national breed societies, although they can take part in other club shows and agility classes.

While the breed has traditionally been less well known in the UK, it is becoming more popular year on year, as news of these little dogs with the big character spreads. It is currently 13th in the Top 20 Breeds, according to The Kennel Club in the UK.

Although the Miniature Schnauzer is a generally robust and sturdy breed which generally remains active even to old age, there are increasing numbers of toy or teacup Schnauzers in the USA.

These have been bred down from Minis and do not conform to breed standards. They are not recognized by the AKC, CKC or KC in the UK, but many people are attracted by their cuteness and love these tiny canines.

If you do decide you want a toy or teacup, make sure you choose a reputable breeder with a proven track record, not a puppy mill or a breeder out to make a fast buck, as this could result in an unhealthy pup and heartache for you and your family. (See Chapter 7 on **Puppies** for help)

Hypoallergenic

The most popular dog breed in the USA, Canada and the UK is the Labrador Retriever. However, Miniature Schnauzers – and their big brothers the Standards and Giants - have two big advantages over the hairy Retriever –
They are non-shedding and hypoallergenic

This makes Schnauzers popular with dog lovers suffering from pet allergies as well as people who don't want to spend all their free time cleaning the carpets and furniture! There is no 100% guarantee that an allergy sufferer

will NOT have a reaction to a Schnauzer, the best way to find out is to spend some time with the puppy or dog before committing to him.

We have an allergy sufferer in our house who experiences no reaction at all to Max, our Mini Schnauzer, but allergic reactions can vary from person to person and from one individual Schnauzer to the next – even in the same litter.

Safe to say that Miniature Schnauzers are GENERALLY a good choice for dog lovers who suffer from pet allergies. To say that a Miniature Schnauzer NEVER sheds a hair would be untrue, but they are certainly classed as minimal shedders.

Our Max loses almost no hair, although we may find the occasional small fur ball on the floor, especially if he is overdue a trip to the groomers. In contrast, when friends visit with their dogs, we find dog hair around the house for weeks afterwards. (See Chapter 9 on **Schnauzers and Allergy Sufferers**).

History

The Schnauzer originated in Germany in the 15th century. In those days tradesmen and farmers travelled the countryside with heavily laden carts selling their wares at markets.

They needed a versatile dog which could guard the cart as well as keep down the vermin back at home. Thus the first Schnauzer was born. The original Schnauzer was a Standard Schnauzer; the Miniature was bred down from this medium-sized dog.

The modern Miniature was recognized as a breed in Germany in 1880. The first ones arrived in the United States in 1924 and the breed was recognized by the American Kennel Club two years later. (See Chapter 4 for the most comprehensive **History of the Schnauzer**).

Appearance

The Miniature Schnauzer is a smallish, yet robust dog with a unique appearance. Like all Schnauzers, the Mini is almost square in shape with the height at the withers (top of the shoulders) being almost the same as length of the body, giving the breed a sharp, "boxy" look.

The official size for a Miniature Schnauzer, as laid down by the breed societies, is to stand 12 inches to 14 inches tall at the withers. Females tend to be slightly smaller than males.

With their bushy eyebrows, trademark beard and moustache, not to mention their cheeky expression and jaunty strides, the Miniature Schnauzer is an instantly recognizable and attractive breed.

Miniature Schnauzers come in a variety of unusual colors, including white and chocolate, and although these Schnauzers are dearly loved by their owners, their colors are not officially recognized by the breed societies.

If you get a purebred Schnauzer in one of the three recognized colors - Salt and Pepper - Solid Black - Black and Silver – from an approved breeder, your dog should come with registration papers from the Kennel Club.

Physical Characteristics

While the breed is known for its strong lines and bearded face, the actual breed standards as laid down by the Kennel Clubs vary from country to country.

In the USA and Canada, the Miniature Schnauzer is classed as a **Terrier.** In the UK the breed comes under the **Utility Group.**

In North America it is common to have both the ears and tail cropped. For showing, the dog must have a docked tail and can have cropped or natural ears.

Since April 2007 it has been illegal to dock any dog's tail - except for working gundogs – in the UK. Dogs born prior to that with docked tails are accepted in the show ring. It is also illegal to crop the dog's ears in the UK.

In continental Europe, most Schnauzers are left natural with long tails and floppy ears.

The breed characteristics are laid down by the Kennel Clubs to maintain standards within the breed. Registration of a purebred or pedigree Schnauzer – or any other breed - encourages breeding from responsible breeders who have gone into the background of their breeding stock.

Responsible breeders select only the best dogs for reproduction, based on factors such as the health, looks, temperament and character of the parents and their ancestors. They do not simply take any available male and female and allow them to breed.

They also aim to reduce or eradicate some illnesses which may affect the breed. In the case of Miniature Schnauzers, this may involve allergies (some Minis have reactions to things like grass, often seasonal) and skin disorders, pancreatitis, diabetes, cataracts, epilepsy, auto-immune diseases and bladder stones.

Just because your dog is not registered with the Kennel Club does not mean that he or she is a bad dog.

But if your dog is registered, it is more likely that the breeder is more experienced and has spent time considering all of these factors before allowing his or her dogs to produce puppies.

American Kennel Club Breed Standard

<u>**Miniature Schnauzer**</u> - Terrier Group

General Appearance
The Miniature Schnauzer is a robust, active dog of terrier type, resembling his larger cousin, the Standard Schnauzer, in general appearance, and of an alert, active disposition. **Faults - Type -** Toyishness, ranginess or coarseness.

Size, Proportion, Substance
Size - From 12 to 14 inches. He is sturdily built, nearly square in proportion of body length to height with plenty of bone, and without any suggestion of toyishness. **Disqualifications -** Dogs or bitches under 12 inches or over 14 inches.

Eyes - Small, dark brown and deep-set. They are oval in appearance and keen in **expression.** **Faults** - Eyes light and/or large and prominent.

Ears - When cropped, the ears are identical in shape and length, with pointed tips. They are in balance with the head and not exaggerated in length. They are set high on the skull and carried perpendicularly at the inner edges, with as little bell as possible along the outer edges. When uncropped, the ears are small and V-shaped, folding close to the skull.

Head - strong and rectangular, its width diminishing slightly from ears to eyes, and again to the tip of the nose. The forehead is unwrinkled. The **topskull** Is flat and fairly long. The foreface is parallel to the topskull, with a slight stop, and it is at least as long as the topskull. The **muzzle** is strong in proportion to the skull; it ends in a moderately blunt manner, with thick whiskers which accentuate the rectangular shape of the head.

Faults - Head coarse and cheeky. The **teeth** meet in a **scissors bite**. That is, the upper front teeth overlap the lower front teeth in such a manner that the inner surface of the upper incisors barely touches the outer surface of the lower incisors when the mouth is closed. **Faults** - Bite - Undershot or overshot jaw. Level bite.

Neck - strong and well arched, blending into the shoulders, and with the skin fitting tightly at the throat.

Body - short and deep, with the brisket extending at least to the elbows.

 Ribs are well sprung and deep, extending well back to a short loin. The underbody does not present a tucked up appearance at the flank.

Backline is straight; it declines slightly from the withers to the base of the tail. The withers form the highest point of the body. The overall length from chest to buttocks appears to equal the height at the withers.

Faults - Chest too broad or shallow in brisket. Hollow or roach back.

Tail - set high and carried erect. It is docked only long enough to be clearly visible over the backline of the body when the dog is in proper length of coat. **Fault** - Tail set too low.

Forequarters - Forelegs are straight and parallel when viewed from all sides. They have strong pasterns and good bone. They are separated by a fairly deep brisket which precludes a pinched front. The elbows are close, and the ribs spread gradually from the first rib so as to allow space for the elbows to move close to the body. **Fault** - Loose elbows.

Shoulders - are sloping, muscled, yet flat and clean. They are well laid back, so that from the side the tips of the shoulder blades are in a nearly vertical line above the elbow. The tips of the blades are placed closely together. They slope forward and downward at an angulation which permits the maximum forward extension of the forelegs without binding or effort. Both the shoulder blades and upper arms are long, permitting depth of chest at the brisket.

Feet short and round (cat feet) with thick, black pads. The toes are arched and compact.

Hindquarters - The hindquarters have strong-muscled, slanting thighs. They are well bent at the stifles. There is sufficient angulation so that, in stance, the hocks extend beyond the tail. The hindquarters never appear overbuilt or higher than the shoulders.

The rear pasterns are short and, in stance, perpendicular to the ground and, when viewed from the rear, are parallel to each other. **Faults** - Sickle hocks, cow hocks, open hocks or bowed hindquarters.

Coat - Double, with hard, wiry, outer coat and close undercoat. The head, neck, ears, chest, tail, and body coat must be plucked. When in show condition, the body coat should be of sufficient length to determine texture. Close covering on neck, ears and skull. Furnishings are fairly thick but not silky.

 Faults - Coat too soft or too smooth and slick in appearance.

Color - The recognized colors are **salt and pepper, black** and **silver and solid black**. All colors have uniform skin pigmentation, i.e. no white or pink skin patches shall appear anywhere on the dog.

Salt and Pepper - The typical salt and pepper color of the topcoat results from the combination of black and white banded hairs and solid black and white unbanded hairs, with the banded hairs predominating. Acceptable are all shades of salt and pepper, from light to dark mixtures with tan shadings permissible in the banded or unbanded hair of the topcoat.

 In salt and pepper dogs, the salt and pepper mixture fades out to light gray or silver white in the eyebrows, whiskers, cheeks, under throat, inside ears, across chest, under tail, leg furnishings, and inside hind legs. It may or may not also fade out on the underbody. However, if so, the lighter underbody hair is not to rise higher on the sides of the body than the front elbows.

Black and Silver - The black and silver generally follows the same pattern as the salt and pepper. The entire salt and pepper section must be black. The black color in the topcoat of the black and silver is a true rich color with black undercoat. The stripped portion is free from any fading or brown tinge and the underbody should be dark.

Black - Black is the only solid color allowed. Ideally, the black color in the topcoat is a true rich glossy solid color with the undercoat being less intense, a soft matting shade of black. This is natural and should not be penalized in any way.

The stripped portion is free from any fading or brown tinge. The scissored and clippered areas have lighter shades of black. A small white spot on the chest is permitted, as is an occasional single white hair elsewhere on the body.

Disqualifications - Color solid white or white striping, patching, or spotting on the colored areas of the dog, except for the small white spot permitted on the chest of the black.

The body coat color in salt and pepper and black and silver dogs fades out to light gray or silver white under the throat and across the chest. Between them there exists a natural body coat color. Any irregular or connecting blaze or white mark in this section is considered a white patch on the body, which is also a disqualification.

AKC Miniature Schnauzer - Gait
The trot is the gait at which movement is judged. When approaching, the forelegs, with elbows close to the body, move straight forward, neither too close nor too far apart. Going away, the hind legs are straight and travel in the same planes as the forelegs.

Note - It is generally accepted that when a full trot is achieved, the rear legs continue to move in the same planes as the forelegs, but a very slight inward inclination will occur. It begins at the point of the shoulder in front and at the hip joint in the rear. Viewed from the front or rear, the legs are straight from these points to the pads. The degree of inward inclination is almost imperceptible in a Miniature Schnauzer that has correct movement. It does not justify moving close, toeing in, crossing, or moving out at elbows.

Viewed from the side, the forelegs have good reach, while the hind legs have strong drive, with good pickup of hocks. The feet turn neither inward nor outward.

Faults - Single tracking, sidegaiting, paddling in front, or hackney action. Weak rear action.

Temperament
The typical Miniature Schnauzer is alert and spirited, yet obedient to command. He is friendly, intelligent and willing to please. He should never be overaggressive or timid.

AKC Miniature Schnauzer – Disqualifications: *Dogs or bitches under 12 inches or over 14 inches. Color solid white or white striping, patching, or spotting on the colored areas of the dog, except for the small white spot permitted on the chest of the black.*

The body coat color in salt and pepper and black and silver dogs fades out to light gray or silver white under the throat and across the chest. Between them there exists a natural body coat color. Any irregular or connecting blaze or white mark in this section is considered a white patch on the body, which is also a disqualification.

Visit the American Kennel Club: **www.akc.org/breeds/miniature_schnauzer**

The Kennel Club (UK) Breed Standard

Miniature Schnauzer - Utility Group

General Appearance
Sturdily built, robust, sinewy, nearly square, (length of body equal to height at shoulders). Expression keen and attitude alert. Correct conformation is of more importance than colour or other purely 'beauty' points.

Characteristics
Well balanced, smart, stylish and adaptable.

Temperament
Alert, reliable and intelligent. Primarily a companion dog.

Head and Skull
Head strong and of good length, narrowing from ears to eyes and then gradually forward toward end of nose. Upper part of the head (occiput to the base of forehead) moderately broad between ears. Flat, creaseless forehead; well muscled but not too strongly developed cheeks. Medium stop to accentuate prominent eyebrows.

Powerful muzzle ending in a moderately blunt line, with bristly, stubby moustache and chin whiskers. Ridge of nose straight and running almost parallel to extension of forehead. Nose black with wide nostrils. Lips tight but not overlapping.

Eyes
Medium-sized, dark, oval, set forward, with arched bushy eyebrows.

Ears
Neat, V-shaped, set high and dropping forward to temple.

Mouth
Jaws strong with perfect, regular and complete scissor bite, i.e. upper teeth closely overlapping lower teeth and set square to the jaws.

Neck
Moderately long, strong and slightly arched; skin close to throat; neck set cleanly on shoulders.

The Kennel Club Picture Library. Copyright David Dalton and Per Unden

Forequarters
Shoulders flat and well laid. Forelegs straight viewed from any angle. Muscles smooth and lithe rather than prominent; bone strong, straight and carried well down to feet; elbows close to body and pointing directly backwards.

Body
Chest moderately broad, deep with visible strong breastbone reaching at least to height of elbow rising slightly backward to loins. Back strong and straight, slightly higher at shoulder than at hindquarters, with short, well developed loins. Ribs well sprung. Length of body equal to height from top of withers to ground.

Hindquarters
Thighs slanting and flat but strongly muscled. Hindlegs (upper and lower thighs) at first vertical to the stifle; from stifle to hock, in line with the extension of the upper neck line; from hock, vertical to ground.

Feet
Short, round, cat-like, compact with closely arched toes, dark nails, firm black pads, feet pointing forward.

Tail
Previously customarily docked.
Docked: Set on and carried high, customarily docked to three joints.
Undocked: Set on and carried high, of moderate length to give general balance to the dog. Thick at root and tapering towards the tip, as straight as possible, carried jauntily.

Gait/Movement

Free, balanced and vigorous, with good reach in forequarters and good driving power in hindquarters. Topline remains level in action.

Coat

Harsh, wiry and short enough for smartness, dense undercoat. Clean on neck and shoulders, ears and skull. Harsh hair on legs. Furnishings fairly thick but not silky.

Colour

All pepper and salt colours in even proportions, or pure black, or black and silver. That is, solid black with silver markings on eyebrow, muzzle, chest and brisket and on the forelegs below the point of elbow, on inside of hindlegs below the stifle joint, on vent and under tail.

Size

Ideal height: dogs: 36 cms (14 ins); bitches: 33 cms (13 ins). Too small, toyish appearing dogs are not typical and undesirable.

Faults

Any departure from the foregoing points should be considered a fault and the seriousness with which the fault should be regarded should be in exact proportion to its degree and its effect upon the health and welfare of the dog.

Note

Male animals should have two apparently normal testicles fully descended into the scrotum.

Visit the Kennel Club website at **www.thekennelclub.org.uk**

Chapter 2. The Standard Schnauzer

Origins

The Standard Schnauzer is known as "the dog with the human brain" and is the original of all three types of Schnauzer.

The Schnauzer, as it is simply called in the UK - or Mittelschnauzer in Germany - has been a celebrated European breed dating back to the 14th or 15th century.

They originated in Southern Germany where they were bred for their versatility. This athletic working dog kept the rats out of the barn, guarded the farmyard and travelling wagons and herded livestock.

During World War I, Standard Schnauzers were used as guard dogs by the German Army and dispatch carriers by the Red Cross. It wasn't until after the war that they were first imported into the USA in any numbers.

Despite being the original, the Standard is not as well known as its cousins the Miniature Schnauzer and Giant Schnauzer. The breed is only the 107th most popular in the USA, compared with the Miniature at number 11 and the Giant at 83.

Appearance

The Standard Schnauzer is an exciting dog to see and own. Bigger and more powerful than the Mini, they are classed as medium-sized dogs. Males stand about 18 to 20 inches high at the shoulders with females being about an inch smaller. They weigh from 30 to 50 pounds.

This is a robust, stocky and sinewy breed with an extremely stylish appearance when properly groomed. A fit Standard is an impressive sight with a powerful, deep chest and sharp body lines. He has the classic 'boxy' shape of the Schnauzer with the height at the shoulders being almost the same as the length of the body. Like all Schnauzers, the Standard also has the trademark full beard and bushy eyebrows.

The amount of facial hair varies from dog to dog. Don't be disappointed if your Schnauzer puppy doesn't grow a full beard right away. Like men, they have to reach maturity before they can grow a bushy beard! It may take them a year or so to develop their full facial hair.

While the breed is universally known for its athletic, square appearance and bearded face, the specific breed standards vary from country to country. In the USA and Canada, the Standard Schnauzer is classed in the **Working Group.** In the UK the dog is shown in the **Utility Group.**

As with Minis, it is common to have both the ears and tail cropped in the USA. For showing the dog must have a docked tail and can have either cropped or natural ears.

Since April 2007 in the UK it has been illegal to dock any dog's tail - except for working gundogs. Dogs born prior to that with docked tails are accepted in the show ring. It is also illegal to crop the dog's ears in the UK. In continental Europe, most Standard Schnauzers are left natural with long tails and floppy ears.

The Coat

The Standard, like the Giant and Miniature Schnauzer, has a double coat. The outer coat is harsh and wiry and covers a softer layer underneath. Like all three types of Schnauzer, they are hypoallergenic and non-shedding.

You should brush your dog at home at least once or twice a week and send

 him to the groomer's to be stripped or clipped about every 8 to 12 weeks, depending on how fast his hair grows. All show Schnauzers are hand-stripped rather than clipped and this preserves the characteristics of their coat.

There is nothing at all wrong with having your Standard Schnauzer clipped, it just means that his or her coat may go a little wavier or, in the case of salt and peppers, lose some of the outer pepper coloring, which would prevent you from showing him or her at Kennel Club events.

Standard Schnauzers only come in two colors –
pepper and salt and **solid black**

Unlike their Mini cousins, there are no whites or different colored Standard Schnauzers.

Temperament

With his clean, sharp lines and lively, individualistic personality, the Standard Schnauzer is a unique individual and can be a joy to live with.

The lively - sometimes comic personality - of the Standard makes him an interesting and entertaining companion. He has a strong - sometimes stubborn - mind and a naturally curious nature. Standards are not usually placid or lazy dogs which are happy sleeping in a corner all day. They want to be involved and can be intense by nature.

They are intelligent, sociable and alert; an excellent watch dog and family companion. If you are looking for a jogging buddy, the Standard might be the dog for you. On the other hand, he may be too lively and powerful to leave with your grandmother while you're on vacation.

The combination of intelligence, creativity and high spirit - as well as sense of fun - has earned him the nickname "the dog with the human brain."

Standards are versatile dogs – robust enough to be a working dog yet not too big and strong to handle when trained.

However, his combination of intelligence, combined with high spirits and a strong-willed nature, can make him a handful if not properly trained and exercised.

With the right education and enough exercise time, the Standard is a super addition to any household. He is a true "people dog" and thrives on the stimulation derived from living with a family.

Schnauzers are not generally one-man dogs. They often have a favorite person, but normally will readily accept all family members. They are noted for guarding the family home and displaying devotion to their immediate circle.

You give the Standard what he needs: exercise, training and being around people, and you will have a devoted friend for life.

Suitability

This is not a breed for those who want a placid, friendly-to-everyone dog that can be fed, walked and forgotten. They like to be involved.

The Standard Schnauzer is a strong, vigorous dog and if you do a lot of outdoor exercise, this would be a breed to consider. They are also alert and reliable.

Raised and trained properly, they are very good with their own family children and most others who respect their high sense of self-dignity. But they usually don't like being teased.

Like its Miniature Schnauzer cousin, the Standard likes to be at the centre of things. He develops to his fullest potential when treated as part of the family. For this reason most Standard Schnauzers - even the top show dogs - are house pets and companions. Generally, a Standard should not be kept in a kennel outside, they want to be inside with you – or outside with you.

Neither does he or she want to be left alone all day. If he is not interested or challenged, he can easily become bored. All three types of Schnauzer love being at the midst of family life.

Exercise

The Standard is a strong dog capable of great endurance and was originally bred as a working dog. Although the UK Kennel Club lists the breed as needing only "moderate exercise", you'd be well advised to get ready to do a fair amount of walking – or even jogging - if you decide to get one.

Just like humans, energy levels will vary from one individual to another. You do get the occasional couch potato Standard Schnauzer.....but generally this breed will require exercising two or three times a day to remain content. They have higher stamina levels and exercise requirements than Miniature Schnauzers.

If you're lucky enough to have a large garden, that's a bonus. However, this should not replace regular daily walks. Regular exercise helps to keep your dog's heart muscles and joints functioning. As with humans, it also helps to keep your dog healthy and free from illness.

As a general rule of thumb, **an absolute minimum** of 45 minutes exercise per day outside the home is recommended. An hour or two is even better. This dog was bred for work and still has that daily need to get rid of energy.

Training

If you're thinking of getting a Standard Schnauzer puppy, proper training is important. A well-trained dog that you can take anywhere without worrying is a marvelous companion.

Due to their intelligence, Standards do learn quickly. They will retain most things they learn – even the bad things sometimes. They therefore need direction that is consistent and firm, but never rough. Don't be surprised if your Standard tries to push the boundaries. He'll rule the house if you let him, so it's important for you to start off on the right foot.

An ideal way to start is to find out if there's a local puppy or dog training class in your area. This not only gives you and your dog an opportunity to learn things the right way, it also enables them to socialize and get used to other puppies.

Your puppy should get used to other dogs as early as possible. Lack of socialization can sometimes lead to aggression or fear with other dogs, although Standards are not by nature aggressive with other dogs.

 Another way of getting yourself up to speed initially is to invest in a dog training book or DVD to learn the training basics, although nothing can replace dog training classes for socializing with other dogs and learning while there are plenty of distractions going on. (See Chapter 11 on **Training.**)

However you decide to train your Standard, it will be time (and even money) well spent. Putting in the effort at the beginning will bring rewards in the long run.

Mentally and physically, the Standard is one of the most versatile breeds of dogs and most are happy to participate in a whole range of activities and sports – even herding

Because of their usually loyal and gentle nature and affinity with humans, Standards like their smaller cousin the Miniature Schnauzer, can also be trained as therapy dogs.

Keep him interested and exercised and a Standard will make a companion second to none.

Health

The Standard Schnauzer is generally a very healthy breed. It doesn't suffer from many of the hereditary diseases which can affect many purebreds.

The two ailments which can affect the breed are **hereditary eye disease** and **hip dysplasia.**

The Standard Schnauzer Club of America recommends that all breeders test their breeding stock for these two ailments and only breeds from stock which is 100% clear.

American Kennel Club Breed Standard

<u>**Standard Schnauzer**</u> – Working Group

General Appearance
The Standard Schnauzer is a robust, heavy-set dog, sturdily built with good muscle and plenty of bone; square-built in proportion of body length to height.

His rugged build and dense harsh coat are accentuated by the hallmark of the breed, the arched eyebrows and the bristly mustache and whiskers.

Faults - Any deviation that detracts from the Standard Schnauzer's desired general appearance of a robust, active, square-built, wire-coated dog.

Any deviation from the specifications in the Standard is to be considered a fault and should be penalized in proportion to the extent of the deviation.

Size, Proportion, Substance - Ideal height at the highest point of the shoulder blades, 18½ to 19½ inches for males and 17½ inches to 18½ inches for females.

Dogs measuring over or under these limits must be faulted in proportion to the extent of the deviation. Dogs measuring more than one half inch over or under these limits must be disqualified.

The height at the highest point of the withers equals the length from breastbone to point of rump.

Head - Head strong, rectangular, and elongated; narrowing slightly from the ears to the eyes and again to the tip of the nose.

The total length of the head is about one half the length of the back measured from the withers to the set-on of the tail. The head matches the sex and substance of the dog.

Expression alert, highly intelligent, spirited.

Eyes medium size; dark brown; oval in shape and turned forward; neither round nor protruding. The brow is arched and wiry, but vision is not impaired nor eyes hidden by too long an eyebrow.

Ears set high, evenly shaped with moderate thickness of leather and carried erect when cropped.

If uncropped, they are of medium size, V-shaped and mobile so that they break at skull level and are carried forward with the inner edge close to the cheek.

Faults - Prick, or hound ears.

Skull (Occiput to Stop) moderately broad between the ears with the width of the skull not exceeding two thirds the length of the skull. The skull must e flat; neither domed nor bumpy; skin unwrinkled. There is a slight stop which is accentuated by the wiry brows.

Muzzle strong, and both parallel and equal in length to the topskull; it ends in a moderately blunt wedge with wiry whiskers accenting the rectangular shape of the head.

The topline of the muzzle is parallel with the topline of the skull. Nose is large, black and full. The lips should be black, tight and not overlapping.

Cheeks - Well developed chewing muscles, but not so much that "cheekiness" disturbs the rectangular head form.

Bite - A full complement of white teeth, with a strong, sound scissors bite.

The canine teeth are strong and well developed with the upper incisors slightly overlapping and engaging the lower. The upper and lower jaws are powerful and neither overshot nor undershot.

Faults - A level bite is considered undesirable but a lesser fault than an overshot or undershot mouth.

Neck, Topline, Body
Neck strong, of moderate thickness and length, elegantly arched and blending cleanly into the shoulders. The skin is tight, fitting closely to the dry throat with no wrinkles or dewlaps.

The **topline** of the back should not be absolutely horizontal, but should have a slightly descending slope from the first vertebra of the withers to the faintly curved croup and set-on of the tail.

Back strong, firm, straight and short. Loin well developed, with the distance from the last rib to the hips as short as possible.

Body compact, strong, short-coupled and substantial so as to permit great flexibility and agility. *Faults* - Too slender or shelly; too bulky or coarse.

Chest of medium width with well sprung ribs, and if it could be seen in cross section would be oval. The breastbone is plainly discernible. The brisket must descend at least to the elbows and ascend gradually to the rear with the belly moderately drawn up.

Fault - Excessive tuck-up. Croup full and slightly rounded.

Tail set moderately high and carried erect. It is docked to not less than one inch nor more than two inches. *Fault*--Squirrel tail.

Forequarters

Shoulders-The sloping shoulder blades are strongly muscled, yet flat and well laid back so that the rounded upper ends are in a nearly vertical line above the elbows.

They slope well forward to the point where they join the upper arm, forming as nearly as possible a right angle when seen from the side. Such an angulation permits the maximum forward extension of the forelegs without binding or effort.

Forelegs - straight, vertical, and without any curvature when seen from all sides; set moderately far apart; with heavy bone; elbows set close to the body and pointing directly to the rear. Dewclaws on the forelegs may be removed. **Feet** small and compact, round with thick pads and strong black nails. The toes are well closed and arched (cat's paws) and pointing straight ahead.

Hindquarters

Strongly muscled, in balance with the forequarters, never appearing higher than the shoulders. Thighs broad with well bent stifles. The second thigh, from knee to hock, is approximately parallel with an extension of the upper neck line.

The legs, from the clearly defined hock joint to the feet, are short and perpendicular to the ground and, when viewed from the rear, are parallel to each other. Dewclaws, if any, on the hind legs are generally removed. Feet as in front.

Coat

Tight, hard, wiry and as thick as possible, composed of a soft, close undercoat and a harsh outer coat which, when seen against the grain, stands up off the back, lying neither smooth nor flat. The outer coat (body coat) is trimmed (by plucking) only to accent the body outline.

As coat texture is of the greatest importance, a dog may be considered in show coat with back hair measuring from 3/4 to 2 inches in length. Coat on the ears, head, neck, chest, belly and under the tail may be closely trimmed to give the desired typical appearance of the breed.

 On the muzzle and over the eyes the coat lengthens to form the beard and eyebrows; the hair on the legs is longer than that on the body.

These "furnishings" should be of harsh texture and should not be so profuse as to detract from the neat appearance or working capabilities of the dog.

Faults - Soft, smooth, curly, wavy or shaggy; too long or too short; too sparse or lacking undercoat; excessive furnishings; lack of furnishings.

Color
Pepper and salt or pure black.

Pepper and Salt -The typical pepper and salt color of the topcoat results from the combination of black and white hairs, and white hairs banded with black. Acceptable are all shades of pepper and salt and dark iron gray to silver gray.

Ideally, pepper and salt Standard Schnauzers have a gray undercoat, but a tan or fawn undercoat is not to be penalized. It is desirable to have a darker facial mask that harmonizes with the particular shade of coat color.

Also, in pepper and salt dogs, the pepper and salt mixture may fade out to light gray or silver white in the eyebrows, whiskers, cheeks, under throat, across chest, under tail, leg furnishings, under body, and inside legs.

Black - Ideally the black Standard Schnauzer should be a true rich color, free from any fading or discoloration or any admixture of gray or tan hairs. The undercoat should also be solid black. However, increased age or continued exposure to the sun may cause a certain amount of fading and burning.

A small white smudge on the chest is not a fault. Loss of color as a result of scars from cuts and bites is not a fault.

Faults - Any colors other than specified, and any shadings or mixtures thereof in the topcoat such as rust, brown, red, yellow or tan; absence of peppering; spotting or striping; a black streak down the back; or a black saddle without typical salt and pepper coloring-and gray hairs in the coat of a black; in blacks, any undercoat color other than black.

Gait

Sound, strong, quick, free, true and level gait with powerful, well angulated hindquarters that reach out and cover ground. The forelegs reach out in a stride balancing that of the hindquarters.

At a trot, the back remains firm and level, without swaying, rolling or roaching. When viewed from the rear, the feet, though they may appear to travel close when trotting, must not cross or strike. Increased speed causes feet to converge toward the center line of gravity.

Faults - Crabbing or weaving; paddling, rolling, swaying; short, choppy, stiff, stilted rear action; front legs that throw out or in (East and West movers); hackney gait, crossing over, or striking in front or rear.

Temperament

The Standard Schnauzer has highly developed senses, intelligence, aptitude for training, fearlessness, endurance and resistance against weather and illness. His nature combines high-spirited temperament with extreme reliability.

Faults - In weighing the seriousness of a fault, greatest consideration should be given to deviation from the desired alert, highly intelligent, spirited, reliable character of the Standard Schnauzer.

Dogs that are shy or appear to be highly nervous should be seriously faulted and dismissed from the ring. Vicious dogs shall be disqualified.

Disqualifications

Males under 18 inches or over 20 inches in height. Females under 17 inches or over 19 inches in height. Vicious dogs.

Visit the American Kennel Club at www.akc.org/breeds/standard_schnauzer

The Kennel Club (UK) Breed Standard

<u>Schnauzer</u> – Utility Group

General Appearance
Sturdily built, robust, sinewy, nearly square, (length of body equal to height at shoulders). Expression keen and attitude alert. Correct conformation is of more importance than colour or purely 'beauty' points.

Characteristics
Strong, vigorous dog capable of great endurance.

Temperament
Alert, reliable and intelligent. Primarily a companion dog.

Head and Skull
Head strong and of good length, narrowing from ears to eyes and then gradually forward toward end of nose.

Upper part of the head (occiput to the base of the forehead) moderately broad between ears. Flat, creaseless forehead; well muscled but not too strongly developed cheeks. Medium stop to accentuate prominent eyebrows.

Powerful muzzle ending in a moderately blunt line, with bristly, stubby moustache and chin whiskers. Ridge of nose straight and running almost parallel to extension of forehead. Nose black with wide nostrils. Lips tight but not overlapping.

Eyes
Medium-sized, dark, oval, set forward with arched bushy eyebrows.

Ears
Neat, V-shaped, set high and dropping forward to temple.

Mouth
Jaws strong, with a perfect, regular and complete scissor bite, i.e. upper teeth closely overlapping.

Eyes
Medium-sized, dark, oval, set forward with arched bushy eyebrows.

Ears
Neat, V-shaped, set high and dropping forward to temple.

Mouth
Jaws strong, with a perfect, regular and complete scissor bite, i.e. upper teeth closely overlapping lower teeth and set square to the neck.

Neck
Moderately long, strong, and slightly arched; skin close to throat; neck set cleanly on shoulders.

Forequarters
Shoulders flat and well laid. Forelegs straight viewed from any angle. Muscles smooth and lithe rather than prominent; bone strong, straight and carried well down to feet; elbows close to body and pointing directly backward.

Body
Chest moderately broad; deep with visible, strong breastbone reaching at least to height of elbow and rising slightly backward to loins.

Back strong and straight, slightly higher at shoulder than at hindquarters, with short, well developed loins. Ribs well sprung. Length of body equal to height from top of withers to ground.

Hindquarters
Thighs slanting and flat but strongly muscled. Hindlegs (upper and lower thighs) at first vertical to the stifle; from stifle to hock in line with the extension of the upper neck line; from hock, vertical to ground.

Feet
Short, round, cat-like, compact with closely arched toes, dark nails, firm black pads, feet pointing forward.

Tail
Previously customarily docked. If docked: Set on and carried high, customarily docked to three joints.
Undocked: Set on and carried high, of moderate length to give general balance to the dog. Thick at root and tapering towards the tip, as straight as possible, carried jauntily.

Gait/Movement
Free, balanced and vigorous, with good reach in forequarters and good driving power in hindquarters. Topline remains level in action.

Coat
Harsh, wiry and short enough for smartness. Closer on neck and shoulders; clean on throat, skull and ears. Harsh hair on legs. Dense undercoat essential.

Colour
Pure black (white markings on head, chest and legs undesirable) or pepper and salt. Pepper and salt shades range from dark iron grey to light grey; good pigmentation. Hairs banded dark/light/dark. Facial mask to harmonise with corresponding coat colour.

Size
Ideal height at withers: dogs: 48 cms (19 Ins); bitches: 45.7 cms (18 ins). Any variations of more than 2.5 cms (1 in) in these heights undesirable.

Faults
Any departure from the foregoing points should be considered a fault and the seriousness with which the fault should be regarded should be in exact proportion to its degree and its effect upon the health and welfare of the dog.

Note
Male animals should have two apparently normal testicles fully descended into the scrotum.

Visit the Kennel Club website at **www.thekennelclub.org.uk**

Chapter 3. The Giant Schnauzer

Powerful Protector

The Giant Schnauzer is a highly intelligent, spirited and energetic dog. He's like Mohammed Ali in his prime – incredibly strong and full of energy. He demands your attention, loves people and has a heart of gold underneath that powerful exterior.

The Giant is loyal, strongly territorial and an instinctive protector of his family. His life revolves around his owners. In return for his devotion, he expects your time.

This is a high maintenance breed that requires a major amount of training, grooming and exercise. However, with the right people he is one of the most rewarding dogs of all to own.

The Giant - or Riesenschnauzer as he's known in Germany - has a long history of training and working alongside humans as companion, assistant and even guardian.

He is the second most popular of the three Schnauzer breeds, after the Miniature. In the US, this is the 83rd most popular dog breed.

Appearance

This is a striking dog and an elegant mover. Once seen, never forgotten. The breed was truly recognized in 2008 when the beautiful black Jafrak Philippe Olivier beat almost 23,000 dogs from 181 breeds to win **Best in Show at Crufts** - the largest dog show in the world.

His owners Kevin and Sandie Cullen of Sussex in the South of England, UK, have written an exclusive article at:
www.max-the-schnauzer.com/giant-schnauzer-champion.html

In appearance The Giant Schnauzer is large and solid, but compact rather than heavy. Like an athlete, he is muscular, fit and very agile.

His shoulder height is almost the same as his body length, giving a neat, square shape. He has the bushy eyebrows, whiskers and full beard typical of the Schnauzer.

Males are 25.5 to 27.5 inches high at the shoulders and weigh anything from 60 to 90 pounds – that's a lot of dog food! Bitches are two or three inches smaller and weigh 55 to 75 pounds.

Jafrak Philippe Olivier

Like the Standard Schnauzer, this athletic breed is classed in the Working Group in North America, as it is in the UK. Although the Standard and Miniature are both included in the Utility Group in the UK.

In North America the tail is docked and the ears may or may not be cropped. Since April 2007 it has been illegal to dock any dog's tail - except for working gundogs – in the UK. Dogs born prior to that with docked tails are accepted in the show ring. It is also illegal to crop the dog's ears in the UK.

The Coat

Solid black or pepper and salt are the only two colors for Giant Schnauzers. They have a harsh, wiry outer coat and dense, soft undercoat. Like all Schnauzers, they are regarded as a non-shedding, hypoallergenic dog breed.

It's a fact that no dog is totally non-shedding and you may find the occasional fur ball in the house, particularly if they are overdue a visit to the grooming salon.

These dogs require regular grooming. Because they are non shedding (and hypoallergenic), they have to be stripped or clipped regularly - about every 8 to 10 weeks. This keeps them looking handsome and elegant and not scruffy and woolly!

Regular weekly brushing and combing help to prevent the legs and the beard from tangling. A word of warning, once your Giant Schnauzer has established a fully grown beard, expect it to be soaked every visit to the water dish....

Temperament

They are NOT a larger version of the Miniature Schnauzer.

There are three distinctive Schnauzer breeds all with very different personalities and characteristics. Giant Schnauzers are physically very strong and usually have extremely high energy levels. They are loud and demanding and require a lot of daily attention and exercise.

As a guard dog they are second to none. Their natural ability to protect their owners and home makes Giant Schnauzers a valuable asset - as long as they are part of the family. They like to be involved with whatever its family is doing, even if it's just sitting watching the TV.

If left alone the Giant becomes bored and frustrated - he may even become unruly and uncontrollable. Due to their intelligence, many have a stubborn streak and require a firm hand when training.

If you decide to get a Giant Schnauzer, you MUST be prepared to devote lots of quality time to your dog - all the way from puppyhood throughout his adult life.

Training

Because Giants can be strong willed, it's especially important for you to start off on the right foot with your puppy or adult dog. This means proper training.

Find out if there's a local puppy or dog training class in your area. A quick and easy way of getting to know the basics is to buy a dog training book or DVD. But these cannot replace training classes with a professional dog handler, as you will learn good practices and your Giant will learn to socialize with other dogs.

As with children, putting the time in at the beginning will be well worth the effort! Teaching good habits from the start will stop your Giant getting into bad habits - like jumping up or barking loudly or pulling on the leash - before they grow up into big powerful animals. Sadly, all too many Giants in the USA end up in rescue centers after they became too much to handle. Yet speak to a responsible owner who devotes plenty of time to this dog and he or she will tell you that they are second to none; the most rewarding breed in the world.

History

All three types of Schnauzer originate from the Standard Schnauzer (or just 'Schnauzer' as it is called in the UK) which has been around for 500 years. However, the Giant didn't arrive on the scene until fairly recently. In 19th century Southern Germany, cattlemen wanted a larger version of the Standard Schnauzer for herding.

They created the Giant by selectively breeding the Standard with several other breeds of dog. As the Giant was bred as a working dog, he still has the capacity for hard work, and a lot of exercise – it's wired into his DNA.

Although the breed has had an excellent reputation for its work with the police and military for nearly a century in Germany, it was still a rarity in the USA and Britain in the 1960's.

Exercise - and plenty of it

If you're a couch potato, then the Giant Schnauzer is definitely NOT the dog for you!

If, on the other hand, you're about to embark on a 10-year fitness program, then he could be the ideal training partner.......

Giants will take as much exercise as they can get. They are energetic dogs which love running free. They were bred as a working dog to run and herd animals all day long. They have to get rid of this excess energy and require exercising for a couple of hours a day.

They need long daily walks, jogs or runs. If you're not that fit yourself, you can cycle a few miles and let the dog run alongside.

If they are not exercised at least twice daily, they can bounce off the walls and become difficult to deal with - even well trained ones. The most common phrase among breeders, owners and trainers is: "A tired Giant is a happy Giant!"

Like all three types of schnauzer, the Giant becomes very attached to people. But he can also become demanding he doesn't get enough exercise or if he is not made aware of the house rules early on. They are naturally protective dogs, generally make excellent watchdogs, but need socializing with other dogs and animals, so they learn to trust others and not become aggressive with outsiders or visitors. Once properly socialized, they will take their cue from you.

Giants often do well with other Giants – provided you've got the space. Owners who have the time to devote to exercising and training these dogs will tell you that, not only are they extremely handsome creatures, but they are also incredibly rewarding.

Like most Schnauzers, Giants love snow and, unlike many Miniatures, many of them also love being in the water.

Given their high energy levels and intelligence, you might think about getting involved in agility classes, advanced obedience training, carting or tracking. These are all activities at which this breed excels.

Supreme Champion of Crufts in 2008, Giant Schnauzer
Philippe Jafrak Olivier with owner Kevin Cullen

In short, the Giant Schnauzer is an extremely rewarding dog for the right owners who are prepared to give him the time and energy he needs. If you think that a couple of hours a day is too big a commitment for you, then think about getting a Standard Schnauzer, which shares many of the traits of the Giant, but requires slightly less of your time.

American Kennel Club Breed Standard

Giant Schnauzer - Working Group

General Description
The Giant Schnauzer should resemble, as nearly as possible, in general appearance, a larger and more powerful version of the Standard Schnauzer, on the whole a bold and valiant figure of a dog.

Robust, strongly built, nearly square in proportion of body length to height at withers, active, sturdy, and well muscled. Temperament which combines spirit and alertness with intelligence and reliability.

Composed, watchful, courageous, easily trained, deeply loyal to family, playful, amiable in repose, and a commanding figure when aroused.

The sound, reliable temperament, rugged build, and dense weather-resistant wiry coat make for one of the most useful, powerful, and enduring working breeds.

Head - Strong, rectangular in appearance, and elongated; narrowing slightly from the ears to the eyes, and again from the eyes to the tip of the nose. The total length of the head is about one-half the length of the back (withers to set-on of tail). The head matches the sex and substance of the dog. The top line of the muzzle is parallel to the top line of the skull; there is a slight stop which is accentuated by the eyebrows.

Skull - (Occiput to Stop). Moderately broad between the ears: occiput not too prominent. Top of skull flat; skin unwrinkled.

Cheeks - Flat, but with well-developed chewing muscles; there is no "cheekiness" to disturb the rectangular head appearance (with beard).

Muzzle - Strong and well filled under the eyes; parallel and equal in length to the topskull; ending in a moderately blunt wedge. The nose is large, black, and full. The lips are tight, and not overlapping, black in color.

Bite - A full complement of sound white teeth (6/6 incisors, 2/2 canines, 8/8 premolars, 4/6 molars) with a scissors bite. The upper and lower jaws are powerful and well formed. **Disqualifying Faults**--Overshot or undershot.

Ears - When cropped, identical in shape and length with pointed tips. They are in balance with the head and are not exaggerated in length. They are set high on the skull and carried perpendicularly at the inner edges with as little bell as possible along the other edges.

When uncropped, the ears are V-shaped button ears of medium length and thickness, set high and carried rather high and close to the head.

Eyes - Medium size, dark brown, and deep-set. They are oval in appearance and keen in expression with lids fitting tightly. Vision is not impaired nor eyes hidden by too long eyebrows.

Neck - Strong and well arched, of moderate length, blending cleanly into the shoulders, and with the skin fitting tightly at the throat; in harmony with the dog's weight and build.

Body - Compact, substantial, short-coupled, and strong, with great power and agility. The height at the highest point of the withers equals the body length from breastbone to point of rump. The loin section is well developed, as short as possible for compact build.

Forequarters
The forequarters have flat, somewhat sloping shoulders and high withers. Forelegs are straight and vertical when viewed from all sides with strong pasterns and good bone. They are separated by a fairly deep brisket which precludes a pinched front. The elbows are set close to the body and point directly backwards.

Chest - Medium in width, ribs well sprung but with no tendency toward a barrel chest; oval in cross section: deep through the brisket.

The breastbone is plainly discernible, with strong forechest; the brisket descends at least to the elbows, and ascends gradually toward the rear with the belly moderately drawn up. The ribs spread gradually from the first rib so as to allow space for the elbows to move close to the body.

Shoulders

The sloping shoulder blades (scapulae) are strongly muscled, yet flat. They are well laid back so that from the side the rounded upper ends are in a nearly vertical line above the elbows.

They slope well forward to the point where they join the upper arm (humerus), forming as nearly as possible a right angle. Such an angulation permits the maximum forward extension of the forelegs without binding or effort. Both shoulder blades and upper arm are long, permitting depth of chest at the brisket.

Back - Short, straight, strong, and firm.

Tail - The tail is set moderately high and carried high in excitement. It should be docked to the second or not more than the third joint (approximately one and one-half to about three inches long at maturity).

Hindquarters - The hindquarters are strongly muscled, in balance with the forequarters; upper thighs are slanting and well bent at the stifles, with the second thighs (tibiae) approximately parallel to an extension of the upper neckline.

The legs from the hock joint to the feet are short, perpendicular to the ground while the dog is standing naturally, and from the rear parallel to each other. The hindquarters do not appear over-built or higher than the shoulders. Croup full and slightly rounded.

Feet - Well-arched, compact and catlike, turning neither in nor out, with thick tough pads and dark nails.

Dewclaws - Dewclaws, if any, on hind legs should be removed; on the forelegs, may be removed.

Gait - The trot is the gait at which movement is judged. Free, balanced and vigorous, with good reach in the forequarters and good driving power in the hindquarters.

Rear and front legs are thrown neither in nor out. When moving at a fast trot, a properly built dog will single-track. Back remains strong, firm, and flat.

Coat - Hard, wiry, very dense; composed of a soft undercoat and a harsh outer coat which, when seen against the grain, stands slightly up off the back, lying neither smooth nor flat. Coarse hair on top of head; harsh beard and eyebrows, the Schnauzer hallmark.

Color - Solid black or pepper and salt.

Black - A truly pure black. A small white spot on the breast is permitted; any other markings are disqualifying faults.

Pepper and Salt - Outer coat of a combination of banded hairs (white with black and black with white) and some black and white hairs, appearing gray from a short distance. Ideally; an intensely pigmented medium gray shade with "peppering" evenly distributed throughout the coat, and a gray undercoat.

Acceptable; all shades of pepper and salt from dark iron-gray to silver-gray. Every shade of coat has a dark facial mask to emphasize the expression; the color of the mask harmonizes with the shade of the body coat. Eyebrows, whiskers, cheeks, throat, chest, legs, and under tail are lighter in color but include "peppering." Markings are disqualifying faults.

Height - The height at the withers of the male is 25½ to 27½ inches, and of the female, 23½ to 25½ inches, with the mediums being desired. Size alone should never take precedence over type, balance, soundness, and temperament.

It should be noted that too small dogs generally lack the power and too large dogs, the agility and maneuverability, desired in the working dog.

Faults - The foregoing description is that of the ideal Giant Schnauzer. Any deviation from the above described dog must be penalized to the extent of the deviation.

The judge shall dismiss from the ring any shy or vicious Giant Schnauzer.

Shyness A dog shall be judged fundamentally shy if, refusing to stand for examination, it repeatedly shrinks away from the judge; if it fears unduly any approach from the rear; if it shies to a marked degree at sudden and unusual noises.

Viciousness A dog that attacks or attempts to attack either the judge or its handler, is definitely vicious. An aggressive or belligerent attitude towards other dogs shall not be deemed viciousness.

AKC Giant Schnauzer Disqualifications
Overshot or undershot. Markings other than specified.

Visit the American Kennel Club website at: www.akc.org/breeds/giant_schnauzer

———————————

The Kennel Club (UK) Breed Standard

Giant Schnauzer - Working Group

Characteristics - Versatile, strong, hardy, intelligent and vigorous. Adaptable, capable of great speed and endurance and resistant to weather.

Temperament - Bold, reliable, good-natured and composed.

Head and Skull - Head strong, of good length, narrowing from ears to eyes and then gradually toward end of nose.

The overall length (from nose to occiput) is in proportion to the back (from withers to set on of tail) approximately 1 : 2.

Upper part of head (occiput to base of forehead) moderately broad between ears – with flat creaseless forehead. Well muscled but not over-developed cheeks. Medium stop accentuated by bushy eyebrows. Powerful muzzle ending in a moderately blunt wedge, with bristly stubby moustache and chin whiskers. Ridge of nose straight, running parallel to extension of forehead. Nose black with wide nostrils.

Eyes - Medium-sized, dark, oval, set forward, with lower lid fitting closely.

Ears - Neat, V-shaped, set high and dropping forward to temple.

Mouth - Jaws strong with a perfect, regular and complete scissor bite, i.e. upper teeth closely overlapping lower teeth and set square to the jaws. Lips black, closing tightly but not overlapping.

Neck - Moderately long, strong and slightly arched, skin close to throat, neck set cleanly on shoulders.

Forequarters - Shoulders flat, well laid back. Forelegs straight viewed from any angle. Muscles smooth and lithe rather than prominent, bone strong, carried straight to feet. Elbows set close to body and pointing directly backward.

Body - Chest moderately broad and deep, reaching at least to height of elbow rising slightly backward to loins. Breast bone clearly extends to beyond joint of shoulder and upper arm forming the conspicuous forechest.

Back strong and straight, slightly higher at shoulder than at hindquarters, with short, well developed loins. Slightly sloping croup. Ribs well sprung. Length of body equal to height at top of withers to ground.

Hindquarters - Strongly muscled. Stifles forming a well defined angle. Upper thighs vertical to stifle, from stifle to hock in line with extension of upper neck line, from hock vertical to ground. When viewed from rear, hind legs parallel.

Feet - Pointing directly forward, short, round, compact with closely arched toes. Deep, dark and firm pads. Dark nails.

Tail - Previously customarily docked.

Docked: Set on high and carried at an angle slightly above topline. Customarily docked to two joints. Undocked: Set on high and carried at an angle slightly above topline. In balance with the rest of the dog.

Gait/Movement - Free, balanced and vigorous, with good reach of forequarters and good driving power from hindquarters. Topline remains level in action.

Coat - Top coat harsh and wiry, just short enough for smartness on body. Slightly shorter on neck and shoulders, but blending smoothly into body coat.

Clean on throat, skull, ears and under tail. Good undercoat. Harsh hair on legs.

Colour
(a) Pure black

(b) Pepper and salt: Shades range from dark iron grey to light grey; hairs banded black/light/black. Dark facial mask essential, harmonising with corresponding body color.

On both colours white markings on head, chest and legs undesirable. Good pigmentation essential.

Size - Height: dogs: 65-70 cms (251/2-271/2 ins); bitches: 60-65 cms (231/2-251/2 ins). Variations outside these limits undesirable.

Faults - Any departure from the foregoing points should be considered a fault and the seriousness with which the fault should be regarded should be in exact proportion to its degree and its effect upon the health and welfare of the dog.

Note: Male animals should have two apparently normal testicles fully descended into the scrotum.

Visit the Kennel Club website at **www.thekennelclub.org.uk**

Chapter 4. The History of Schnauzers

There is no precise written record of Schnauzer history. Over the years dog breed experts have discussed many theories, but nobody knows *exactly* how and when the first Schnauzer came into being.

Many ill-informed articles have appeared, particularly on websites. After much research covering many sources, here is the most credible version of the true history of the Schnauzer:

Birth of a Breed

The Schnauzer originated in Southern Germany in the 14th or 15th century. In those days farmers and trades people travelled around the countryside with heavily laden carts selling their skills and produce at markets.

They needed a medium-sized and versatile dog, strong enough to guard the cart, but small enough to easily fit into that same cart. These practical men also wanted a good ratter to keep down the vermin back at home.

Wire-haired Pinschers

The breeders involved in Schnauzer history probably crossed the black German Poodle and the gray Wolfspitz with more than a pinch of Wire-Haired Pinscher (aka Rough Pinscher) to create the first Schnauzer.

This medium-sized 'prototype' most closely resembled today's Standard Schnauzer and established the breed as a working dog.

Origin of the Name

The word **Schnauzer** should be pronounced **"sh-now-tser"** with the German **Z** sounding like **TS** - as in Mozart, which is spoken "Motsart."

It comes from the German word "Schnauze" meaning snout. This obviously refers to the wonderful whiskers on the muzzle - often described as the beard and moustache - which are the trademark of all Schnauzers and give them such an unforgettable look.

Miniature Pinscher

In the early days of Schnauzer history in Germany, the first Schnauzers as we know them were referred to as Wire-Haired Pinschers.

At the 3rd German International Show in 1879, three Wire-Haired Pinschers, owned by C. Berger from Wurtemburg, were entered.

The winner was a dog called "Schnauzer". And from then on, all dogs of this breed were called Schnauzers.

The Schnauzer Family Tree

This is shown on page 49, courtesy of the American Kennel Club, and outlines the different dog breeds used to develop the three types of Schnauzer.

It's interesting that although they look nothing alike now, the modern Schnauzers and Pinschers share the same ancestors.

The original smooth coated Pinschers were bred with each other to give the sleek coat of today's Miniature and Doberman Pinschers.

The Wire-Haired Pinschers were specifically bred to give the rough coat of modern Schnauzers. It is interesting to see how selective breeding, albeit over a long period of time, could produce such different dogs – in terms of appearance, temperament and size.

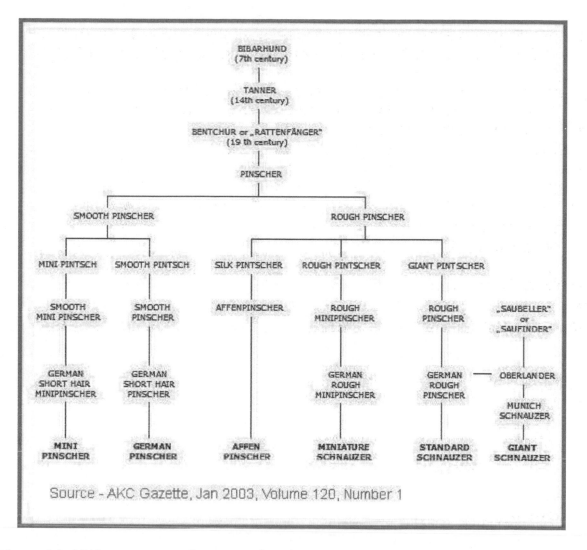

Source - AKC Gazette, Jan 2003, Volume 120, Number 1

In the mid-19th century, German dog breeders began to show an interest in this versatile native breed. At this time, the medium-sized dogs were also being crossed with other breeds to create the Miniature and later the Giant.

Although there may have been an odd one imported earlier, the first Schnauzers were brought into the UK and America around 1900. They were probably brought to England and the New World as beloved pets of immigrant families as well by travelers and traders returning home.

Champion Standard Nero de Grisons, born 1943

During World War I, Standard Schnauzers were used as guard dogs by the German Army and dispatch carriers by the Red Cross.

It was, however, soldiers returning from the First World War who brought back Schnauzers in greater numbers. The fighting men greatly admired the courage and spirit of these dogs.

Standard Schnauzer History

The Standard Schnauzer is the original. It is the oldest of the three distinct Schnauzer breeds and the one from which Miniatures and Giants originate. The breed is known at the Mittelschnauzer (Middle Schnauzer) in Germany and simply as the Schnauzer in the UK.

It was a combination of working, hunting and terrier stock. Historically the breed was employed as an all-rounder on farms. This job included getting rid of vermin and guarding the family and their property as well as herding sheep and cattle. This versatile dog would also provide protection for the families on their travels to and from market.

In the mid-1800s, fanciers of the Standard Schnauzer crossed it with the black German Poodle and the gray Wolfspitz to get the rough coat and salt-and-pepper color of the breed today.

Miniature Schnauzer History

The Miniature Schnauzer was exhibited as a distinct breed at early as 1899. It's thought to have been derived from breeding the smallest of the Standard Schnauzers with Affenpinschers, gray Spitz and black Poodles in a highly selective breeding program.

Four Miniatures imported by Mrs. M. Slattery of the Marienhof Kennels in 1924 were the foundation stock for the breed in America.

Miniature Schnauzers were first registered as a separate breed in 1926. The following year the first American champion was Mrs. Slattery's Ch. Moses Taylor. This was an honor shared with Don v. Dornbusch, since both won on the same day - but at different shows.

Jocco-Fulda-Lilliput 1899

Since then the Miniature Schnauzer's popularity has soared, elevating the dog to one of the most loved breeds in America.

Giant Schnauzer History

The Giant Schnauzer was the last of all three breeds of Schnauzer to be created.

In Germany the **"Riesenschnauzer"** (which literally means **Giant Snouter** in German!) was initially bred and used to drive cattle and sheep. It was also used as a guard dog.

In the 1928 book on German dog breeds, E. von Otto says the father of the Giants was the great **"bear Schnauzer"** of Munich. This was a dog breed with long shaggy hair related to the Old German Shepherd dog.

This was probably crossed with the black Great Dane, giving strength and power to the Giant, as well as the instinct to protect.

Von Otto also wrote: "In his general appearance and wonderful nature he bears a very strong resemblance to the Bouvier des Flandres." This was another dog breed developed to drive cattle, but whose intelligence, strength and versatility have been put to many uses since then.

The Odivane Kennel of Mary Moore was one of the first importers of Giants into the UK, whilst the breed was imported into the USA in the 1930's.

However, until the 1960's there were still less than 50 Giant Schnauzers a year registered in America.

With selective breeding and importing from successful kennels as well as word of mouth endorsements of the breed, the popularity of the Giant Schnauzer has increased considerably over the last 40 years.

A modern black American Giant Schnauzer

Schnauzers in Art

There is a statue in Mecklenburg, Germany, dating from the 14th century, of a hunter with a Schnauzer crouching at his feet. The Schnauzer again appears in a 1620 statue called "The Night Watchman" in Stuttgart, Germany.

It's a fact that the breed also featured in several paintings by Albrecht Durer (1471-1528). He probably owned a Schnauzer himself, as he made several paintings of what looks like the same dog at different stages of its life.

A tapestry from 1501 called Crown of Thorns - by Lucas Cranach the Elder - also contained a dog looking suspiciously like a Schnauzer. Other famous artists, such as the Dutch master Rembrandt (17th Century) and English painted Joshua Reynolds (1723-1792) also painted Schnauzers.

The first time that the word *Schnauzer* is mentioned in literature is in the book "*Les Races des Chien*" by Count Henri van Bylandt in 1894. He writes that the smaller version of the wire-haired pinscher is called the Zwergschnauzer (which literally means dwarf schnauzer).

In more modern times, many people will have seen the iconic Schnauzer poster for chocolate bars, which came in three energy-packed sizes: Giant, Standard and Miniature!

Chapter 5. The Schnoodle

Some people, particularly breeders, have asked why we have included Schnoodles in this book ,as they are not pure Schnauzers. Our aim is to provide comprehensive information on all aspects of the breed and we believe that to omit discussing the Schnauzer crossbreed would have been a mistake. So here's the facts:

A Schnoodle is a cross between a Schnauzer and a Poodle. It's hard to say what a typical one looks like as they range in size from very small to very large and their coats come in a variety of colors.

There are three types of Poodle – **Standard, Miniature** and **Toy** and three types of Schnauzer - **Giant , Standard** and **Miniature.** A Schnoodle can be any combination of these.

There are four types of Schnoodle: **Giant, Standard, Miniature** or **Toy**. The most common of these used to be the Miniature, which usually weighs between 10lbs and 16lbs. However, Giant Schnoodles are becoming more popular and these can weigh up to 80lbs.

Can I Get a Purebred?

No, a Schnoodle is a Poodle-Schnauzer crossbreed or a hybrid. Puppies are not eligible for registration with purebred or pedigree registries such as the American, Canadian or UK Kennel Clubs. However, in the USA they can be registered with the American Canine Hybrid Club.

The Schnoodle is not considered a purebred. It doesn't 'breed true', meaning that it doesn't display a consistent set of characteristics. That's why Schnoodles come in all shapes and sizes.

One of the hottest arguments you'll ever hear between dog lovers is the one between the owner of a purebred (or pedigree in the UK) - with papers showing an impressive lineage - and the owner of a common or garden mongrel or crossbreed who thinks that his dog is better.

Some dog owners do not want a pedigree or pure-bred dog. The Kennel Clubs in various countries lay down a strict set of guidelines as to how a particular breed should look. When pedigree dogs are responsibly bred with other pedigree dogs, the best traits of the breed are reproduced.

Unfortunately, sometimes faults creep into a breed and these can also be passed on. Some people believe that crossbreeds or even mongrels have a more robust and healthy nature, as they are taking their characteristics from a bigger and more varied gene pool.

Some of the different faces of the Schnoodle

With a Schnoodle, you will generally get a non-shedding dog with the characteristics of either a Schnauzer or a Poodle or – more likely – a combination of the two. Make sure you check out both these breeds before you get a Schnoodle.

"Hybrid Vigor"

Schnoodle puppies and other so-called 'designer dogs' are causing a big debate in the canine world at the moment. If you're thinking about getting a Schnoodle, read the facts and then make up your own mind.

Some think it's a great idea to create a dog by crossing two existing breeds. When done responsibly, breeding is **by design**. In other words it is breeding between a **deliberately chosen sire and dam**.

This proper parentage can give the crossbreed puppy the advantage of **hybrid vigor** – or robustness.

The theory is that the puppy may be stronger and healthier as he is less likely to inherit the genetic faults of either purebred parent. Many purebred breeds have problems which have been bred in over the years.

For example, some Dalmatians are deaf, some Labradors have hip problems and Dachshunds may suffer from back problems. This is because as well as breeding the good points into a pedigree or purebred, the faults have also been inadvertently passed on.

It's often thought that the best crossbreed is a first generation - or F1 - cross. This applies to Schnoodles too. An F1 Schnoodle puppy is the product of a purebred Schnauzer and a purebred Poodle.

An F2 – or second generation cross – might be a cross between two Schnoodles. These puppies may also be good, healthy dogs but the further away from the original breeds the puppy is, the less likely it is that you will know what his or her characteristics will be.

One thing is certain - NOTHING is 100% certain with a crossbreed.

Most Schnoodles are non-shedding and hypoallergenic, but NO breeder can give you a cast-iron guarantee. They are, however, more likely to be non-shedding than some other crossbreeds, such as the Labradoodle or Cockapoo (a cross between a Poodle and a Cocker Spaniel), where the puppy may take after the shedding parent and molt.

Odds are that even the other littermates didn't turn out looking and acting exactly the same as your dog. On the other hand, with a crossbreed you have the true designer original!

The idea of **hybrid vigor** is that a crossbred dog will be healthier than a purebred **as** it is created from a bigger and more diverse gene pool. Of course, this only applies if both parents are from healthy stock and do not carry any inherent defects.

How wonderful it would be if you could take any two purebred dogs, cross breed them and automatically ensure a 100% healthy dog. Unfortunately, it is not as simple as that.

Some say hybrid vigor is a result of carefully planned breeding based on studying the health and personality histories of the parent dogs going back several generations. They also believe that it occurs only in first generation, or F1, crosses.

Others are sure that hybrid vigor does not exist in crossbred dogs. They think that in fact the dog might inherit the health problems of either or both parents.

It's fair to say the jury's still out on this one - you'll have to make up your own mind. If you do decide to get a Schnoodle, the most important thing you can do is to select a good, responsible breeder.

Like many other crossbreeds, Schnoodles can and do make really wonderful pets. Get to know the facts and if you decide a Schnoodle or other crossbreed is just the dog you're looking for, here are some points to bear in mind when selecting a puppy:

Schnoodle Tips

* Schnoodles do tend to have the personality type of one or the other of their parent breeds.

*Read all you can about the characteristics of the Schnauzer and the Poodle - your dog will be a mixture of these.

* Choose a responsible breeder and ask lots of questions.

* Make sure you see both parents (of the puppy, not the breeder!) Look at their size, coat and temperament.

* Find out whether the Schnoodle puppies are First Generation (F1) crosses. If not, what crosses are the parents?

Allergy Sufferers

With more than 10% of Americans suffering from allergies, there are a lot of dog lovers out there searching for a pet that won't make them sneeze.

All three types of Schnauzer and three types of Poodle and **most** Schnoodles are considered to be non-shedding and hypoallergenic. That means they are

LESS likely to cause an allergic reaction.

While there is no 100% guarantee, Schnoodles are generally non-shedding, as they take after one of their parents. Neither the Schnauzer nor the Poodle sheds hair. The Schnauzer has a double coat and the Poodle's coat is actually a type of wool.

On the whole, Schnoodles are likely to be less shedding than other crossbreeds like the Yorkipoo (Yorkshire Terrier/Poodle), Labradoodle (Labrador/Poodle), Goldendoodle (Golden Retriever/Poodle) or Cockapoo (Cocker Spaniel/Poodle). All of these breeds have one parent (or grandparent if they are F2 second generation crosses) which sheds hair.

Like humans, Schnoodle puppies inherit characteristics from their parents. If two Miniature Schnauzers breed, you can be pretty sure what the pups will look like.

When a Poodle and a Schnauzer breed, the resulting Schnoodle will probably look more like one parent that the other - just like we do.

The puppy may have a wiry coat like the Schnauzer, a softer woolly coat like the Poodle or often a combination of the two.

However, because **both parents are hypoallergenic** the probability is that the Schnoodle will be too.

Physical Characteristics

How Big Are Schnoodles?

This is not an easy question to answer because of the many different sizes and variations of the Poodle-Schnauzer crosses that might be involved.

* A Toy Schnoodle is 10 inches or under at the shoulders and under 10 pounds in weight. This is a cross between a Toy Poodle and a small Miniature Schnauzer.

* A Giant is a cross between a Standard Poodle and a Giant Schnauzer. A fully grown one will weigh as much as 65-80lbs and stand 24 to 27 inches high at the shoulders.

Some breeders think the Poodle takes the chunkiness out of the Schnauzer, while the Schnauzer takes the pointed head away from the Poodle.

Although there are no written breed characteristics, The Schnoodle should be well-proportioned and athletic. He should have a keen, bold, and lively expression.

Breeders

The Schnoodle is in high demand and can cost anywhere from $500 to $1,200, depending on the parents. Some of Schnoodles' popularity is due to the fact that MOST of them are hypoallergenic and non-shedding.

If you're thinking of getting a Schnoodle, the importance of finding a good, reputable breeder cannot be stressed enough.

The high price that Schnoodles fetch has triggered puppy mills. These are puppy factories where the prime aim is to make money, not to produce healthy puppies. You may find that although you save money on your puppy in the short term, you will be faced with an unhealthy pup bred from poor stock, costing a lot of money on vets' bills in the long run.

There are, however, responsible Schnoodle breeders. Do some research to find a suitable one, then make a visit. It is not a good idea to buy a dog over the internet. You're making a decision which will affect your life for the next decade or more, so making the time and effort to pick the right puppy is important. It IS a good idea to ask to speak to some people who have already bought puppies from your selected breeder.

Visit Chapter 7 on **Puppies** to read our Top Ten Tips.

Schnoodle Coat & Colors

The coat can come in many colors -

- **Black**
- **White**
- **Grey**
- **Apricot**
- **Chocolate**
- **Black with white markings**
- **Wheaten**
- **Sable**
- **Parti** (white with patches of color)
- **Phantom** (black and tan like the Doberman)

Although there are a variety of colors, the Schnoodle coat is almost always curly or at least wavy.

A puppy can take on the coat characteristics of either breed and Schnoodle puppies in the same litter may have differing coat qualities.

Schnauzers and Poodles are both regarded as non-shedding and hypoallergenic dog breeds.

The chances are that your Schnoodle will also be a non-shedding dog.

As the puppy matures it may develop the rough, wirier hair of the Schnauzer, the softer hair of the Poodle or something in between.

Some develop coarser Schnauzer-like hair in places - most notably the back - with softer Poodle hair on other parts of the body.

Like Schnauzers and Poodles, the Schnoodle should not shed hair, although you might find the occasional fur ball on the floor when he's ready for a trim.

This means that Schnoodles are fairly high maintenance as far is grooming is concerned. They need regular brushing to stop their coat from matting and a visit to the grooming parlor for a trim every eight to 12 weeks. When you budget how much your dog will cost you, don't forget to add the trips to the groomers.

There is no defined breed cut for this crossbreed. Most of them get a general groom - with, say, a #7 shear - with rounded semi-long hair left on the face. For a more terrier-like look, have a squarer trim around the face.

Owners should also make sure that the area inside their Schnoodle's ears does not become matted with fur and hot, this is a potential breeding ground for bacteria. Like Schnauzers and Poodles, the inside of Schnoodles' ears should be plucked regularly – either by you or your groomer.

We recommend at least once a month or more to get rid of unwanted hair and allow air to circulate, keeping them clean and healthy. Ask your groomer to pay particular attention to the inside of your dog's ears.

Ears and Tails

You often see Schnauzers with cropped ears, but Schnoodles' ears are left naturally uncropped.

They may have a long ear flap that lays closer to their head and hangs down – like a Poodle - or a shorter ear that stands upright at the base and folds over midway toward the front - like the uncropped ears of a Schnauzer.

Some Schnoodle breeders dock their puppies' tails - usually to the same length as a Schnauzer, which is 3 joints. More often Standard Schnoodles are seen with their tail left naturally long.

You can consult with the breeder about this. However, as tail docking is done to conform to breed standards and the Schnoodle is a crossbreed, there is little point in having the tail docked. One of the usual reasons for getting a crossbreed is because the new owners don't want a pedigree dog – so why try to imitate them?

In the UK it is now illegal to dock any dog's tail unless it is a working dog or hound.

Temperament

The Schnoodle temperament will vary from one dog to the next. However, there are some general characteristics that are common with many, if not most, Schnoodles.

Generally, Schnoodles are happy and playful by nature. Provided they get enough exercise, they are sociable, fun dogs and are becoming increasingly popular as they are usually hypoallergenic and make good companions for humans.

The Schnoodle is an intelligent crossbreed which often has high energy levels and loves playtime. They usually interact well with other dogs and are not normally aggressive by nature.

However, as with all puppies, early socialization with other dogs as well as a wide range of people is important. This teaches your dog to trust and be trusted.

The Schnoodle temperament mixes the intellect of the Poodle with the companionship and devotion of the Schnauzer. If treated well when young, Schnoodles make loving, loyal and amusing companions.

Being eager to please, they are relatively easy to train. Training should be done in short bursts and efforts should be made to keep it interesting, as it may not be easy to keep their concentration for a long period.

They love playing and distractions. Smaller Schnoodles may be happy as lapdogs, whereas the larger ones are friskier and will require more of your time and attention.

Like Schnauzers, Schnoodles like being with people and involved at the center of family life. They are not happy when left alone for long periods. If you are out at work all day, a Schnoodle may not be a suitable choice.

To learn more about Schnoodle character traits, read about the breeds they come from.

Poodles and Schnauzers

The Poodle is fun and full of character and so is the Schnauzer.

Both breeds are intelligent and good natured dogs that enjoy the company of people and respond well to training. Both breeds are also sociable and can be stubborn!

The Schnoodle temperament varies from one individual to another depending on which traits it has inherited from which parent. A good idea is to look up the characteristics of both the Schnauzer and the Poodle; your Schnoodle will be a mixture of these.

Here's a brief profile of the 2 breeds - **Poodles** are highly intelligent dogs. They are obedient and active - Standard Poodles tend to be calmer than the Miniatures and Toys. They are good with children and other pets and are often shy with strangers.

Schnauzers are devoted and loving. They generally make good watchdogs. The Standard Schnauzer is known as "the dog with the human brain". The Miniature is alert and playful, sometimes almost childlike. The Miniature can also be an attention-seeker and is often happiest when with humans.

The Giant is bold, loyal and often very protective of his owner. It is probably true to say that all Schnauzers enjoy being with humans and this is a trait often reported by Schnoodle owners.

Training

With the right education, Schnoodles are usually easy to train. They also LOVE being with people – they are not going to be happy and content if you're intending leaving them home alone all day.

These are intelligent, alert and sociable dogs. Boredom or loneliness has been known to cause them to become destructive or bark all the time if left for long periods.

By nature they are generally affectionate, devoted to the family and have a great sense of fun. They are also gaining a growing reputation in agility and fly ball competitions. Most of them love water.

Due to their intelligence, high trainability and love of humans, some Schnoodles are now being used as therapy dogs in hospitals, schools and nursing homes.

As far as exercise goes, they are very adaptable. Of course, a Giant Schnoodle will need a lot more exercise than a Toy. They are not usually known for their stamina, but more for their sense of fun and playfulness.

If you get a Giant Schnoodle and want to train him or her properly, make sure they get enough daily exercise, otherwise they may become bored and unresponsive.

Schnoodles do not have a long attention span. The trick is to keep them interested and stimulated. They love a challenge, so try and combine training with some fun.

Giant Schnoodles

The Giant Schnoodle could be just the dog for you if:

- You like big dogs
- You like Giant Schnauzers
- You like Standard Poodles
- You have allergies
- You don't like vacuuming
- You take lots of daily exercise

Big and Bubbly

The Giant Schnoodle is a cross between a Standard Poodle and a Giant Schnauzer and is definitely in the LARGE category of dog breeds.

A fully grown adult will weigh 65 to 80lbs - the average is around 70lbs. Like Giant Schnauzers, Schnoodle males will measure 25½ to 27½ at the withers (where the neck joins the back) and females will be a couple of inches shorter.

The Giant Schnoodle combines the characteristics, temperament and coat of both the Giant Schnauzer and the Standard Poodle. He or she will usually be black in color, as most Giant Schnauzers are black.

A Giant Schnoodle often looks similar to a Giant Schnauzer that is overdue a trip to the grooming parlor. The coat has a wavy, shaggy – and some would say more natural - appearance when untrimmed.

Both Poodles and Schnauzers are intelligent, loyal, love being with people and are generally easy to train, although some Giants do require a firm hand.

You could expect your dog to be similar to this. Because they are so intelligent, they can get easily bored so exercise and training is the answer.

They can be protective of the family - like the Giant Schnauzer - and are usually very good with children. If you ask Giant Schnoodle owners to describe their pets, three words keep cropping up -

- playful
- loving
- intelligent

"Playful" may sound quite cute, but if you have a frustrated 80lb pet bouncing round the house, it may not be quite so charming!

Exercise

To keep your Giant Schnoodle happy, you DEFINITELY need to give him plenty of daily exercise. Don't think about getting one unless you're prepared to take him out for at least an hour a day.

Many Schnoodles - especially the smaller ones - are fairly adaptable when it comes to exercise. But the **Giant** is a very large dog (the clue is in the name!) and will require regular daily exercise if he or she is not to become bored or frustrated.

If you like Schnoodles but are not keen on the idea of hours and hours of exercise every week, then a smaller Schnoodle from a Miniature Schnauzer or Miniature Poodle might well be more suitable for you.

Many big Schnoodles do well in agility classes and competitions. Their boisterous nature and active minds love the challenge of racing round that course!

Most giants are definitely water dogs, they also love the snow and do well in almost any climate.

Chapter 6. Schnauzer Colors

The Different Colors

This topic has caused much debate over the last few years. Whichever side of the fence you sit on, there is no denying that white and different colored Schnauzers, such as partis, are becoming increasingly popular.

We're really only talking about Miniature Schnauzers here, as Giants and Standards are virtually always **pepper and salt** (or salt and pepper) or **black**. We're also talking mainly about the USA where white and colored Schnauzers are growing in significant numbers. Today there are breeders producing Mini Schnauzer puppies in all sorts of colors, including:

- **White**
- **False white**
- **Wheaten**
- **Platinum**
- **Platinum silver**
- **Liver**
- **Liver pepper**
- **Liver tan**
- **Chocolate**
- **Chocolate phantom**

Then there's all the parti Miniature Schnauzers. "Parti" comes from the French word for *divided* and means two colors - like piebald or skewbald (pinto) for a horse. Generally all parti Schnauzers have patches of white on them. Here are some:

- **Black parti**
- **Salt and pepper parti**
- **Liver parti**
- **Liver tan parti**
- **Liver pepper parti**
- **Black and silver parti**

There are even more, but you get the picture - there are many different Schnauzer colors currently being bred.

The Great Debate

So why the great debate? If people love the look of a white, chocolate, parti or any other color of Schnauzer – and many do – what's the problem?

Here are both sides of the debate for you to make up your own mind.

On one side of the fence are the Kennel Clubs and breed societies. They only accept the Miniature Schnauzer colors of **pepper and salt, black** or **black and silver** in their shows.

On the other side are the breeders and owners of colored Schnauzers.

A white or colored Schnauzer CAN have registered American Kennel Club purebred papers (or a Kennel Club pedigree in the UK) if both parents were registered with the American Kennel Club.

But even if a colored Schnauzer has papers, he or she may not be entered into conformation shows under AKC or AMSC (American Miniature Schnauzer Club) rules. They can, however, compete in other events such as Agility, Canine Good Citizen, Obedience and Earth Dog Trials.

Colored Schnauzers can also be shown in rare breed classes organized by the IABCA (International All Breed Canine Association). In fact there are some highly successful white Schnauzer champions from these events.

Due to genetics it also means that if, for example, two white Schnauzers breed, **their puppies will not necessarily be white**. There may be some white puppies in the litter, but the colors of the puppies will depend on the genes of both parents.

There are quite complicated and scientific reasons (related to genetics and recessive and dominant genes) as to why there are so many possible Schnauzer colors.

For the technically minded, there's an interesting research article on dog colors by Professor Sheila Schmutz of the University of Saskatchewan at
http://homepage.usask.ca/~schmutz/dogcolors.html
For the rest of us lesser mortals, here's the discussion on Schnauzer colors in a nutshell –

Against: On one side of the debate are the Kennel Clubs and breed societies. They only accept the Miniature Schnauzer colors of pepper and salt, black or black and silver.

One of the main aims of the AKC and breed clubs - most notably the AMSC in the USA - is to try and protect the breed and keep it healthy by laying down a set of definitions or **breed standards**.

They also claim that the rarity of colored Schnauzers has led to high prices and puppy farms producing unusual colors to make a fast buck - without any regard for genetics or the future health of the Schnauzer puppy. This is what AKC Licensed Show Judge Marcia Feld has to say -

"This definition is what makes a Great Dane a Great Dane, a Poodle a Poodle, a Dalmatian a Dalmatian, etc.

"It is not up to each of us to decide that we would like to change each of these breeds because we like It or find it appealing. Adhering to these definitions is what retains the individuality of the breed. Breeding to the definition is the challenge for the breeder.

"A brown Dalmatian might be cute - but he is no longer a Dal; a tiny

Great Dane would be more easily kept - but he is no longer a Great Dane, and a hard coated Poodle would be easier to groom, but he wouldn't be a Poodle. And in that same light, a white (or colored) Schnauzer is no longer a Schnauzer; he Is disqualified because he does not meet the definition of that breed.

"The little white (or colored) Schnauzer is not 'bad'. He is simply not a good specimen of the breed. I would suggest that the person who likes a small white terrier seriously considers the purchase of a Westie. (By the way, the Westie wouldn't be a Westie if he were any color other than white!)"

A further argument against breeding different Schnauzer colors is that the parents are selected purely for the color of the resulting puppies, rather than taking other important issues - such as health and lineage – into account.

On its website, the Miniature Schnauzer Club of Canada provides a detailed answer to the question: Why Not White Miniature Schnauzers? You can read the full article here: www.mscc.ca/white.html

For: Breeders of colored Miniature Schnauzers claim that -

*One of the original colors in Germany, where Schnauzers originate, was "gelb" - literally yellow - but more commonly taken to mean white.

*In the early Miniature Schnauzer studbooks from Germany, the pepper and salt color was actually was recorded less often than other colors, including red, yellow and blue, which are no longer seen today.

*Black and silver Miniature Schnauzers were originally classified as pepper and salt and, by the time the mistake was realized, it was too late to take back all of their registration papers.

When breeders realized that this color bred "true", in other words black and silver parents could produce black and silver puppies, the color became accepted by the breed societies.

*For several years, the Canadian Kennel Club has been accepting the registrations of black Mini Schnauzers born to non-black parents. Why not accept white schnauzers, ask some owners.

*Colored Schnauzers - particularly white Schnauzers - occur naturally. They are part of nature and should be fully accepted.

*All Mini Schnauzers carry the genes to be pepper and salt, but if they inherit the white genes from both parents, the pepper and salt is covered or "hidden" and the dog's coat is white. (This does not mean that if you breed from two white parents all the puppies are guaranteed to be white.)

*Breeders of colored Schnauzers say that they are responding to a market created not by themselves, but by pet lovers who are looking for that "rarity factor".

*Many claim that their multicolored puppies ARE recognized by the AKC in the sense that they are bred from purebred parents registered with the AKC.

*A colored or white Schnauzer may be registered with the AKC as long as both parents are also AKC registered.

Our Advice

We are not here to tell you whether or not to get a white or colored Schnauzer, we're here to give you the independent facts and let you make up your own mind.

Some white and colored Schnauzer breeders are now well established, but there are others out there who are looking to make a fast profit from these "designer dogs" which sell for several hundred dollars each (see photo, left, of a puppy mill).

The argument against the whites and colors is all to do with breeding. The suggestion from those opposed to Schnauzer colors is that some breeders are breeding from inferior stock. This leads to health problems for the dog and vets, bills and heartache for the owner later on.

Our advice is this: If you do want a white or colored Schnauzer, **spend time finding the right breeder.** See Chapter 7 on **Puppies** and our top ten tips for selecting the right breeder. Your puppy's health will largely depend on the quality of her parentage.

Don't buy a puppy unseen on the internet. A puppy will become a part of your family for many, many years. Spend a little time before you take the plunge to find and then visit a recommended breeder.

If you pick a Schnauzer bred from good stock, you have more chance of having a happy, healthy puppy for many years to come – whatever the color.

The White Schnauzer

A white Schnauzer is virtually always a Miniature Schnauzer - there are almost no white Standards or Giants.

They are NOT albinos, as their skin has pigment. For those of you interested in the technical reason for whites, they are Schnauzers which carry the double recessive e/e gene.

Some people think that Miniature Schnauzers were bred with Westies (West Highland Terriers) to create the white color - that's not true either.

How White is White? If you buy a nice white car and are unlucky enough to have a bump in it – you will realize there's lots of different types of white paint when you come to do the repairs.... Well, white Schnauzers are a bit the same!

There are quite a few different types of white -

*A **no color** is a dog with a pure white coat. They are born with pink lips, pads and noses which later turn the base color. The usual base color of Schnauzers is black or brown.

 *A **true white** is also known as black-nosed white - no prizes for guessing why - see photo on right.

*A **white chocolate** is also called a brown-nosed white (the clue is in the name again!) This is genetically the same coat is the black-nosed white, only the base color is brown, not black.

*False white, platinum, platinum silver** and **wheaten** are all variations of white Schnauzers. False whites are born a tan color, but lighten to white when they are fully grown. Wheaten minis are more of a yellowy white (with a brown base color) and platinum miniatures have more of a silver colored coat with a black base color. The wheaten, platinum and platinum silver minis are true no-whites.

By the way, if you do buy a white Schnauzer with a light skin or nose, you may also need to buy sun cream. Like pale skinned horses and other animals, white Schnauzers can also suffer from sunburn. And just as with humans, a lighter skin does has less of the pigment melanin to protect against the sun's harmful rays.

Keep an eye out for reddish or inflamed skin. If your white Schnauzer does suffer from sunburn, there are a number of soothing natural products which can be applied to good effect.

White Schnauzer History

Miniature Schnauzers were first created by reducing the size of (or "breeding down") the Standard Schnauzer. German breeders did this by crossing the Standard with various other breeds of dog, such as the Affenpinscher.

The breeders wanted to produce a smaller version of the Standard Schnauzer in every way - same appearance, temperament and color. The Standard Schnauzer only has two colors, **salt & pepper** and the less common **black**.

In the late 19th century, breeders had far less understanding of genetics than they do now. By crossing the Standard with different colored dogs, they actually produced Miniature Schnauzers in a third color - **black and silver**.

These were originally classed as salt and pepper. Breeders then realized that the black and silver color bred 'true' when both parents had this color. By then it was too late to unregister all black and silver dogs, so this third color was created and accepted.

The same universal acceptance has not, however, been given to whites.

Yellow Schnauzers

Early German breed records record a "gelb" (German for yellow) color. This was introduced into the breed through German black champion Miniature Schnauzer Peter V Westerberg, born in 1902.

Peter was mated to a female called Gretel and they produced a "yellow" pup named Mucki VD Werneburg in 1914. (Nice to know Peter was still going strong and 'producing the goods' at 12 years old - which is the equivalent of 84 in human years!!)

Two years later, Mucki gave birth to German Champion Peterle VD Werneburg.

Almost every Miniature Schnauzer line researched in AKC records can be traced back to Peterle or his grandfather Peter V Wersterberg.

It's often said that **gelb** meant **white**, but there is no definite proof of this. But when hand stripped, most white Schnauzers with the proper wiry coats have a yellowish streak on their backs and heads.

It's thought this is why they were originally called "yellow" in German records.

Owning a White Schnauzer

Over the last decade or so, white Schnauzers have become ever-more popular, especially in the USA where there are lots of breeders and countless owners.

If you do decide to get a white one, they you will probably have to spend a little bit more time than other Schnauzer owners keeping your white white!

One of the most common problems is staining on the face. This usually shows as tear staining below the eyes or the beard turning a reddish-brown color as it becomes discolored with food.

There are several products on the market which help with this. One is called Angel Eyes. We cannot say if it works, as our Schnauzer Max is salt and pepper and we have never used it, but many readers of our website at www.max-the-schnauzer.com have reported that they use it.

Changing Color

Another worry for white Schnauzer owners is that sometimes their dog changes color! If you read above about the different colors of whites, you will see that some of them change color from puppyhood to adulthood – it's in their genes and perfectly normal.

Sometimes a white Schnauzer's nose will turn pink or will get pink spots. This can be perfectly natural or there may be a reason for it.

One of the most common causes of a fading nose is called "snow nose" or "winter nose," because the dog's nose will fade to pink or white during the winter months, and return to black once summer arrives.

A nose turning pink can also be a sign of an allergic reaction to plastic. If you think this may be the case, switch plastic dog bowls for metal ones.

It can also be a sign of illness in your dog, but will usually be accompanied by other signs.

If your dog's nose is changing color, but he is otherwise happy, healthy and active, he is probably fine. If his nose is blistering, or seems chapped or dry, consult a vet to see if there is a health reason behind it.

Some owners have found that by changing their dog food, their white Schnauzer's nose has gone darker. One method of helping to keep your dog's nose black is to add a natural sea kelp (seaweed) supplement to his food.

If your white Schnauzer's nose is pink, make sure that he is protected in summer by putting sunscreen on his nose. While the pigment protects black noses, pink ones may get sunburn.

The White Schnauzer in Events

Even though White Schnauzers may have AKC papers - if both of their parents are registered - they are not accepted in shows under AKC or AMSC (American Miniature Schnauzer Club) rules.

They CAN compete in other events such as Agility, Canine Good Citizen, Obedience and Earth dog trials. A white Schnauzer can also be shown in rare breed classes organized by the IABCA (International All Breed Canine Association).

Traditionally, all three types of Schnauzer do well in agility and similar classes. Not only are they good at them, but they love competing, dashing around and showing off! There is no reason why a white Schnauzer can't compete and enjoy the classes too.

White Schnauzers can tend to be a little larger than some Miniature Schnauzers and so would have the added advantage of size.

White Initiative

The White Miniature Schnauzer Initiative was established in 2006 in Germany for worldwide friends and breeders of whites.

Their aim is to provide a network for sharing ideas and information and to give breeders the opportunity expand the gene pool of the white Miniature Schnauzers internationally.

There is some talk of a similar organization being formed in the USA, but nothing has come of it so far.

Whatever the color of your Schnauzer, spend time to choose the right puppy for you and your family – and ENJOY!

Chapter 7. Puppies

Are You Ready?

Apart from having a baby, getting a puppy is one of the most important, demanding, expensive and life-enriching decisions you will ever make.

Just like babies, puppies will love you unconditionally. But there is a price to pay. In return for their loyalty and devotion, you have to fulfill your part of the bargain.

You have to be prepared to devote several hours a day to your new puppy, especially in the beginning. You have to feed, exercise and train them EVERY DAY as well as take care of their health and welfare. You have also to be prepared to part with hard cash for regular healthcare and even more money in veterinary bills if they fall ill.

If you are not prepared, or are unable, to devote this amount of time and money to a new arrival – or if you are out at work all day – then now might not be the right time for you to consider getting a puppy.

Schnauzers, more than most dogs, <u>love</u> being with people. To leave a Schnauzer, like the black Standard pictured, on his or her own all day long is not fair on this naturally sociable animal whose greatest wish is to be by your side.

Some Schnauzers may become badly behaved or even destructive if they are left on their own too long. Rescue homes are full of cute Schnauzer puppies which grew up and became too demanding for their owners.

If you are determined to have a dog even if you are out at work all day, then consider getting a breed which is not so emotionally dependent on humans and survives better without much attention.

Schnauzers don't. They want to be with you and in the thick of things. The same goes for Schnoodles; these are also extremely sociable dogs.

Schnauzers – particularly Miniature Schnauzers - may live to be well into their teens, so getting a puppy is definitely a long-term commitment. Before getting a puppy, ask yourself some questions:

Have I Got Enough Time?

In the first days after leaving his or her mother and littermates, a puppy will feel very lonely and maybe even a little afraid. You and your family will have

to spend time with your new arrival to make him or her feel safe and sound.

Ideally, for the first few days, you will be around all of the time to help your puppy settle into his new home and to start bonding with him. Book time off work in the beginning if necessary, but don't just get a puppy and leave him or her alone in the house a couple of days later.

After that, you will need to spend time house-training and then good behavior training. You'll have to make time every day (mo matter what the weather) for exercise. This is important, as many behavior problems are a result of a dog having too much energy and intelligence and not enough exercise.

You'll also have to feed your dog daily, in fact several times a day with a young puppy. He or she will also require regular grooming. Schnauzers don't shed hair, but they do need regular brushing to stop their hair from matting.

Don't forget you will also need to take time to visit the veterinary for regular healthcare visits, such as annual inoculations.

How Long Can I Leave Him For?

This is a question we get asked all of the time and one which causes a lot of debate among owners and prospective Schnauzer owners on our website.

Schnauzers have been described as "Velcro" dogs. In other words, they like to stick to their owners. These are very sociable dogs - sociable with humans, that is.

Some of them prefer to spend their time with humans rather than play with other dogs.

Having said that, Schnauzers often do well with other Schnauzers and many owners have more than one, so that they keep each other company while their beloved owner is away.

All dogs are pack animals. Their natural state is to be with others. Being alone is not natural for a dog, although many have to get used to it.

So how many hours can you leave a dog alone for?

Well, a useful guide comes from the rescue organizations. In the UK, they will not allow anybody to adopt a dog if they are intending leaving that dog alone for more than four or five hours a day.

Dogs left at home alone all day become bored and, in the case of Schnauzers and other breeds which are highly dependent on human company for their happiness, they may well become sad or depressed.

Some of it will, of course, depend on the character and temperament of your dog. But a lonely Schnauzer may display signs of unhappiness by making a mess in the house, being destructive, behaving badly when you return or barking all of the time. Others may adapt better to being left alone.

We do not recommend leaving a Schnauzer alone for longer than five hours maximum. Even Giant Schnauzers have smaller bladders than humans.

Forget the emotional side of it, how would you like to be left for eight hours without being able to visit the bathroom?

A puppy or fully-grown dog must NEVER be left shut in a crate all day.

It is OK to leave a puppy or adult dog in a crate if they are happy there, but the door should never be closed for more than two or three hours. A crate is a place where a puppy or adult should feel safe, not a prison.

Ask yourself why you want a dog – is it for selfish reasons or can you really offer a good home to a young puppy and then adult dog for the next decade and more? Would it be more sensible to wait until you are at home more?

Is My Home Suitable?

If you have decided to get a puppy, then choose one which will fit in with your living conditions.

If you live in a small apartment on the 10th floor of a high rise, then a Giant Schnauzer would not be a good choice. They love bounding around and need tons of exercise.

If your home is small, then of all three types of Schnauzer, a Miniature would be most suitable. Also, if you have less time to devote to your pet, a Mini would be a better choice than a Standard or Giant, which are both robust dogs and will certainly need more exercise.

Family and Neighbors

What about the other members of your family, do they all want the puppy as well? A puppy will grow into a dog which will become a part of your family for many years to come.

If you have children, they will, of course, be delighted. Make sure your puppy gets enough time to sleep – which is most of the time in the beginning.

He doesn't want to be constantly pestered by young children. Sleep is very important to puppies, just as it is for babies.

Remember that dogs are very hierarchical, in other words, there is pecking order. There is always one person that the puppy will regard as pack leader, usually the person who feeds him or who spends most time with him.

Puppies will often regard children as being on their own level, like a playmate, and so they might chase, jump and nip at them with sharp teeth. This is not aggression; this is normal play for puppies. Be sure to supervise play time and make sure the puppy doesn't get too boisterous.

What about the neighbors? You may think that it is none of their business, but if your dog is out in the yard or garden barking his head off all day, you can be sure they will have something to say about it.

One way to prevent this is to make sure your dog gets plenty daily exercise, so he'll be too tired to bark all day.

Older People

If you are older or have elderly relatives living with you, the good news is that Schnauzers are very sociable pets and great company. They love to be

involved with people and generally have gentle temperaments.

Bear in mind that larger dogs may be too difficult to handle for a senior citizen, especially if they haven't been trained not to jump up at people, or if they pull on the leash.

If you are older, make sure your energy levels are up to those of a young puppy. Ask yourself if you are fit enough to take your dog for at least one walk every day.

My father is in his early 80's but takes Max, our Mini, out for over an hour every day – even in the rain or snow. It's good for him and it's good for Max, helping to keep both of them fit and socialized! They get fresh air, exercise and the chance to communicate with other dog walkers and their pets.

Some smaller dogs survive perfectly well by only going put into the garden or yard, but there is really no substitute in a dog's mind for a good walk away from the home at least once a day – or more with a larger dog. Just get out the leash and see how your dog reacts, you'll soon see if he'd rather go for a walk or stay in the house or yard.

Many older people get a puppy after losing a loved one (either a husband, wife or previous much-loved dog). A dog gives them something to care for and love, as well as a constant companion. Lots of people find that Miniature Schnauzers in particular make excellent companion dogs.

 It goes without saying that they require less space and less exercise than a Standard or a Giant Schnauzer and so are more suitable for elderly people.

Single People

Many single adults own dogs, but if you live alone, having a puppy will require a lot of dedication from you.

There will be nobody to share the tasks of daily exercise, grooming and training, so taking on a dog requires a huge commitment and a lot of your time if the dog is to have a decent life.

If you are out of the house all day as well, it is not really fair to get a puppy, or even an adult dog. Left alone all day, they will feel isolated and sad.

However, if you work from home or close to home or are at home all day and you can spend considerable time with the puppy every day, then great! All three types of Schnauzers make wonderful companions.

Deciding on which type of Schnauzer will depend on factors such as the time you have to give to a dog, the size of your house and yard and your energy levels. The bigger the dog, the more exercise and space they will need.

Other Pets

If you already have other pets in your household, spend time to introduce them to each other.

If you have other dogs, supervised sessions from an early age will help the dogs to get along and chances are, they will become the best of friends.

Cats may be more of a problem; most Schnauzers' natural instinct is to chase a cat. But again, supervised sessions are the answer.

A Schnauzer's instinct is usually to chase small furry mammals and birds. They were originally bred as ratters and this trait is still strong in some of them. A lot will depend on the temperament of the individual dog and at what age he is introduced to the other animal(s).

Introduce other pets to your puppy at the earliest possible age. If a cat is already in the household, the pup may tease the cat, but in the end will probably learn to live with it.

It is much harder to get an adult Schnauzer to get used to cats or other animals in the house, especially if he has been used to chasing cats, squirrels, birds and generally any critter smaller than himself on his daily walks.

Until you know that the animals will get on together, do not leave them unsupervised. For a dog to get on with a cat, you are asking him to forget his natural instincts and to respond to your training. But it can be done successfully with many Schnauzers.

There are, however, limits. Don't expect your Schnauzer to become best friends with your pet bunny!

If you are still determined to have a Schnauzer even when you are out all day, or for several hours at a time, here are some useful points:

Top Ten Tips For Working Schnauzer Owners

1. Either come home during your lunch break to let your dog out or employ a dog walker (or neighbor) to take him out for a walk in the middle of the day.

2. Do you know anybody you could leave your dog with during the day? Consider leaving the dog with a relative or elderly neighbor who would welcome the companionship of a dog without the full responsibility of ownership.

3. Take him for as long a walk as possible before you go to work – even if this means getting up at the crack of dawn – and walk him as soon as you get home.

Exercise generates serotonin in the brain and has a calming effect. A dog that has had a good run for half an hour before you leave home will be less anxious and more ready for a good nap.

4. Leave him in a place of his own where he feels comfortable. If you use a crate, leave the door open, otherwise his favorite dog bed or basket.

 If possible, leave him in a room with a view of the outside world. This will be more interesting for him than staring at four blank walls.

5. Make sure that there are no cold draughts in the place where you leave him – or that it does not get too hot during the day.

6. Leave toys available for him to play with. Stuff a Kong toy with his favorite treats and this will keep him occupied for a while. Choose the right size of Kong for your dog and then put a treat inside. You can even smear the inside with peanut butter or another treat to keep your dog occupied for longer.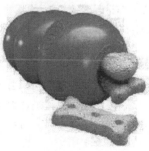

7. Remove his food and put it down at specific meal times. If the food is there all day, he may become a fussy eater or "punish" you for leaving him alone by refusing to eat.

Make sure he has access to water at all times. Dogs **cannot cool down by sweating;** they do not have many sweat glands (which is why they pant, but this is much less efficient than perspiring) and can die without sufficient water.

8. Have you got a fenced-in garden or yard? Can you fit a dog flap to one of your doors to allow your Schnauzer to go in and out of the house during the day? You can buy door flaps which respond to an electronic signal on your dog's collar so that only he is allowed in and out of the house.

If you do use a dog flap, here's a couple of warnings: firstly make sure that your garden is dog-proof so he can't wander off. Secondly, we would not advise one if the garden or yard is visible from the sidewalk. Schnauzers are very handsome dogs and there's always a risk of them being dognapped

9. Consider leaving a radio or TV on very softly in the background. The "white noise" can have a soothing effect on some pets.

 If you do this, select your channel carefully – try and avoid one with lots of bangs and crashes or heavy metal music!

10. Stick to the same routine before you leave your dog home alone. This will help your dog feel secure. Before you go to work, get into a daily habit for getting yourself ready, then feeding and exercising your Schnauzer. Dogs love routine.

You could consider getting two Schnauzers to keep each other company while you are out. But remember, this will involve even more of your time

and twice the expense.

And finally, when you come home your Schnauzer will be ecstatically pleased to see you. Greet him normally, but try not to go overboard by making too much of a fuss of him as soon as you walk through the door.

Give him a pat and a stroke then take off your coat and do a few other things before turning your attention back to your Schnauzer.

Lavishing your Schnauzer with too much attention the second you walk through the door may encourage separation anxiety or demanding behavior.

Puppy Stages

It is important to understand how a puppy develops into a fully grown dog. This knowledge will help you to be a good owner to your puppy.

The first few months and weeks of a puppy's life will have an effect on his behavior and temperament for the rest of his life. This Puppy Schedule will help you to understand the early stages:

Birth to seven weeks	A puppy needs sleep, food and warmth. He needs his mother for security and discipline and littermates for learning and socialization. The puppy learns to function within a pack and learns the pack order of dominance. He begins to become aware of his environment. During this period, puppies should be left with their mother.
Eight to twelve weeks	A puppy should not leave his mother before eight weeks. At this age the brain is fully developed and he now needs socializing with the outside world. He needs to change from being part of a canine pack to being part of a human pack. This period is a fear period for the puppy, avoid causing him fright and pain.
13 to 16 weeks	Training and formal obedience should begin. He needs socializing with other humans, places and situations. This period will pass easily if you remember that this is a puppy's change to adolescence. Be firm and fair. His flight instinct may be prominent. Avoid being too strict or to soft with him during this time and praise his good behavior.
Four to eight months	Another fear period for a puppy is between 7 to 8 months of age. It passes quickly, but be cautious of fright or pain which may leave the puppy traumatized. The puppy reaches sexual maturity and dominant traits are established. Your dog should now understand the commands 'sit', 'down', 'come' and 'stay'.

Plan Ahead

Puppies usually leave the litter for their new homes when they are eight weeks or older. Toy breeds may stay with the mother for up to 12 weeks. Like all dogs, Schnauzer puppies learn the rules of the pack from their mothers. Most continue teaching their pups the correct manners and do's and don'ts until they are around eight weeks old.

Breeders who allow their pups to leave before this time may be more interested in a quick buck than a long-term puppy placement.

Top breeders often have waiting lists. If you want a well-bred Schnauzer puppy, it pays to plan ahead.

If you have decided you are definitely going to have a puppy, and you have decided on which type of Schnauzer to get, then the next step is one of the most important decisions you will make: choosing the right breeder.

Like humans, your Schnauzer puppy will be a product of his or her parents and will inherit many of their characteristics. How healthy your puppy will be now and throughout its life will to a large extent depend on the health and genes of its parents.

It is essential that you select a good, responsible breeder. They will have checked out the temperament and health records of the parents and will only breed from suitable stock.

There are many Schnauzer and Schnoodle breeders on the internet - especially those breeding Miniature Schnauzers - and many are trustworthy and conscientious.

However, with the cost of a purebred Schnauzer puppy rising to several $100s or £100s, some unscrupulous breeders have been tempted by the money. You wouldn't order a best friend without screening them first, so why buy an unseen puppy?

At the very minimum you MUST visit the breeder personally. We'd also recommend following our Top Ten Tips to help you make the right decision.

Buying a poorly-bred puppy may save you a few bucks (or quid in the UK) in the short term - but could cost you a fortune in extra veterinary bills or dog training lessons in the long run.

The Schnauzer rescue groups know only too well the dangers of buying a poorly-bred dog. Many years of problems – either health or behavior – can follow, causing pain and distress for both dog and owner. All rescue groups strongly recommend taking the time to find a good breeder.

There are lots of really good Miniature, Standard and Giant Schnauzer breeders who have the right puppy for you - but how do you find them?

Everybody knows you should get your puppy from "a good breeder." But how can you tell the good guys from the bad guys? A good starting point if you are looking for a pedigree Schnauzer is the Kennel Club in your country. Each Kennel Club normally has a list of approved breeders and you can find details of ones in your area on their websites.

If that's not an option and you've never bought a Schnauzer puppy before, how do you avoid buying one from a "backstreet breeder" or puppy mill? These are people who just breed puppies for profit and sell them to the first person who turns up with the cash.   Unhappily, this can end in heartbreak for a family months or years later when their puppy develops health or temperament problems due to poor breeding.

Good Schnauzer breeders will only breed from dogs which have been carefully selected for size, temperament, health and lineage. There are plenty out there - it's just a question of finding one. The good news is that there are signs that can help the savvy buyer spot a good breeder.

Top Ten Tips for Selecting a Good Breeder

1. They keep the dogs in the home and as part of the family - not outside in kennel runs. You should also make sure the area where the puppies are kept is clean.

2. They have Schnauzers which appear happy and healthy. The dogs are excited to meet new people, and don't shy away from visitors.

3. A good dog breeder will encourage you to spend time with the puppy's parents - or at least the pup's mother - when you visit. They want your entire family to meet the puppy and are happy for you to make more than one visit.

4. They breed only one or two types of dogs, maybe Miniature Schnauzers and Giants - or Miniature Schnauzers and another small dog breed, and they are very familiar with the "breed standards".

See our information on **Breed Standards** in Chapters 1, 2 and 3 to find out exactly how all three types of Schnauzer should look if they are purebred.

5. All purebreds and pedigrees have some potential genetic weaknesses. A good breeder should explain these and should have documents to prove that both parents are free from any genetic defects.

For example, a small number of pedigree Miniature and Giant Schnauzers in the UK have suffered with hereditary cataracts. Veterinarians and breeders are working on ridding the breeds of this problem. Eye test certificates are available for healthy breeding dogs.

6. Responsible Miniature Schnauzer breeders should provide you with a written contract and health guarantee and allow you plenty of time to read it. They will also show you records of the puppy's veterinary visits and explain what vaccinations your new puppy will need.

7. They give you guidance on caring and training for your puppy and are available for your assistance after you take your puppy home.

8. They feed their dogs high quality 'premium' dog food.

9. They don't always have puppies available, but will keep a list of interested people for the next available litter.

10. And finally... good Schnauzer breeders will provide references of other families who have bought their puppies. Make sure you call at least one. A good breeder will also agree to take a puppy back within a certain time frame if it does not work out for you, or if there is a health problem.

Happy, healthy puppies are what everybody wants. Taking the time now to find a responsible Schnauzer breeder is time well spent.

It could save you a lot of time, money and worry in the future and help to ensure that you and your chosen puppy are happy together for many years.

Schnauzer Litter Size

Depending on which type of Schnauzer you are getting, litter size will vary. Miniature Schnauzers will generally have a litter of 3 to 5 or 6 puppies.

Standard Schnauzers have larger litters with six to 10 puppies, while the Giant will generally have five to eight puppies.

A good breeder with many years' experience may well help you decide which Schnauzer puppy will grow up to be best for you and your family.

He or she will observe the pups several times a day for the first few weeks of their lives and will have a good idea of each puppy's character and temperament.

You do, however, want to make sure that the puppy you choose is fit and healthy.

Twelve Top Tips for Selecting a Healthy Puppy

1. Schnauzers are sturdy dogs and your puppy should have a well-fed appearance. They should NOT, however, have a distended abdomen (pot belly) as this can be a sign of worms.

2. The ideal Schnauzer puppy should not be too thin either. You should not be able to see his ribs.

3. The puppy's eyes should be bright and clear with no mucus or discharge.

4. His nose should be cool, damp and clean with no discharge.

5. The pup's ears should also be clean and again there should be no discharge or dirty build-up.

6. His gums should be clean and a healthy pink color.

7. Check the puppy's bottom to make sure it's clean and there are no signs of diarrhea.

8. A Schnauzer's coat should be clean and shiny with no signs of ticks or fleas. Red or irritated skin or bald spots could be a sign of infestation or a skin condition

9. The puppy should breathe normally with no coughing or wheezing.

10. When the puppy is distracted, clap or make a noise behind him (not too loud) to make sure he's not deaf.

11. Choose a puppy that is solid in build and moves well without any sign of injury or lameness.

12. Finally, ask to see veterinarian records to make sure your puppy has been wormed and has had his first injections.

If you are unlucky enough to have a health problem with your puppy in the first few months, a reputable breeder will allow you to return the pup.

Also, if you get the Schnauzer puppy home and things don't work out for whatever reason, good breeders should also take the puppy back. Make sure this is the case before you commit.

Choosing the Right Temperament

If you've decided that a Schnauzer is the ideal dog for you, then here are two important points to bear in mind at the outset:

- Find a responsible breeder with a good reputation. We can't stress that enough.

- Take your time. Choosing a puppy which will share your home and your life for the next 10 to 15 years is an important decision. Don't rush it.

You've picked a Schnauzer because of their size and temperament. You (like us) might also have allergies.

Presumably you're planning on spending a lot of time with your new puppy, as all Schnauzers are "people" dogs and love being with humans. If you've chosen a Giant Schnauzer, then be sure you're prepared for lots of daily exercise as well.

Individuals

The next thing to remember is that while the breeds share many characteristics and temperament traits, Schnauzer puppies also have their own individual characters, just like humans.

Are you fit and active - do you want a lively, energetic dog? Or are you older and maybe live alone? If so, a smaller, more placid Schnauzer will suit you better, maybe an older dog which needs re-homing.

If possible, visit the puppy at the breeder's more than once. This will give you an idea of the puppy's character in comparison to his or her littermates.

Some Schnauzer puppies will run up to greet you, pull at your shoelaces and playfully bite your fingers. Others will be more content to stay in the basket sleeping. Watch their behavior and energy levels. Which puppy will be suitable?

Submissive or Dominant?

A submissive dog will by nature be more passive, less energetic and also possibly easier to train.

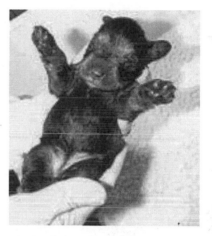

A dominant dog will usually be more energetic and livelier. They may also need a firmer hand when training or socializing with other dogs.

There is no good or bad, it's a question of which type of character will best suit you and your lifestyle.

Here are a couple of tests to try at the breeder's to see if your puppy has a submissive or dominant personality:

> * Roll the Schnauzer puppy gently on to his or her back in the crook of your arm (or on the floor). Then rest a hand on the pup's chest and look into his eyes for a few seconds. If he immediately struggles to get free, he is considered to be dominant. A puppy that doesn't struggle but is happy to stay on his or her back has a more submissive character.

> * A similar test is the suspension test. Gently lift the puppy at arm's length under the armpits for a few seconds while allowing his hind legs to dangle free. A dominant pup will kick and struggle to get free. A puppy that is happy to remain dangling is more submissive.

Useful Tips

Here are some other useful signs to look out for –

* Watch how he interacts with other Schnauzer puppies in the litter. Does he try and dominate them, does he walk away from them or is he happy to play with his littermates?

This may give you an idea of how easy it will be to socialize him with other dogs.

* After having contact with the puppy, does he want to follow you or walk away from you? Not following may mean he has a more independent nature.

* If you throw something for the puppy is he happy to retrieve it for you or does he ignore it?

This may measure their willingness to work with humans.

* If you drop a bunch of keys behind the Schnauzer puppy, does he act normally or does he flinch and jump away? The latter may be an indication of a timid or nervous disposition.

(Our Mini Schnauzer Max is frightened of loud noises but is lively and playful in other ways. This is not uncommon with Miniatures.) Not reacting could also be a sign of deafness.

Decide which type of temperament would fit in with you or your family and the rest is up to you!

A Schnauzer that has constant positive interactions with people and other animals during the first three to four months of life will be a more stable, happier dog.

In contrast, a puppy plucked from its family and isolated at home alone for weeks on end will be less happy, less socialized and may well have behavior problems later on.

Puppies are like children. Being properly raised contributes to their confidence, sociability, stability and intellectual development.

The bottom line is that a pup raised in a warm, loving environment with people is likely to be more tolerant and accepting and less likely to develop behavior problems.

For those of you who want to take a scientific approach to choosing the right puppy, we are including the full *Volhard Puppy Aptitude Test.*

This test has been developed by the highly respected Wendy and Jack Volhard who have built up an international reputation over the last 30 years for their invaluable contribution to dog training, health and nutrition.

They have written eight books and the Volhard PAT is regarded as the premier method for evaluating the nature of young puppies.

Jack and Wendy have also written the excellent Dog Training for Dummies book. Visit their website at www.volhard.com for details of their upcoming Dog Training Camps, as well as their training and nutrition groups.

The Volhard Puppy Aptitude Test

Here are the ground rules for performing the test:

- The testing is done in a location unfamiliar to the puppies. This does not mean they have to taken away from home. A 10-foot square area is perfectly adequate, such as a room in the house where the puppies have not been.
- The puppies are tested one at a time.
- There are no other dogs or people, except the scorer and the tester, in the testing area
- The puppies do not know the tester.
- The scorer is a disinterested third party and not the person interested in selling you a puppy.
- The scorer is unobtrusive and positions him or herself so he or she can observe the puppies' responses without having to move.
- The puppies are tested before they are fed.
- The puppies are tested when they are at their liveliest.
- Do not try to test a puppy that is not feeling well.
- Puppies should not be tested the day of or the day after being vaccinated.
- Only the first response counts!

Top Tip: During the test, watch the puppy's tail. It will make a difference in the scoring whether the tail is up or down.

The tests are simple to perform and anyone with some common sense can do them. You can, however, elicit the help of someone who has tested puppies before and knows what they are doing.

----

1. Social attraction - the owner or caretaker of the puppies places it in the test area about four feet from the tester and then leaves the test area. The tester kneels down and coaxes the puppy to come to him or her by encouragingly and gently clapping hands and calling. The tester must coax the puppy in the opposite direction from where it entered the test area. Hint: Lean backward, sitting on your heels instead of leaning forward toward the puppy. Keep your hands close to your body encouraging the puppy to come to you instead of trying to reach for the puppy.
2. Following - the tester stands up and slowly walks away encouraging the puppy to follow. Hint: Make sure the puppy sees you walk away and get the puppy to focus on you by lightly clapping your hands and using verbal encouragement to get the puppy to follow you. Do not lean over the puppy.
3. Restraint - the tester crouches down and gently rolls the puppy on its back and holds it on its back for 30 seconds. Hint: Hold the puppy down without applying too much pressure. The object is not to keep it on its back but to test its response to being placed in that position.
4. Social Dominance - let the puppy stand up or sit and gently stroke it from the head to the back while you crouch beside it. See if it will lick your face, an indication of a forgiving nature. Continue stroking until you see a behavior you can score. Hint: When you crouch next to the puppy avoid leaning or hovering over the puppy. Have the puppy at your side with both of you facing in the same direction.

    Top Tip: During testing maintain a positive, upbeat and friendly attitude toward the puppies. Try to get each puppy to interact with you to bring out the best in him or her. Make the test a pleasant experience for the puppy.

5. Elevation Dominance - the tester cradles the puppy with both hands, supporting the puppy under its chest and gently lifts it two feet off the ground and holds it there for 30 seconds.
6. Retrieving - the tester crouches beside the puppy and attracts its attention with a crumpled up piece of paper. When the puppy shows some interest, the tester throws the paper no more than four feet in front of the puppy encouraging it to retrieve the paper.

7. Touch Sensitivity - the tester locates the webbing of one the puppy's front paws and presses it lightly between his index finger and thumb. The tester gradually increases pressure while counting to ten and stops when the puppy pulls away or shows signs of discomfort.
8. Sound Sensitivity - the puppy is placed in the center of the testing area and an assistant stationed at the perimeter makes a sharp noise, such as banging a metal spoon on the bottom of a metal pan.
9. Sight Sensitivity - the puppy is placed in the center of the testing area. The tester ties a string around a bath towel and jerks it across the floor, two feet away from the puppy.
10.   Stability - an umbrella is opened about five feet from the puppy and gently placed on the ground.

During the testing make a note of the heart rate of the pup, this is an indication of how it deals with stress, as well as its energy level.

Puppies come with high, medium or low energy levels. You have to decide for yourself, which suits your life style. Dogs with high energy levels need a great deal of exercise, and will get into mischief if this energy is not channeled into the right direction.

Finally, look at the overall structure of the puppy. You see what you get at 49 days age (seven weeks). If the pup has strong and straight front and back legs, with all four feet pointing in the same direction, it will grow up that way, provided you give it the proper diet and environment in which to grow. If you notice something out of the ordinary at this age, it will stay with puppy for the rest of its life. He will not grow out of it.

Scoring the Results
Following are the responses you will see and the score assigned to each particular response. You will see some variations and will have to make a judgment on what score to give them –

Test	Response	Score
SOCIAL ATTRACTION	Came readily, tail up, jumped, bit at hands	1
	Came readily, tail up, pawed, licked at hands	2
	Came readily, tail up	3
	Came readily, tail down	4
	Came hesitantly, tail down	5

	Didn't come at all	6
FOLLOWING	Followed readily, tail up, got underfoot, bit at feet	1
	Followed readily, tail up, got underfoot	2
	Followed readily, tail up	3
	Followed readily, tail down	4
	Followed hesitantly, tail down	5
	Did not follow or went away	6
RESTRAINT	Struggled fiercely, flailed, bit	1
	Struggled fiercely, flailed	2
	Settled, struggled, settled with some eye contact	3
	Struggled, then settled	4
	No struggle	5
	No struggle, strained to avoid eye contact	6
SOCIAL DOMINANCE	Jumped, pawed, bit, growled	1
	Jumped, pawed	2
	Cuddled up to tester and tried to lick face	3
	Squirmed, licked at hands	4
	Rolled over, licked at hands	5
	Went away and stayed away	6
ELEVATION DOMINANCE	Struggled fiercely, tried to bite	1
	Struggled fiercely	2
	Struggled, settled, struggled, settled	3
	No struggle, relaxed	4
	No struggle, body stiff	5
	No struggle, froze	6
RETRIEVING	Chased object, picked it up and ran away	1
	Chased object, stood over it and did not return	2
	Chased object, picked it up and returned with it to tester	3
	Chased object and returned without it to	4

	tester	
	Started to chase object, lost interest	5
	Does not chase object	6
TOUCH SENSITIVITY	8-10 count before response	1
	6-8 count before response	2
	5-6 count before response	3
	3-5 count before response	4
	2-3 count before response	5
	1-2 count before response	6
SOUND SENSITIVITY	Listened, located sound and ran toward it barking	1
	Listened, located sound and walked slowly toward it	2
	Listened, located sound and showed curiosity	3
	Listened and located sound	4
	Cringed, backed off and hid behind tester 5	5
	Ignored sound and showed no curiosity	6
SIGHT SENSITIVITY	Looked, attacked and bit object	1
	Looked and put feet on object and put mouth on it	2
	Looked with curiosity and attempted to investigate, tail up	3
	Looked with curiosity, tail down	4
	Ran away or hid behind tester	5
	Hid behind tester	6
STABILITY	Looked and ran to the umbrella, mouthing or biting it	1
	Looked and walked to the umbrella, smelling it cautiously	2
	Looked and went to investigate	3
	Sat and looked, but did not move toward the umbrella	4
	Showed little or no interest	5
	Ran away from the umbrella	6

The scores are interpreted as follows:

Mostly 1's
Strong desire to be pack leader and is not shy about bucking for a promotion
Has a predisposition to be aggressive to people and other dogs and will bite
Should only be placed into a very experienced home where the dog will be trained and worked on a regular basis

Top Tip: Stay away from the puppy with a lot of 1's or 2's. It has lots of leadership aspirations and may be difficult to manage. This puppy needs an experienced home. Not good with children.

Mostly 2's
Also has leadership aspirations
May be hard to manage and has the capacity to bite
Has lots of self-confidence
Should not be placed into an inexperienced home
Too unruly to be good with children and elderly people, or other animals
Needs strict schedule, loads of exercise and lots of training
Has the potential to be a great show dog with someone who understands dog behavior

Mostly 3's
Can be a high-energy dog and may need lots of exercise
Good with people and other animals
Can be a bit of a handful to live with
Needs training, does very well at it and learns quickly
Great dog for second time owner.

Mostly 4's
The kind of dog that makes the perfect pet
Best choice for the first time owner.
Rarely will buck for a promotion in the family
Easy to train, and rather quiet.
Good with elderly people, children, although may need protection from the children
Choose this pup, take it to obedience classes, and you'll be the star, without having to do too much work!

Top Tip: The puppy with mostly 3's and 4's can be quite a handful, but should be good with children and does well with training. Energy needs to be dispersed with plenty of exercise.

Mostly 5's
Fearful, shy and needs special handling
Will run away at the slightest stress in its life
Strange people, strange places, different floor or surfaces may upset it

Often afraid of loud noises and terrified of thunder storms. When you greet it upon your return, may submissively urinate. Needs a very special home where the environment doesn't change too much and where there are no children. Best for a quiet, elderly couple
If cornered and cannot get away, has a tendency to bite

Top Tip: Avoid the puppy with several 6's. It is so independent it doesn't need you or anyone. He is his own person and unlikely to bond to you.

Mostly 6's
So independent that he doesn't need you or other people
Doesn't care if he is trained or not - he is his own person Unlikely to bond to you, since he doesn't need you.
A great guard dog for gas stations!
Do not take this puppy and think you can change him into a lovable bundle - you can't, so leave well enough alone.

Interpreting the Scores
Few puppies will test with all 2's or all 3's, - there'll be a mixture of scores.

For that first time, wonderfully easy to train, potential star, look for a puppy that scores with mostly 4's and 3's. Don't worry about the score on Touch Sensitivity - you can compensate for that with the right training equipment.

It's hard not to become emotional when picking a puppy - they are all so cute, soft and cuddly. Remind yourself that this dog is going to be with you for eight to 16 years. Don't hesitate to step back a little to contemplate your decision. Sleep on it and review it in the light of day.

Avoid the puppy with a score of 1 on the Restraint and Elevation tests. This puppy will be too much for the first-time owner.

It's a lot more fun to have a good dog, one that is easy to train, one you can live with and one you can be proud of, than one that is a constant struggle.

Getting a Dog From a Shelter
Don't overlook an Animal Shelter as a source for a good dog. Not all dogs wind up in a shelter because they are bad. After that cute puppy stage, when the dog grows up, it may become too much for its owner. Or, there has been a change in the owner's circumstances forcing him or her into having to give up the dog.

Most of the time these dogs are housetrained and already have some training. If the dog has been properly socialized to people, it will be able to adapt to a new environment. Bonding may take a little longer, but once accomplished, results in a devoted companion.

A Dog or a Bitch?

When you have decided to get a Schnauzer puppy and know how to find a good breeder, the next decision is whether to get a male or female.

The differences within the sexes are greater than the differences between the sexes. In other words, you can get an aggressive female and a submissive male, or vice versa.

There are, however, some general traits which are more common with one sex or another.

Male Schnauzers– usually just referred to as "dogs" – are more likely to be more aggressive towards other males. Most males will not deliberately start a fight, but an unneutered one is more likely to defend whatever he regards as his territory – and this may include you!

An entire (un-neutered) male is also more likely to go wandering off on the scent of a female. This happened with our Miniature Schnauzer Max several times. On walks he sniffed out the trail of a bitch "on heat" (the time on her menstrual cycle when she is ready for mating). Although normally fairly obedient, our calls for him to come back fell on deaf ears – Max had other things on his mind - and disappeared over the fields.

We were lucky, Max was brought back home by strangers. After the third time, we had him neutered and he has never run off since. According to our vet, Max is much more content now, as he is not thinking about sex all of the time!

Female Schnauzers, or bitches, tend to be less aggressive towards other dogs, except if they are raising puppies. You might want to consider a female if you have young children and are looking for a family companion. A bitch may be more tolerant toward young creatures, including your children.

Bear in mind that when you select your puppy, you should also be looking out for the right temperament as well as the right sex.

Unless you bought your Schnauzer specifically for showing or breeding, it is recommended you have your dog neutered, or spayed if she is a female. If you plan to have two or more Schnauzers living together, this is even more highly recommended.

It is generally thought that spaying and neutering may also reduce the risk of certain types of cancer and lead to a longer lifespan in some cases. But there are always two sides to every argument, see Chapter 8 on **The Birds and The Bees.**

Puppy Checklist

Here's a list of things you ought to think about getting before bringing your puppy home:

- A dog bed or basket
- Bedding – old towels or a blanket which can easily be washed
- If possible, a towel or piece of cloth which has been rubbed on the puppy's mother to put in his bed
- Collar and leash
- Identification tag for the puppy's collar
- Food and water bowls
- A puppy coat if you live in a cold climate
- Lots of newspapers for house training
- Poop bags
- Possibly a crate
- Some old towels for cleaning your puppy and covering the crate if you decide to use one.
- Puppy food – find out what the breeder is feeding
- Puppy treats
- Toys and chews suitable for puppies
- PLENTY OF TIME!

Later on you'll also need a larger collar, a longer leash, grooming brushes, dog shampoo and flea and worming products and maybe other items such as a harness or a travel crate.

Vaccinations

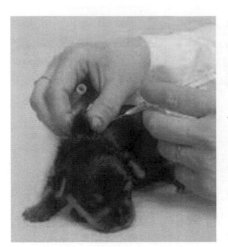

When he arrives home, you need to make an appointment with your veterinarian to complete your puppy's vaccinations if he hasn't already had them all. All puppies need these shots.

The usual schedule is for the pup to have his first vaccination at or after seven weeks old. This will protect him from a number of diseases in one shot. These may include Canine Parvovirus (Parvo), Distemper, Infectious Canine Hepatitis (Adenvirus), Leptospirosis and Kennel Cough. In the USA, puppies may also need vaccinating separately against Rabies and Lyme Disease.

Your puppy will need a second and maybe a third vaccination a few weeks later to complete his immunity. Consult your vet to find out exactly what injections are needed for the area you live in.

Diseases such as Parvo and Kennel Cough are highly contagious and you should not let your puppy mix with other dogs - unless they are your own and have already been vaccinated - until he has completed his vaccinations, otherwise he will not be fully immunized. You also shouldn't take him to places where unvaccinated dogs might have been, like the park.

Your dog will need a booster injection every year of his life. Your vet should give you a record card or send you a reminder, but it's a good idea to keep a note of the date in your diary.

Vaccinations are generally quite safe and side effects are uncommon. If your puppy is unlucky enough to be one of the few that does have an adverse reaction to his shots, here are the signs to look out for:

Mild reaction – sleepiness, irritability and not wanting to be touched, sore or a small lump at the place where he was injected, nasal discharge or sneezing, puffy face and ears.

Severe reaction – anaphylactic shock. A sudden and quick reaction, usually before leaving the vet's, which causes breathing difficulties. Other symptoms may include vomiting, diarrhea, staggering and seizures. This type of reaction is extremely rare. There is a far, far greater risk of your puppy being ill and spreading disease if he does not have the vaccinations.

Bringing a New Puppy Home

First of all, make sure that you have puppy-proofed your home!

Remember that most puppies are nosy little chewing machines and so remove anything breakable within the puppy's reach.

You may also want to remove your precious oriental rugs and keep the puppy off your expensive carpets until he is fully house-trained and has stopped chewing everything in sight.

Designate a place within your home which will be the puppy's area. An area with a wooden or tiled floor would be a good start until he or she is house-trained.

Make sure that the area is warm enough - but not too warm. It should not take a puppy too long to get used to his new surroundings, but the first few days will be very traumatic for him and he will probably whine a lot.

Imagine a small child being taken away from his or her mother, and that is how your Schnauzer puppy will feel.

If you have a garden or a yard that you intend letting your puppy roam in, make sure that every little gap has been plugged. You'd be amazed at the tiny holes they can escape through.

In order for your puppy to grow into a well-adjusted dog, he has to feel comfortable and relaxed in his new surroundings.

He is leaving the warmth and protection of his mother and littermates and so for the first few days at least, your puppy will feel very sad. It is important to make the transition from the birth home to your home as easy as possible.

His life is in your hands. How you react and interact with him in the first few days and weeks will shape your relationship for the years ahead.

The First Few Days

This can be a very stressful time for a tiny Schnauzer puppy and a worrying time for new owners. Your puppy has just been taken away from her mother and brothers and sisters and is feeling very sorry for herself.

Our website receives many emails from worried new Schnauzer owners. Here are some of the most common concerns:

* My puppy sleeps all the time, is this normal?

* My puppy won't stop crying or whining.

* My puppy is shivering.

* My puppy won't eat.

* My puppy is very timid.

* My puppy follows me everywhere, she won't let me out of her sight.

What is Normal?

If you work and will be out of the house for most of the day, then get your puppy on a Friday or Saturday so she has at least a couple of days to adjust to her new surroundings. A better idea is to book a week off work to help your puppy settle in.

If you don't work, leave your diary free for the first few days. Getting a new pup and helping her settle in properly is almost a full-time job for the first few days.

Before you collect your Schnauzer puppy, let the breeder know when you are coming and ask him not to feed her for three or four hours beforehand. She will be less likely to be car sick and she should be hungry when she arrives in her new home.

It is normal for a new puppy to sleep for most of the time when you bring her home. Make sure she gets plenty of rest. If you have children, don't let them constantly waken the pup, she needs her sleep.

Don't invite friends round to see your new puppy for at least 24 hours – however excited you are, she needs a quiet 24 hours with you or you and your family members.

It is a frightening time for your puppy. Talk softly to your new pup and gently stroke her. If you can, bring home a piece of cloth which has been rubbed with her mother's scent and put it in her bed.

Is your puppy shivering with cold or nerves? Make sure she is in a warm, safe, quiet place away from any draughts and loud noises. Talk to her and stroke her gently, she needs plenty of reassurance.

If your puppy won't eat, spend time gently coaxing her to eat something. If she leaves her food, take it away and try it later. Do not leave it down for her all of the time or she may get used to turning her nose up at food. The next time you put something down for her, she is more likely to be hungry.

The puppy is following you as you have taken the place of her Mom. Encourage her to follow you by patting your leg and calling her and when she does, praise her for doing so.

If your puppy is crying, it is probably for one of the following reasons:

* she's hungry or lonely

* she wants attention from you

* she needs to go to the bathroom.

If it is none of these, then check her body to make sure she hasn't picked up an injury. Schnauzers have a strong instinct to want to bond with humans. That emotional attachment between you and your Schnauzer may grow to become one of the most important aspects of your – and certainly your Schnauzer's - life.

The strongest bonding period for a puppy is between eight and 12 weeks of age. The most important factors in bonding with your puppy are TIME spent with her and PATIENCE, even when she makes a mess in the house or chews your furniture.

Remember, she is just a baby and it takes time to learn not to do these things. Spend the time to love and train your Schnauzer pup and you will have a loyal friend for life who will always be there for you and never let you down.

Crates

If you are unfamiliar with them, crates may seem like a cruel punishment for a dog. On the other hand many people, including some trainers, breeders and people who show dogs, recommend their use to train a puppy and make him feel secure. It's true to say they are used more in the USA than elsewhere.

If you do use a crate, then remember that it is NOT a prison to restrain the dog. It should only be used in a humane manner and time should be spent to make the puppy feel like the crate is his own safe little haven.

If the door is closed on the crate, your Schnauzer must ALWAYS have access to water while inside his crate. He also needs bedding in there and it's a good idea to put a chew in as well.

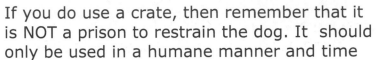

We tried our Mini Schnauzer Max with a crate when he was a young puppy and he howled and whined every time he went in. In the end, we couldn't bear to hear the noise and so we abandoned the crate. It is now in the porch at our house and makes a very useful storage place for Wellington boots and running shoes!

Now, several years later, having heard from so many of our American readers about how much their Schnauzers love their crates, I think perhaps we gave up too easily.

If used correctly and if time is spent getting the puppy used to the crate, it can be a valuable tool. But crates are not for every Schnauzer and they should NEVER be used as a means of imprisoning the dog because you are out of the house all day.

Schnauzers are not like hamsters or pet mice which can adapt to life in a cage. These dogs thrive on interaction with their human owners and being caged all day is a miserable existence for them.

The best place for a crate is in the corner of a room, away from cold draughts or too much heat. Schnauzers like to be near their pack - which is you. Leave him where he can see and hear you. It's a good idea for the crate to be your dog's only bed.

The crate should be large enough to allow your dog to stretch out flat on his side without being cramped, be able to turn round easily and to sit up without hitting his head on the top.

If you are buying a crate that is big enough for your fully-grown Schnauzer, block off part of it while he is small so that he feels safe and secure. You can also buy adjustable crate dividers.

Crates aren't for every owner or dog. But, used correctly, a crate can help to:

- Housetrain your dog
- Keep your dog safe when travelling
- Create a doggie bedroom or place where your Schnauzer feels safe

---

Crate Training a Puppy

If you do decide to use a crate, here's one method of getting your puppy firstly to accept it, and then to actually want to spend time in there.

A puppy might not be very happy about going into a crate at first, but he will be a lot easier to crate train than an adult dog, which may have got used to having the run of your house.

1. Drop a few tasty puppy treats around and then inside the crate.

2. Put your puppy's favorite bedding in there. Keep the door open.

3. Give all of your puppy's meals to him inside the crate. Again, keep the door open.

4. Place a chew or treat INSIDE the crate and close the door while your puppy is OUTSIDE the crate. He will be desperate to get in there. Open the door, let him in and praises him for going in.

5. Fasten a long-lasting chew inside the crate and leave the door open. Let your puppy go inside to spend some time eating the chew.

6. After a while, close the crate door and feed him some treats through the mesh while he is in there. At first just do it for a few seconds at a time, then gradually increase the time. If you do it too fast, he will become distressed.

7. Slowly build up the amount of time he is in the crate. For the first few days, stay in the room, then gradually leave the room for a short time, first one minute, then three, then 10, 30 minutes and so on.

Next Steps
* Put your dog in his crate at regular intervals during the day - up to a maximum of two hours.

* Don't crate only when you are leaving the house. Place the dog in the crate while you are home as well. Use it as a "safe" zone

* By using the crate both when you are home and while you are gone, your dog becomes comfortable in the crate and not worried that you won't come back, or that you are leaving him alone. This helps to prevent separation anxiety later in life.

* Give him a chew and be sure to remove collar and tags which could become caught in an opening.

* Make it very clear to children that the crate is NOT a playhouse for them, but a "special room" for the dog,

* Although the crate is your dog's haven and safe place, it must not be off-limits to humans. You should be able to reach inside at any time.

The next points are important if crate training is to succeed:

* Do not let the dog immediately out of the crate while he is barking or he will think that barking is the key to opening the door to the crate.

* Wait until the barking or whining has stopped for at least 10 seconds before letting him out.

If you do decide to use a crate, remember that a dog is not normally a caged animal. Use the crate for limited periods and only if your dog is comfortable in there. NEVER force a dog to go in and then lock him in for hours on end. Better to find him a new, happier home.

Following our guidelines on selecting the right breed, then breeder, then puppy is a good start – but it is only the beginning! Read the other chapters on how to care for and train your puppy so that you and your new best friend can have many years of happiness together.

Chapter 8. Schnauzers for Allergy Sufferers

Hypoallergenic

The Miniature, Standard and Giant Schnauzer are all hypoallergenic dogs, but what does this mean exactly?

The official definition of the word hypoallergenic is *"having a decreased tendency to provoke an allergic reaction"*.

In other words there is **no cast iron guarantee** that an allergy sufferer won't suffer a reaction to a certain type of dog. But if you do choose a hypoallergenic dog, the chances are greatly reduced.

From personal experience and from numerous comments on our website, we can say that many people who normally suffer from allergies are perfectly fine with Schnauzers.

My partner is allergic to horses, cats and usually dogs, but has no reaction whatsoever to our Miniature Schnauzer, Max.

In this chapter we look at which breeds of dogs are hypoallergenic and what you can do to make sure that you are not going to be allergic to the puppy or dog that you choose.

Amazingly, 50 million Americans suffer from allergies, according to the Asthma and Allergy Foundation of America. One in five of these - 10 million people - are pet allergy sufferers.

Most people think that people are allergic to animal hair, but that's not true. What they are actually allergic to are proteins - or allergens.

These are secreted by the animal's oil glands and then shed with the dander, which is actually dead skin cells. These proteins are also found in dog saliva and urine.

The good news for dog lovers is that there are more people allergic to cats!

The Facts

It IS possible for pet allergy sufferers to enjoy living with a dog without spending all of their time sneezing, wheezing, itching or breaking out in rashes. Millions of people are proving the case - including our family.

There are some types of dog which are definitely better for allergy sufferers, and all three types of Schnauzer – and the Schnoodle crossbreed - are most certainly within that group.

Indeed, according to our research, many people choose Schnauzers either because they have allergies themselves or because the dogs are largely non-shedding and therefore easy to clean up after.

However, it is not completely straightforward and you DO have to put in extra time to make sure that you pick the right dog and maybe make a few adjustments to your home as well.

Firstly, choose a dog from a **non-shedding and hypo-allergenic** breed. Let's clear up a couple of points right away:

- No dog is totally non-shedding
- No dog is totally hypoallergenic

Here are two more very important points to remember:

- People's pet allergies vary greatly.
- Pet allergy sufferers may react differently to different breeds **as well as individual dogs within that breed.**

All dogs - even so-called "hairless" dogs - have hair, dander (dead skin cells, like dandruff), saliva and urine. Therefore all dogs *can* cause allergic reactions. But not all dogs do.

Some hypoallergenic dog breeds do not affect pet allergy sufferers as much because of the type or amount of hair that they shed.

All Schnauzers and virtually all Schnoodles are considered to be non-shedding and hypoallergenic dogs. Schnauzers have a double coat and it is the case that generally they do not molt.

They might lose the occasional little fur ball, but the dog generally does not shed. If a Schnauzer brushes up against you or the furniture, his hair will not fall out.

This is largely due to the double coat. The outer coat is hard and wiry and the undercoat is softer and close to the skin. The outer coat traps the inner coat and the dander.

This type of coat sheds only when the dog is left ungroomed for several months. Hypoallergenic dogs virtually do not molt. (You might find the *occasional* dog hair around the house).

Other Ways to Reduce Pet Allergies

Non-shedding (or hypoallergenic) puppies are a popular choice for people with allergies.

If you are thinking of getting one, try and spend some time alone with the specific pup you are thinking of getting at the breeder's to determine what - if any - reaction you have.

Allergic symptoms do not always happen immediately, sometimes there can be a couple of days' delay.

Everyone with pet allergies can tolerate a certain amount of allergens (things they are allergic to). If that person is just below his or her tolerance, any additional allergen will push him over the edge, triggering a reaction.

So, if you reduce the general allergen load in the home, you'll be much more successful when you bring a non-shedding dog home.

A couple of very successful ways of reducing the allergen load inside the house are to -

- Get a **HEPA** air cleaner in the bedroom and/or main living room. HEPA stands for High Efficiency Particle Air - a type of air filter that removes 99.97% of all particles.
- Use a HEPA vacuum cleaner.

These are not cheap, but if you suffer allergies and you really want to share your life and home with a dog, they are worth considering. Both will dramatically improve the quality of the air you breathe in your home.

Of course, the only sure-fire way to 100% GUARANTEE no allergic reaction is not to have a dog!

Which Breed?

If you - like us –are determined to go ahead and share your home with the best, most loyal and devoted friend you'll ever have, then you must pick a hypoallergenic (non-shedding) breed.

Of course, we all know and love Schnauzers..... But you MIGHT want to look at other breeds before you decide to get a Schnauzer.

Many new types of crossbreed dogs are springing up and some breeders are making claims about them being *guaranteed* non-shedding. Be warned, there is no such thing – even with a purebred or pedigree dog. But with a Schnauzer or a Schnoodle, there is an extremely good chance that your dog will be a non shedder.

Of all the crossbreeds, the ones which are bred from two non-shedding purebred parents represent the best chance of getting a non-shedding dog.

Labradoodles (a cross between a Labrador Retriever and a Poodle) are becoming increasingly popular, especially in Australia and the UK, but many of these DO shed hair, as their coat may take on more of the characteristics of the Labrador, which molts.

Top of the list of a non-shedding crossbreed has to be the **Schnoodle,** as the dog is a product of a Schnauzer and a Poodle and both are non-shedding.

We would always recommend getting a first generation cross – that is one from a purebred Schnauzer and a purebred Poodle, rather than from two Schnoodles.

Schnoodle

In terms of purebreds, the UK and American Kennel Clubs do not make any claims about hypoallergenic dogs or breeds. But they both publish details of **"breeds that generally do well with people with allergies."**

List of Hypoallergenic Dogs

Here is a list of hypoallergenic dogs from both the American Kennel Club (AKC) and The Kennel Club (UK). These are all purebred dogs.

While the Kennel Clubs do not guarantee that you will not have an allergic reaction to a particular dog, certain hypoallergenic and non-shedding dog breeds are generally thought to be better for allergy sufferers.

American Kennel Club List

The American Kennel Club's list of **"breeds that generally do well with people with allergies"** is:

Bichon Frise

Bedlington Terrier

Bichon Frise

Chinese Crested

Irish Water Spaniel

Kerry Blue Terrier

Maltese

Poodle (Toy, Miniature and Standard)

Portuguese Water Dog

Schnauzer (Giant, Standard and Miniature)

Soft Coated Wheaten Terrier

Xoloitzcuintli (FSS Breed)

Wheaten Terriers

Kennel Club (UK) List

The KC has this to say about hypoallergenic and non-shedding dog breeds:

"For those owners who wish to obtain a dog which SUPPOSEDLY does not shed its coat, one of these listed breeds may be a suitable choice:"

Gundog Group
Lagotto Romagnolo

Irish Water Spaniel

Spanish Water Dog

Working Group
Bouvier des Flandres

Giant Schnauzer

Portuguese Water Dog

Russian Black Terrier

Pastoral Group
Hungarian Puli

Komondor

Toy Group
Bichon Frise

Bolognese

Chinese Crested

Coton de Tulear

Havanese

Maltese

Yorkshire Terrier

Portuguese Water Dog

Yorkshire Terrier

Lhasa Apso

Utility Group

Lhasa Apso

Intermediate Mexican Hairless

Miniature Mexican Hairless

Standard Mexican Hairless

Miniature Schnauzer

Standard Poodle

Toy Poodle

Miniature Poodle

Shih Tzu Tibetan Terrier

Mexican Hairless

Terrier Group

Bedlington Terrier

Dandie Dinmont Terrier

Glen of Imaal Terrier

Sealyham Terrier

Soft Coated Wheaten Terrier

Bedlington Terrier

Remember:
  * No breed is totally non-shedding
  * No breed is totally hypoallergenic

Try and spend some time with the individual dog beforehand to see if you have any reaction. Then wait a couple of days.

If there's no reaction, then you could join the countless allergy sufferers who are lucky enough to share their home with Man's Best Friend.

Chapter 9. Feeding Your Schnauzer

Choices

Whole books have been written on this single topic. It is a bit of a minefield as pet owners are bombarded with endless choices as well as countless  adverts from dog food companies, who all claim that theirs is the best.

Basically there are many different types of food to choose from: dry complete diets, semi-moist or tinned food (with or without a biscuit mixer), dog foods containing only natural ingredients and home-made food.

Within that list, there are many different qualities. Usually you get what you pay for, so a more expensive food is more likely to provide better nutrition for your dog - in terms of minerals, nutrients and high quality - meats than a cheap one, which will probably contain a lot of grain.

Dried foods (also called kibble in the USA) tend to be less expensive than semi-moist or tinned foods. They have improved a lot over the last few years and some of the more expensive ones are now a good choice for a healthy, complete diet.

Dried foods also contain the least fat and the most preservatives. Our Miniature, Max, is on a quality dried food diet (called James Wellbeloved), but not all dogs thrive on them.

In general, tinned foods are 60-70% water. Often semi-moist foods contain a lot of sugar, which is maybe why some dogs seem to love them. Always check the ingredients on any food packet or tin and see which ingredients are listed first.

Choosing the right food for your dog is very important. It will have an influence on his health, coat and even temperament.

There are also three stages of your dog's life to consider when feeding: puppy, adult and senior or veteran. Each of these represents a different physical stage of life for your dog and you need to choose the right food to cope with his body during that particular phase of life.

Also, a pregnant female will require a special diet to cope with the extra demands on her body. This is especially important as she nears the latter stages of pregnancy.

We are not about to recommend on brand of dog food over another, but we do have some general tips to give on feeding your Schnauzer before we look at different types of food in more detail.

---

13 Top Tips for Feeding your Schnauzer

1.   Some Schnauzers – particularly Miniatures – have sensitive skin, allergies or skin problems. A cheap dog food will only make this worse, so we recommend that you bite the bullet and choose a high quality – usually more expensive - dog food. You'll save money in vets' bills in the long run and your dog will be happier.

Don't pick one where the meat or poultry content is NOT the first item listed on the bag. Foods which have been bulked up with cheap cereals or are full of sugar are not the best choice for purebred Schnauzers.

2.   Frequency of feeds should be based on size. Small dogs like Miniature Schnauzers have a fast metabolism and burn off their food calories quicker than large breeds like the Giant Schnauzer.

Generally, adult Miniature and Standard Schnauzers should be fed twice a day, while Giant Schnauzers only need to be fed once a day, although many Giant owners prefer to give two smaller feeds to avoid **bloat** - see Chapter 13 on **Health**. Puppies of all breeds need to be fed more often.

3.   Establish a feeding regime and stick to it. Dogs like routine. If you are feeding twice a day, feed once in the morning and then again at tea-time. Stick to the same times of day.

4.   Do not give the last feed too late in the evening, or your Schnauzer's body will not have chance to process or burn off the food before sleeping. Feeding at the same times every day will also help your dog establish a toilet regime.

5.   Take away the food between meals. The easiest way for your Schnauzer to become a fussy eater is for you to leave the food down all day.

The dog sees the food and it doesn't look so appetizing when it is there all the time. Then he starts to leave the food and you are at your wits' end trying to find a food that your dog will actually eat.

Put the bowl with the food down twice a day and then take it up after 20 minutes – even if he has left some. If he is healthy and hungry, he will look forward to his next meal and soon stop leaving food. If your dog does not eat anything for days, then it is probably a sign that something is wrong with him.

6.   Do not feed too many tidbits between meals. This is unhealthy for the dog, affects his balanced diet and can lead to obesity. Stick to regular mealtimes. Don't feed your dog from the table or your plate, as this encourages attention-seeking behavior such as begging, barking and drooling.

7.   NEVER feed the following items to your dog: grapes, raisins, chocolate, onions, Macadamia nuts, any fruits with seeds or stones, tomatoes, avocadoes, broccoli, rhubarb, tea, coffee or alcohol. ALL of these are poisonous to dogs.
(See our section later in this chapter on poisonous items for dogs.)

8.   If you feed leftovers to your dog, feed them INSTEAD of a balanced dog food meal, not as well as. High quality dog foods are already made up to provide all the nutrients, vitamins, minerals and calories that your dog needs.

Feeding tidbits or leftovers may be too rich for your dog in addition to his regular diet and cause him to scratch or have other problems. Feed leftovers as a meal, not in addition to a meal.

9.   If you decide to switch to a new dog food, do the transition over a week. Unlike humans, dogs' digestive systems cannot handle sudden changes in diet.

Begin by gradually mixing some of the new food in with the old and increase the proportion so that after several days, all the food is the new one.

10.   Check your dog's weight regularly. Obesity in Schnauzers, as well as being generally unhealthy, can lead to the development of some serious health issues such as diabetes, pancreatitis or bladder stones.

 Although the weight will vary from one dog to another and from Miniature to Standard and Giant, a good rule of thumb is that your Schnauzer's tummy should be higher than his rib cage. If his belly hangs down below the level of his rib cage, he is overweight.

11.   Check your dog's poop! If his diet is suitable, the food should be easily digested and produce dark brown, firm, formed stools. If your dog produces soft or light stools, or has wind or diarrhea, then the diet may not suit him, so consult your vet for advice.

12.   If you have a Giant Schnauzer, put his feeding and bowls on a small stand or bench so they are at shoulder height. Giants are susceptible to bloat, a serious condition which occurs when they take in too much air while feeding.

13.   And finally, always make sure that your Schnauzer has access to clean, fresh water. Change the water every day.

Dog Food Allergies

Symptoms

Dog food allergies affect about one in 10 dogs. They are the third most common allergy for our canine companions - after flea bite allergies and atophy (inhaled allergies).

If your dog is not well, how do you know if the problem lies with his food or not? Here are some common symptoms:

- Itchy skin (this is the most common)
- Excessive scratching
- Ear infections
- Hair loss
- Hot patches of skin
- Recurring skin infections
- Increased bowel movements (maybe twice as often as usual)

Schnauzers are no more or less likely to suffer from them than other breeds. There's no strong link between specific breeds and food allergies.

They equally affect males and females as well as neutered and intact animals. They can show up when your dog is five months or 12 years old - although the vast majority of allergies related to dog food start when the dog is between two and six years old.

Many dogs with food allergies also have other types of allergies.

Allergies or Intolerance?

There's a difference between **dog food allergies** and **dog food intolerance**.

Typical reactions to allergies are skin problems and/or itching

Typical reactions to intolerance are diarrhea and/or vomiting

Dog food intolerance can be compared to people who get diarrhea or an upset stomach from eating spicy food. The good news is that both can be cured by a change in diet to the correct food for your particular dog. As they say in the canine world:

"One dog's meat is another dog's poison".

Causes

Certain ingredients are more likely to cause allergies than others. In order of the most common triggers for dogs they are:

Beef

Dairy products

Chicken

Wheat

Eggs

Corn

Soy

Unfortunately, these most common offenders are also the most common ingredients in dog foods!

By the way, don't think that if you put your dog on a rice and lamb dog food diet that will automatically cure the problem. It MIGHT, but then again there's a fair chance it won't.

The reason lamb and rice were thought to be less likely to cause allergies is simply because they have not traditionally been included in dog food recipes - therefore less dogs had reactions to them.

Diagnosis

As you can see from the symptoms listed above, the diagnosis for food allergies is fairly straightforward.

The problem is that these conditions may also be symptoms of other problems such as atophy (breathed-in allergies), flea bite allergies, intestinal problems, mange and yeast or bacterial infections.

You can have a blood test on your dog, but many veterinarians now believe that this is not accurate enough.

If you can rule out all of the above, then you might want to start a food trial with your dog. This, also called an exclusion diet, is the only truly accurate way to find out if your dog has a food allergy.

The problem is that it takes 12 weeks of 100% strict control for it to work properly, during which time you should also keep an allergy diary.

You could skip the food trial altogether and, if you think your Schnauzer is allergic to his or her food, try a hypoallergenic dog food, either commercial or home-made.

There are a number of these on the market and they all have the word **hypoallergenic** in the name.

Although usually more expensive, hypoallergenic dog food ingredients do not include common allergens such as wheat protein or soya, thereby minimizing the risk of an allergic reaction.

How Much Food?

This is a question which we are constantly asked on the website: "How much food should I feed my X-year-old Schnauzer?"
The answer is…..there is no easy answer!

The correct amount of food for your dog depends on a number of factors:

- Breed
- Gender
- Age
- Energy levels
- Amount of daily exercise
- Health
- Environment
- Number of dogs in house
- The quality of the food

Some breeds have a higher metabolic rate than others. Generally smaller dogs have faster metabolism so will require a higher amount of food per pound -or kilo –of body weight.

Female dogs are slightly more prone to putting on weight than male dogs. Some people say that dogs which have been spayed or neutered are more likely to put on weight, although this is disputed by others.

Growing puppies and young dogs need more food than senior dogs with a slower lifestyle.

Every dog is different, you can have two Schnauzers and one may be very energetic while the other has a more placid temperament. The energetic dog will burn off more calories.

Maintaining a healthy body weight for dogs – and humans – is all about balancing what you take in with what you burn off.
 If your dog is exercised three times a day and allowed to run and play off the leash, he will need more calories than a Schnauzer which gets one walk on the leash every day.

Certain health conditions such as an underactive thyroid, diabetes, arthritis or heart disease can lead to dogs putting on weight, so their food has to be adjusted accordingly.

Just like us, a dog kept in a very cold environment will need more calories to keep warm than a dog in a warm climate. They burn extra calories in keeping themselves warm.

Here's an interesting fact: a dog kept on his own is more likely to be overweight than a dog kept with other dogs, as he receives all of the food-based attention.

Cheaper foods usually recommend feeding more to your dog, as much of the food is made up of cereals, which are not doing much except bulking up the weight of the food – and possibly triggering allergies in your Schnauzer.

Because there are so many factors involved, there is no simple answer to how much to feed.

 However, below we have listed a broad guideline of the average amount of **calories** a Schnauzer with medium energy and activity levels needs.

Thanks to *Better Food for Dogs - A Complete Cookbook and Nutrition Guide by D Bastin et al, published by Robert Rose, Inc* for the following information and feeding guide:

"The standard weight of each Schnauzer breed is stated in brackets.

If your Schnauzer falls beyond the standard weight due to under or overfeeding, take the opportunity of diet change as part of your dog's weight management program. Target your dog at the highest acceptable weight of his breed class to begin with if he or she is overweight.

On the other hand, if your Schnauzer is underweight, target your dog at the lowest weight acceptable weight of his breed class to begin with.

Adjust the energy level gradually toward the middle of the range.

Note: if your dog's weight problems are caused by certain health problems, pregnancy or other conditions, consult your vet before implementing any weight management program as this must be supervised by your vet."

Canine Calorie Counter

BREED	WEIGHT	ENERGY
Miniature	10 lb / 4.5 Kg	341 - 411 Kcal
Schnauzer	15 lb / 6.8 Kg	463 - 556 Kcal
5 – 9 kg	20 lb / 9.0 Kg	575 - 690 Kcal
	25 lbs / 11.3 Kg	680 - 816 Kcal
Standard	30 lbs / 13.6 Kg	779 - 935 Kcal
Schnauzer	35 lbs / 15.8 Kg	875 - 1050 Kcal
20 – 27 kg	40 lbs / 18.1 Kg	965 - 1158 Kcal
	45 lbs / 20.4 Kg	1056 - 1267 Kcal
	50 lbs / 22.6 Kg	1143 - 1327 Kcal
	55 lbs / 24.9 Kg	1228 - 1437 Kcal

	60 lbs / 27.2 Kg	1310 - 1537 Kcal
	65 lbs / 29.5 Kg	1392 - 1670 Kcal
Giant	70 lbs / 31.7 Kg	1471 - 1766 Kcal
Schnauzer	75 lbs / 34.0 Kg	1549 - 1859 Kcal
36 – 50 kg	80 lbs / 36.27 Kg	1626 - 1951 Kcal
	85 lbs / 38.6 Kg	1701 - 2042 Kcal
	90 lbs / 40.8 Kg	1776 - 2132 Kcal
	95 lbs / 43.1 Kg	1850 - 2220 Kcal
	100 lbs / 45.3 Kg	1922 - 2307 Kcal
	110 lbs / 49.8 Kg	2065 - 2478 Kcal
	120 lbs / 54.4 Kg	2204 - 2645 Kcal

We feed our Schnauzer a dried hypoallergenic dog food made by James Wellbeloved in England. Max has seasonal allergies which make him scratch, but he seems to do pretty well on this food, which contains natural ingredients.

Here are the manufacturer's recommended feeding amounts for dogs in grams. They are listed in kilograms and grams. (**28.3 grams = one ounce and 1kg = 2.2 lbs).**

The number on the left is the dog's **adult weight** in kilograms. So an adult Miniature Schnauzer would be somewhere between 5kg (11lbs) and 10kg (22lbs), depending on how big the parents were and whether the dog is a male or female.

The numbers on the right are the amount of daily food in grams that an average dog with average energy levels requires, measured in grams (divide this by 28.3 to get the amount in ounces).

For example, a 3-month-old puppy which will grow into a 5kg to 10kg adult dog would require somewhere from 115 – 190 grams of food per day (4 to 6.7 ounces).

NOTE: These are only very general guidelines, your dog may need more or less than this. For example, we feed our seven-year-old Mini Schnauzer more than the recommended amount, but he is active and exercised three times a day and is not at all overweight. Use the chart as a guideline only and if your dog appears to lose or gain weight on the prescribed amount, adjust his or her feeds accordingly.

Dog Feeding Chart

Puppy

Size	expected adult body weight (kg)	Age of Puppy and daily Serving (g)					
		2 mths	3 mths	4 mths	5 mths	6 mths	> 6 mths
Toy	2	50	60	60	60	60	change to adult
Small	5	95	115	120	115	115	change to adult
Medium	10	155	190	195	190	190	change to junior
Medium/Large	20	240	305	325	320	315	change to junior or large breed junior
Large	30	300	400	435	435	430	change to large breed junior
Large/Giant	40	345	480	530	540	530	change to large breed junior
	50	390	550	615	630	630*	change to large breed junior
	60	430	610	690	720*	720*	change to large breed junior
Giant	70	460	675	765*	800*	810*	change to large breed junior
	90	550	810*	920*	960*	970*	change to large breed junior

Junior

Size	expected adult body weight (kg)	Age of Puppy and daily Serving (g)						
		6 mths	7 mths	8 mths	10 mths	12 mths	14 mths	16 mths
Medium	10	200	195	185	175	change to adult		
Medium/Large*	20	330	325	310	290	300	change to adult/large	

Size	Age of Puppy and daily Serving (g)							
	expected adult body weight (kg)	6 mths	7 mths	8 mths	10 mths	12 mths	14 mths	16 mths
Large*	30	455	440	430	400	400	breed adult	
	40	565	555	540	520	485	495	change to large breed adult

Adult

Size	Body Weight (kg)	Daily Serving (g)
Toy	2-5	55-115
Small	5-10	115-190
Medium	10-20	190-320
Medium/Large	20-30	320-430
Large*	30*-40*	430*-520*
Large/Giant*	40*-50*	520*-620*
Giant*	50*-60*	620*-710*
	60*-70*	710*-790*
	70*-90*	790*-950*

Overweight Dogs

Overweight dogs are sadly susceptible to a range of illnesses. According to James Howle, Veterinary Advisor to Lintbells, some of the main ones are:

Joint disease – excessive bodyweight may increase joint stress which is a risk factor in joint degeneration (arthrosis), as is cruciate disease (knee ligament rupture).

Joint disease tends to lead to a reduction in exercise which then increases the likelihood of weight gain which reduces exercise further. A vicious cycle is created.

Overfeeding large breed dogs whilst they are growing can lead to various problems including worsening of hip dysplasia. Weight management may be the only measure required to control clinical signs in some cases.

Heart and lung problems – fatty deposits within the chest cavity and excessive circulating fat play important roles in the development of cardio-respiratory and cardiovascular disease.

Diabetes – resistance to insulin has been shown to occur in overweight dogs, leading to a greater risk of diabetes mellitus.

Tumors – obesity increases the risk of developing mammary tumors in female dogs.

Liver disease – fat degeneration may result in liver insufficiency.

Reduced Lifespan - one of the most serious findings in obesity studies that has been proven to be related to being overweight in both humans and dogs is a reduced lifespan. An overweight dog is more likely to die younger than a dog of normal weight.

Exercise intolerance – this is also a common finding with overweight dogs, which can compound an obesity problem as less calories are burned and therefore are stored, leading to further weight gain.

Schnauzers are particularly attached to humans. However, beware of going too far in regarding your dog a member of the family.

It has been shown that dogs that are perceived to be 'family members' (i.e. anthropomorphosis) by the owner are at greater risk of becoming overweight. This is because attention given to the dog often results in food being given as well. Are you guilty of this?

The important thing to remember is that many of the problems associated with being overweight are reversible. Increasing exercise increases the calories burned, which in turn reduces weight.

Feeding Puppies

Feeding your puppy correctly is very important to help his young body and bones grow strong and healthy.

A dog does most of his growing during the first year of life, so it's worth spending some time to choose the right fuel to power his healthy development.

Think of it as a foundation stone towards future health.

Establishing a regular feeding routine is a good idea, as this will help to toilet train your pup. Get him used to regular mealtimes and then let him outside to do his business. Puppies have fast metabolisms, so the results may be pretty quick!

Generally, Schnauzers have healthy appetites and will eat most things put in front of them. Check the manufacturers' guidelines to check how much to feed your puppy. This will depend on his age and weight.

Stick to the correct amount. You are doing your puppy no favors by overfeeding him. Unless he is thin, don't give in - no matter how much he pleads with you with his big brown eyes. You must be firm and resist the temptation to give him extra food or treats. Obesity in dogs is one of the main causes of health problems.

Types of Food

Many veterinarians and breeders recommend high quality dry food (also called kibble). Chewing the hard kibble also helps to keep the dog's teeth clean and healthy. And the bonus is that it is easy on your pocket – dried foods are normally cheaper than other dog foods.

Choosing the right food can be difficult – you can ask your vet for suggestions when you take him for his inoculations. Initially it is a good idea to continue the food being given by the breeder.

If you intend to change his diet, do it over a week or so, gradually adding a bit more of the new food until you have completely switched over.

Dogs' digestion systems cannot cope with a rapidly changing diet of various different foods like ours can.

Some Schnauzers are prone to skin conditions or allergies and this is sometimes triggered by food.

For this reason alone, we believe that it is worth spending the extra money on a high quality puppy food, which will be less likely to create an adverse reaction in your Schnauzer puppy or adolescent dog.

Schnauzer puppies should stay on puppy food until they are about 9 or 10 months old and then gradually introduced to an adult diet. Check with your vet for the best age to switch for your pup.

Here are some things to look out for on the manufacturers' labels:

* Is there a variety of ingredients? The top ones should be the main content, don't pick one with a lot of grain as many Schnauzers can develop intolerances or allergies.

* There should be proteins listed. Check the percentage of proteins to fats. Is sugar listed? Many semi-moist foods contain sugar, which is not a natural ingredient to feed to a dog.

* Does the food contain a lot of additives and preservatives? Some may be necessary, but too many can be a bad thing.

If you feed a high quality dog food, you should not need to add supplements. Check with your vet before adding any supplements to your puppy's diet.

Once you have decided on a food, monitor your puppy. The best test of a food is how well your puppy is doing on it. If he eats it all up and is lively and his stools look healthy, then he is thriving on his diet.

Feeding Habits

As well as sticking to regular mealtimes to promote easier housetraining, the question of WHO feeds the puppy also needs to be decided.

Schnauzers are particularly loyal dogs and the person who feeds the puppy will probably become their pack leader. In other words, this is the person to whom the dog will probably show most loyalty – and affection.

If your dog is not responding well to a particular family member, a useful tactic is to get that person to feed the dog every day. The way to a dog's heart is often through his or her stomach!

Another important thing to remember is that if your mealtimes coincide with those of your puppy or adult dog, you should ALWAYS eat something from your plate before feeding your Schnauzer.

Dogs are very hierarchical; they respect the pecking order. In the wild the top dogs eat first. If you feed your puppy before you, he will think that he is higher up the pecking order than you.

If allowed, some Schnauzers – especially Minis – can develop a "cocky" attitude and think that they rule the roost. So feeding your dog AFTER

yourself is an important part of training and discipline.

Your dog will not love you any less because you are the boss – in fact, just the opposite.

Incidentally, here's another tip: always walk through open doors BEFORE your dog for the same reason. It shows him that you are the boss.

How Often?

For the first six weeks, puppies need to be given milk about five to seven times a day. Generally they will make some sound if they want to feed. Puppies take this milk from their mother.

The frequency is reduced when the pup reaches six to eight weeks old. Puppies should stay with their mothers until seven or eight weeks of age before leaving the litter.

Once your Schnauzer puppy arrives home with you, he will need to eat three times a day. Generally, a big morning and evening meal with a smaller lunch will suit an eight to 12-week-old puppy.

After this, mealtimes can be cut down to two a day for all breeds of Schnauzer. Giants only need feeding once a day, but many owners feed twice a day to help prevent bloat.

Seniors

Once he reaches eight to 10 months old, your adolescent Schnauzer can switch to an adult diet, which he will eat for most of his life. Owners of some breeds then switch their dogs from an adult to a senior diet as early as seven years of age. Schnauzers are fairly robust dogs that stay active longer than most breeds and they may not need to change so early.

Nine or 10 years is a more common age for Schnauzers to start a senior diet, but it all depends on the individual dog. It may be even later. It is likely that a Giant Schnauzer, which has a shorter lifespan than a Miniature or Standard Schnauzer, will switch to a senior dog food at an earlier age.

Look for signs of your dog slowing down or having joint problems. That may be the time to talk to your vet about switching to a senior diet. You can do this at his annual vaccination appointment, rather than having the expense of a separate appointment.

As a dog grows older, his metabolism slows down, his energy levels decrease and he needs less exercise, just like with humans. You may notice in middle or old age that your dog starts to put weight on. The adult diet he is on may now provide too many calories, so now may be the time to consider switching to a senior diet.

Even though he is older, try and keep his weight in check as obesity in old age only puts strain on his body, especially joints and organs, and makes any health problems even worse.

Other changes which take place are again similar to humans; your dog may move more slowly and sleep more. His organs don't all work as well as they used to, the kidneys slow down and the intestines become less efficient.

When this starts to happen, it is time to feed your old friend a senior diet, which will take these changes into account. You may also consider feeding supplements if your Schnauzer has stiff joints or a touch of arthritis.

As already mentioned, rather than suddenly changing your dog's diet, we recommend discussing the changes in your Schnauzer with your vet when you take him for his annual vaccinations or check up.

If you describe the change in your pet, your vet will be able to tell you if it is time to change his diet.

Feeding your dog the right amount of food, particularly young dogs, is one of the most common questions we get on our website. We also get many questions on the right kind of diet for Schnauzers, especially those with allergies.

In short, the correct diet and amount of food and the right diet depends on a number of factors, including:

* Energy levels
* Amount of daily exercise
* Age
* Whether the dog is pregnant
* Whether the dog has allergies or other medical problems

If your dog is happy and healthy, interested in life, has enough energy, is not too fat and not too thin, then...

Congratulations, you've got it right!

Chapter 10. Schnauzer Training

Training a Schnauzer is like bringing up a child. Put in the effort early on and you will be rewarded with a well-mannered individual who will be a joy to spend time with for years to come. But let your youngster do what he wants, allow him to think he's the boss and you may well finish up with a headstrong adult with some unpleasant behavior traits.

Schnauzers are intelligent, some of them come to regard themselves as almost human; a true member of the family. This is very endearing, but be careful. If not put in their place, they may end up ruling you and your household. The good news is that most Schnauzers are eager to please their owners, which makes training easier.

Schnauzers are not fierce by nature. Most do not show aggression towards other dogs or humans. If they start to do this, or to bark incessantly, then firm training is required. The first two years are his formative years and the most important time for the development of his character and behavior.

You have to show your dog that you are pack leader, not a playmate, otherwise he may push the boundaries. It's your house, you set the rules and, with proper training, your Schnauzer will learn to follow them. Be firm, but **never** be aggressive with your dog. You will either frighten him or teach him to be aggressive back.

Schnauzers, particularly Minis, are not known for their powers of concentration. You could never train a Mini, for example, to be a police dog, there are simply too many distractions. When giving him a command, you may sometimes see your Schnauzer torn between doing what you say or running after that dog/squirrel/human he has just spotted. Keep training short and fun, especially at the beginning.

If you have adopted an older dog, you can still train him. But it will take a little longer to get rid of bad habits and instil good manners. Patience and persistence are the keys here. As the saying goes:

"It's usually pretty easy to train a Schnauzer – it's the owners that take a little longer!"

12 Top Tips for Training Your Schnauzer

1. **Start training your Schnauzer puppy early on.** Like babies, puppies learn quickly and it's this learned behavior which stays with them through adult life. Old dogs CAN be taught new tricks, but it's a lot harder to unlearn bad habits. It's best to start training with a clean slate. Puppy training can start from as early as a few weeks old.

2. **Your voice is your most important training tool.** Your dog has to learn to understand your language and you have to understand him. Your voice and the tone you employ are very important.

    Commands should be issued in a calm, authoritative voice, not shouted. Praise should be given in a happy, encouraging voice, accompanied by stroking or patting. If your dog has done something wrong, use a firm, stern voice, not a harsh shriek. This applies even if your Schnauzer is unresponsive at the beginning.

3. **Avoid giving your dog commands you know you can't enforce.** Schnauzers are intelligent dogs. Every time you give a command that you don't enforce, he learns that commands are optional.

4. **Train your dog gently and humanely.** Teach him using positive, motivational methods. Keep training sessions upbeat so that the whole experience is enjoyable for you and him.

    If obedience training is a bit of a bore, pep things up a bit by "play training". Use constructive, non-adversarial games such as Go Find, Hide and Seek or Fetch the Ball.

5. **Begin your training around the house and garden** (if you've got one). How well your dog responds to you at home affects his behavior outdoors as well. If he doesn't respond well at home, he certainly won't respond any better outdoors where there are 101 distractions, such as other dogs, people, food scraps, cats, birds, etc.

6. **One command equals one response.** Give your dog only one command - twice maximum - then gently enforce it. Repeating commands or nagging will make your Schnauzer tune out.

They also teach him that the first several commands are a bluff. Telling your dog to "SIT, SIT, SIT, SIT!" is neither efficient nor effective. Simply give your dog a single "SIT" command, gently place him in the sitting position and then praise him.

7.   **It's all about good communication**. It's NOT about getting even with the dog. If you're taking an "it's-me-against-the-dog, I'll soon whip him into shape" approach, you may eventually force your dog into submission.

But a relationship based on fear is not a successful one and it will undermine your relationship with him - do you want a dog that flinches when you approach him? You'll also miss out on all the fun that a positive training approach can offer.

8.   **Use your Schnauzer's name in a positive manner.** When training, try not to use it when you are reprimanding, warning or punishing him. He should trust that when he hears his name, good things happen. His name should always be a word your dog responds to with enthusiasm, never hesitancy or fear.

9.   **Don't give your dog lots of attention (even negative attention) when he misbehaves.** Schnauzers LOVE attention. If he gets lots of attention and handling when he jumps up on you, that bad behavior is being reinforced and is therefore likely to be repeated. If he jumps up, push him away, use the command "NO" or "DOWN" and then ignore him.

10.   **Timing is critical to successful training.** When your puppy does something right, praise him immediately. Similarly, when he does something wrong, correct him straight away. Praise and corrections given later do not work as the dog does not know what he has done wrong – or right.

11.   **Have a 'No' sound.** When a puppy is corrected by his mother – for example if he bites her with his sharp baby teeth – she growls at him to warn him not to do it again. When your puppy makes a mistake, make a short sharp sound like **"ACK!"** to tell the puppy not to do that again. This works surprisingly well.

12.   **Be patient.** Rome wasn't built in a day and a Schnauzer won't be trained in 24 hours either. But you'll reap the rewards of a few weeks of regular training sessions for the rest of the dog's life when you have a happy, well-behaved friend and loving companion for life.

Miniature Schnauzer Training

Starting Off on the Right Foot

Despite what you may think, training a Miniature Schnauzer can be a pleasure of toil. Properly done it is a rewarding experience, a learning curve and a lot of fun - for both you and your dog.

Although Miniature Schnauzers share some of their character traits with terriers, they are generally considered to be easier to train than many of the terrier breeds. (In the UK, the Mini is classed by the Kennel Club in the Utility Group, in the USA it is in the Terrier Group).

No matter how easy-to-please your Mini is, obedience training is an absolute must for every dog. Most Minis are pretty smart and will try and push the boundaries - like jumping up at people, ignoring your call or sitting on your comfy armchair - if you'll let them.

If you DO allow them to get away with these and other bad habits, this poor behavior will soon become ingrained - Minis soon work out what is and what is not permitted. Unless you want a cocksure little dog ruling your house, start your training early and stick with it.

Attention Seekers

Miniature Schnauzers love to be at the center of life - they are attention seekers. They are also enthusiastic and eager to please, which are two main reasons why they generally respond well to training.

They thrive on attention, so praise for a job well done has a powerful effect on Miniatures during training. Like most dogs, they don't respond well to negative reinforcement, which only increases stress and anxiety.

Incidentally, if your Mini is behaving badly, once you have given him the "NO!" command and he has stopped, don't give him any more of your time - even bad attention is some attention for him.

Some dogs, just like children will act up in order to get attention. What often happens is that the owners start to yell at the dog, so he soon realizes that shouting means he get attention, which makes his behavior worse.

If your dog tries this on, you should:

1. Give him lots of attention for good behavior
2. Ignore bad behavior – however difficult this might be

When he sees that he gets all the attention for being a good boy and none when he is naughty, his behavior should improve. Most Miniatures have a mind of their own and often a short attention span. This is certainly the case with ours. I really have to make him focus when training or he wanders off to sniff or follow something more interesting than me.

The key to successful training with Minis is **variety** rather than repetition. Try and keep training interesting and fun. Too much repetition will cause them to get bored and lose concentration.

Daily Routine

As with a puppy of any breed, training your Miniature Schnauzer is a must-do. A well-behaved dog that you can take anywhere without worrying is a marvelous companion.

Try and do a little bit of training every day. On our daily walks I still reinforce some of the commands 7-year-old Max learned as a puppy. Occasionally (but not always) I reward him with a treat for sitting or staying - unfortunately his repertoire is somewhat limited!

Without discipline and guidelines, the Mini's energy and playfulness can occasionally turn to stubbornness. If you want to avoid having a "Little Emperor" or "Little Princess" on your hands, we recommend signing up for local dog training classes.

Not only will your Mini learn obedience, but he or she will also learn to socialize with other dogs and humans. Socialization is an important part of dog training.

You could also think about getting a dog training DVD - the beauty of this is that it brings training techniques right into your home – but it should not replace classes with other dogs.

If you start your Miniature Schnauzer training early enough, and then take a few minutes in your normal daily routine to reinforce what your dog has learned, you'll end up with a wonderful little dog that is not only well behaved but also the envy of all your friends.

Standard Schnauzer Training

Although all three types of Schnauzer share some traits, such as their good looks and love of humans, each breed also has its own characteristics.

The Standard is the original of all three Schnauzers. They a medium-sized and robust, energetic dog. The dog's combination of intelligence, energy and high spirit can become a handful for some owners.

Time spent with the dog and proper training are the keys to a successful relationship with your Standard.

The Standard Schnauzer is considered one of the most intelligent of all the breeds. This is a good point, but can be troublesome if not channeled in a positive way through good training.

Time and effort should be put into training when the dog is a pup – this can start as early as a few weeks old. But, with Standards, that training should be reinforced throughout his life to make sure that you, not he, remains top dog.

It's important that he does not become bored through getting too little exercise. Being bred from a working dog, the Standard definitely needs more exercise than a Mini Schnauzer, with the minimum guideline being an hour a day spread over at least two walks. More is, of course, better if you can spare the time.

If you don't have an hour a day to devote to exercising your dog, you might consider getting a Mini Schnauzer instead, as they require less exercise.

Ideally, you should be able to let your Standard off the leash to run free and burn off some of his energy. To make sure that you can do this, your Standard should be socialized with other dogs from an early age. A series of puppy or dog training classes is just the thing for a young dog. Not only will your Standard enjoy them, but you will too.

We loved taking Max to puppy classes. As the proud owners attempted to train their unruly charges walk to heel or ignore the other puppies, the antics of the young dogs were hilarious.

But at the end of the eight weekly classes - coupled with the short and regular training sessions we did at home – we were surprised at the progress made in such a brief space of time. Our dogs were coming back to us, responding to commands and walking nicely on the leash.

Standards (or just plain Schnauzers as they are called in the UK) are not usually aggressive towards other dogs. Like all breeds, they need introducing to other dogs in a neutral, safe and unthreatening environment. Again, puppy socialization or training classes are ideal for this.

As Standards are also good watch dogs, you should also get him or her socialized with other humans from an early age. Encourage friends to come to visit and interact with the dog from an early age. You don't want your Standard to become too territorial and to regard anybody outside the family as a threat.

Out on your walks, let your Standard interact with other dogs and humans. This will not stop him barking when people knock on your door back home. Although he may not do this as a puppy, most Standards make excellent watch dogs and he will alert you to any new arrivals at the house. When socialized with other people, he will follow your lead and be able to tell the difference between a friend and a foe.

The Standard is a highly intelligent dog, "the dog with the human brain". With the right owners who are prepared to spend time training and exercising, these dogs become fantastic, affectionate pets and companions.

Like Miniatures, Standards can have a stubborn streak as well as a mischievous sense of humor. Proper training will teach your dog good manners and that you are the boss, not him.

Dogs are pack animals and need a leader, otherwise they will assume that role. Make sure you establish yourself as pack leader. A Standard's natural inquisitiveness and tendency to push the boundaries will test your resolve. Do not cave in to this stunning looking breed, but hold your ground – and advise other members of the family to do the same.

Establish a single set of ground rules for your dog. If you don't allow the dog to sit on the sofa, make sure that nobody else in the house allows it either. Don't sense mixed messages to this intelligent dog, they will soon find the weak link. Decide your rules, and train your dog to stick to them.

Dogs are hierarchical. They like to know where they stand in the pecking order – make sure that it is below you!

If allowed, they will get away with whatever they can and will rule the house if you let them. They need firm discipline, but should not be treated in a rough manner.

Like all Schnauzers, Standards are people-oriented and sensitive to your reaction. Warm words of praise will be lapped up, while rough treatment, shouting or aggression may lead in turn to bad behavior back, like an unruly child.

Here are a couple of tips to help establish dominance over your dog in a natural manner:

* Feed your dog twice a day, but make sure he receives his food AFTER you have begun your meal. In the wild the dominant animals eat first.

* When you open a door, make sure that you go through bEFORE your dog.

Another tip (and this one sounds a bit odd) which can be used if your dog is becoming too dominant: Get into his basket or bed and trample around in it for a while. Do this every day and it will help to assert your dominance.

Generally, when training your Standard, try and avoid monotonous and repetitive routines, as his enquiring mind will soon become bored and he will switch off. Keep training short, interesting and fun wherever possible.

Because the Standard is agile, bright and quick to learn, it often does well in conformation, obedience, agility, tracking and herding events. These activities appeal to the Standard's energy levels and love of a challenge.

TIME + TRAINING = SUPER STANDARD SCHNAUZER

Early training shapes a dog's personality. What sort of dog do you want?

Giant Schnauzer Training

Most Giant Schnauzer owners will tell you that these are the best dogs in the world.

Kevin Cullen, who won Crufts, the biggest dog show on earth, with his Giant Jafrak Philippe Olivier, told us: *"Giant Schnauzers are addictive. You start with one and end up with two or more – like us.*

"They know every move you make and everything you say. They are creatures of habit and know what time of day it is and what gets done at that time - and you had better be there to do it!

"In return you get the most loyal companion you could ever wish to own. He will guard you and your home with his life. There is no other breed for us."

Yet countless Giant Schnauzers finish up in animal rescue centers, especially in the USA. How can this be?

The answer lies in two words: **training** and **exercise**.

If a Giant is physically and mentally unstimulated, he will become bored, and unresponsive and lose respect for his owners. Eventually, this can lead to him becoming rebellious and difficult to control. This is why some Giants are eventually rejected by their owners and end up in rescue centers.

The Giant Schnauzer is an extremely rewarding dog to own – not to mention strikingly handsome. But you have to put **time** in to get the best out of this breed. But be careful not to over-exercise or rough play with Giant puppies when training, as this can damage their fast-growing joints. Keep training fairly gently in the beginning.

Although Giant puppies love to running around, playing and roughhousing, care should be taken to ensure that the exercise is not too vigorous. Too much strain on joints when young can lead to problems such as hip dysplasia later in life.

Here's that saying again:

"It's usually pretty easy to train a Schnauzer – it's the owners that take a little longer!"

Despite their size, Giants are relatively easy to train and the results achieved are well worth the effort put in by the owner. They are extremely loyal and intelligent dogs, although, like all Schnauzers, they can have a stubborn streak.

Although not aggressive dogs by nature, Giants can be dominant if they are not made aware of their place. Young puppies can try and throw their weight around, so socialization with other dogs from an early age is especially important with Giants. They often co-exist happily with other Giants in the same household, or you might want to think about puppy classes.

A Giant may also try to dominate you, so you have to show authority when you train him. At all times remain calm and firm, but do not shout or screech, Giants are sensitive dogs and do not respond well to harsh treatment.

Because of their intelligence and energy, they can become bored or destructive if not properly trained or exercised.

Giants make excellent guard dogs, as they are very territorial and protective

of the family. You don't want your dog to regard every visitor to your house as an intruder. Proper training and socialization ensures that they do not become suspicious and aggressive towards other people or dogs.

Once trained, they will follow your lead and learn to welcome friends, while still protecting your house.

Think of your Giant puppy as a highly intelligent, demanding and loving child which needs lots of your time and a firm hand to help him or her grow up into an outstanding adult. Establish the ground rules early on and this breed will become a much-loved and uniquely loyal member of the family.

Keep the training going throughout the life of your dog. Take a treat out on walks and keep giving him occasional commands to reinforce what he learned as a puppy.

Giant Schnauzers love learning new tasks and are good at agility, obedience, carting and schutzhund events, and any training should be kept interesting and fun. Too much ordering about and repetition and you'll lose his interest and willingness to learn.

Training should begin in the home and garden or yard where there are less distractions. But it should also be carried on outdoors where there are distractions. Giants love to run and romp around and you can use this time to teach your dog new commands.

These dogs enjoy being at the centre of family life. A Giant is definitely a sociable member of the family and does not appreciate being left alone for long periods. If you are out at work all day or live in an apartment, the Giant is not the right dog for you.

Extremely loyal dogs, they will often bond with one member of the family who they will recognize as pack leader.

 If you want your Giant to respond to all family members, get them involved in training too. Giants are usually very good with children.

Another method of diluting the Giant's loyalties is to allow other members of the family to feed the dog, rather than the same person all the time.

To sum up:

If allowed, the Giant may try and dominate humans and other dogs. Be sure to start training and socialization early, puppy classes are recommended, as is getting out on a leash and meeting other dogs and humans as soon as he is clear after his puppy vaccinations.

Early introduction to others is a must to help him or her learn to accept people and dogs from outside the immediate family. Be firm and consistent when training.

Channel his active mind and body by ensuring he gets plenty of daily exercise on and off the leash. Get all family members to give commands and treats and rotate who feeds him to build loyalty throughout the family.

With the right training and socialization and a lot of daily time from the owner, the Giant is a truly outstanding dog and will become a devoted companion for life.

Chapter 11. Schnauzer Behavior

Treated well and exercised daily, all three types of Schnauzer make wonderful pets. That's why so many Schnauzer owners get a second one (or even more) either as a companion dog or after their dog has passed away. As they say: Once smitten, never forgotten.

Some owners would say that Schnauzers regard themselves as part of the household. They certainly like love to be with people and taking part in our daily lives. But sometimes dogs can develop behavior problems and Schnauzers are no different from any other breed in this respect. There are numerous reasons why a dog might behave badly. Every dog is an individual and every case is different.

Cause and Effect

Poor behaviour may result from a number of factors. These include:

- Poor breeding
- Being badly treated
- Boredom due to lack of exercise
- Being left alone too long
- A change in living conditions
- Anxiety or insecurity
- Lack of socialization
- Fear

Bad behaviour may show itself in a number of different ways, such as:

- Barking
- Growling at people or dogs
- Nipping
- Biting
- Aggression towards other dogs
- Jumping up
- Chewing or destructive behavior
- Soiling inside the house

In this chapter, we look at some of the more common behavior problems affecting owners who have contacted our website at **www.max-the-schnauzer.com**

Although every dog is different and requires individual assessment and treatment, we outline some common causes of bad behavior and offer general pointers to help improve the situation. The best way to avoid it is to put in the time early on to try and nip the problem in the bud. If the bad behavior persists, you should consult a canine professional.

Personality

Just like humans, a dog's personality is made up of a combination of temperament and character. **Temperament** is the nature the dog is born with and it is inherited.

This is why getting your puppy for a good breeder is so important. Not only will a responsible breeder produce puppies from physically healthy dams and sires, but they will also look at the temperament of their dogs and only breed from those with good temperament traits.

Character is what develops through the dog's life and is formed by a combination of temperament and environment. How the dog is treated will have a great effect on his or her personality and behaviour.

Starting off on the right foot with good routines and training for your puppy is very important. Treat your dog well, spend time with him or her, exercise regularly, praise good behavior and be firm when he or she needs discipline. These measures will all help your Schnauzer to grow into a happy and well-behaved adult dog.

If you adopt a rescue Schnauzer, you may need a little extra patience. These people-loving dogs may arrive with some baggage. They have been abandoned by their previous owners for a variety of reasons and some still carry the scars of that trauma.

They may feel insecure or fearful. Your time and patience is needed to teach these dogs to trust again and to become happy in their new forever homes.

Nine Ways to Avoid Bad Behavior

Different dogs have different reasons for exhibiting bad behaviour. There is no simple cure for everything. Your best chance of ensuring your Schnauzer does not become badly behaved is to start out on the right foot and follow these simple guidelines:

1. **Buy from a good breeder**. A good breeder will only breed Schnauzers and one other type of dog maximum. They will use their expertise to match suitable breeding couples, taking into account factors such as good temperament and health.

2. **Start training early.** You can't start too soon, like babies, puppies have enquiring minds which can quickly absorb a lot of new information. You can start teaching your puppy to learn his own name a well as some simple commands from as early as two months old.

Basic training should cover house training, fear and aggressiveness control, chew prevention, simple commands like sit, come, stay and familiarizing him with leash and collar. Adopt a gentle approach when your dog is young. He will lose attention and get frightened if you are too harsh. Start with 10 minutes a day and build up.

Often the way a dog responds to his or her environment is a result of owner training and management – or lack of it.

3. **Take the time to learn what sort of temperament your dog has** – and train him accordingly. Is he by nature a nervous type or a confident chap? What was he like as a puppy, did he rush forward or hang back? Did he fight to get upright when you turned him on his back or was he happy to lie there?

Your puppy's temperament will affect his behavior and how he reacts to the world around him. A timid Schnauzer will not respond well to being shouted at, whereas a dominant, boisterous one will need more effort on your part as well as more discipline and exercise.

4. **Socialize your dog with other dogs and people.** Lack of interaction with people and other canines is one of the major causes of bad behaviour. Puppy classes or adult dog obedience classes are a great way to start, but make sure you do your homework afterwards.

Spend a few minutes each day reinforcing what you have both learned in class. Owners need training as well as Schnauzers!

Socialization does not end at puppyhood. Dogs are social creatures which thrive on seeing, smelling and even licking their fellow canines.

While the foundation for good behavior is laid down during the first few months, good owners will reinforce social skills and training throughout a dog's life.

Exposing your dog to different kinds of people, animals and environments - from dog obedience classes to visits to the vet and walks in the park - helps them develop confidence and ease. This goes a long way in helping them become a more stable, happy and trustworthy companion and reduces their chances of developing bad behavior traits.

5. **Lots of exercise.** Lack of exercise can be another major reason why some dogs behave badly, especially Standard and Giant Schnauzers, which are athletic dogs. All three types of Schnauzer are intelligent breeds and a lack of mental and physical stimulation can result in poor behaviour, such as excessive barking, chewing or ignoring commands as the dog becomes bored or frustrated.

   As the saying goes: "A tired Schnauzer is a happy Schnauzer". See Chapter 12 **Exercise** on how much daily exercise your Schnauzer needs outside the home.

6. **Reward your dog for good behaviour.**
   All training should be based on positive reinforcement; praising and rewarding your dog when (s)he does something good, like responding to a command. Generally, Schnauzers are keen to please their owners but can resort to bad behavior when something is amiss.

   The main aims of training are to build better relationship between your dog and you, his or her master, and to make him feel secure. Dogs often become stubborn and don't obey commands when there is not much interaction between them and their owners. Make sure you take the time to train him and tell him what a good boy he is when he behaves well.

7. **Ignore bad behavior**, no matter how hard this may be. If, for example (s)he is chewing his or her way through your kitchen units, remove the dog from the situation and then ignore him or her.

For some dogs, even negative attention such as shouting is some attention. The more time you spend praising and rewarding good behavior while ignoring bad behavior, the more likely (s)he is to respond to you.

8. **Learn to leave your dog.** Just as leaving your dog alone for too long can lead to behavior problems, so can being with him 100% of the time. The dog becomes over-reliant on his owner and then gets stressed when left. This is known as separation anxiety and usually results in the dog barking or whining incessantly when separated from his owner. It is a stressful situation for both owner and dog.

When your dog is a puppy, or when he arrives at your house as an adult, start by leaving him for a few minutes every day and gradually

build it up so that after a few weeks or months you can leave him for up to four hours. See our sections on **Separation Anxiety** and **Remedies** later in this chapter.

9. **Love your dog – but don't spoil him.** Miniature Schnauzers can develop into "Little Emperors" If allowed to rule the roost. They may become stubborn and resort to barking, growling or nipping if they think that they are in charge.

Giants and Standards have natural protective tendencies. They can become over-protective or too territorial if they are not taught their position in the household. They have to respect you and learn that YOU are the alpha, not them. Failure to train or exercise them properly can result in aggression towards people and other dogs.

You don't do your dog any favors by giving him too many treats either. Obesity in Schnauzers can be a contributory factor to a number of health problems, including diabetes and bladder stones.

Dogs don't just suddenly start behaving badly for no reason. As with humans, there's usually a trigger. Get to know the breed's temperament and your own dog's individual personality and develop a loving, trusting relationship with your dog.

Puppy Biting

Biting is one of the ways in which a puppy explores the world. But a puppy which is allowed to nip people and clothes can grow up to have other behavioral issues as an adult, so one of the most important aspects of puppy training is to teach bite inhibition.

A puppy has to learn what is and what is not acceptable. You don't want an adult dog mauling family, friends and strangers like a young puppy does. For the first few weeks of life, the pup's mother will discipline her litter. When the pup arrives at your home, you have to take her place and teach your new arrival some manners.

This should always be done in a gentle and positive manner. Aggression from you can result in aggression from the dog, as he becomes afraid and tries to overcome this by being combative towards other dogs or people.

Techniques

The first step is to teach your puppy not to hurt people by reducing the force of his play bites. You have to let your puppy know that these can hurt without resorting to physical punishment. A simple "Ouch!" is usually enough. When the puppy backs off, take a short time-out to recover. Then tell your pup to come, sit, and lie down to make up before resuming play.

If your puppy does not respond to your yelp and time-out, one effective technique is to call the puppy a "Bully!" and then leave the room and shut the door. Allow the pup a minute or two to reflect on the connection between his painful bite and the immediate departure of his favorite human playmate. Then return to make up.

It's important to show that you still love your puppy, only that his painful bites are objectionable. Puppies thrive on attention, so their playmate leaving is punishment enough. After a few minutes, have your pup come and sit and then start playing once more.

It is much better for you to walk away than to physically restrain him or remove him from his confinement area at a time when he is biting too hard.

Make a habit of playing with your puppy in his long-term confinement area. This technique is remarkably effective with dominant dogs, as it is the way puppies learn to inhibit the force of their bites when playing with each other.

If one puppy bites another too hard, the bitten pup yelps and playing is postponed while he licks his wounds. The biter soon learns that hard bites interrupt an otherwise enjoyable play session. He learns to bite more softly once play resumes.

The next step is to eliminate bite pressure entirely, even though the bites no longer hurt. While your puppy is chewing his human, wait for a bite that is harder than the rest and respond as if it really hurt, even though it didn't: "Ouch, that really hurt me, you bully!"

Your puppy begins to think: "Wow, these humans are SO sensitive! I'll have to be so careful when mouthing their delicate skin."

That's precisely what you want him to think: that he needs to be extremely careful and gentle when playing with humans.

Your pup should learn not to hurt people well before he is three months old. Ideally, by the time he is four-and-a-half months old, before he develops strong jaws and adult canine teeth, he should no longer be exerting any pressure when mouthing.

When you decide to stop the mouthing session altogether, say "Off" and then offer your puppy a treat, such as a Kong stuffed with kibble.

If ever your pup refuses to release your hand, say, "Bully!" or another sharp word, rapidly take your hand from his mouth, storm out of the room and shut the door. Again, give the pup a couple of minutes on his own to reflect on his loss and then go back to call him to come, sit and make up before continuing the game.

Another technique is to shake a can of coins when your Schnauzer pup starts nipping you. Many Schnauzers are sensitive to loud noises and this type of treatment may startle your pup. Over time, your dog will start to recognize that biting results in that awful sound and will try to avoid it.

Be consistent. If your Schnauzer nips other members of the household, it is important that they react the same way as you during a biting episode. Inconsistency results in confusion on the puppy's part and he may well continue to bite.

Aggression

This can occur for a number of different reasons and before you can remedy your dog's aggression, you have to find the cause.

One of the most common triggers is fear. This fear often comes from a bad experience the dog has suffered or from lack of proper socialization. Another form of fear-aggression is when a dog becomes over-protective of his owner.

Schnauzers are by nature good watchdogs, especially Giants and Standards. This is a positive trait; we want the dog to bark and alert us when somebody arrives unexpectedly at our home. It only becomes a negative trait when this natural instinct to protect turns aggressive.

An owner's treatment of a dog can be another reason. If the owner has been too harsh with the dog, such as shouting, using physical violence or reprimanding the dog too often, this can cause the dog to become aggressive. Again this is fuelled by fear.

Dogs can also become aggressive if they are consistently chained, under-fed or under-exercised. A bad experience with another dog or dogs can be a further cause.

Most dogs are more combative on the leash. This is because once on a leash, a dog cannot run away and escape. He therefore becomes more aggressive, barking and growling to warn off the other dog or person. The dog knows he can't run off, so tries to make himself as frightening as possible.

Socializing your puppy when young is very important. Many dog trainers believe that the first six months of a puppy's life is the critical time for socialization and during that early period they should be introduced to as many different situations, people and dogs as possible.

Techniques

Teaching your dog what is unacceptable behavior in the first place is the best preventative measure. Early training, especially during puppy years and before he or she develops the habit of biting, can save a lot of trouble in the future. Professional dog trainers employ a variety of techniques with a dog which has become aggressive. Firstly they will look at the causes and then they almost always use reward-based methods to try and cure fearful or aggressive dogs.

Counter conditioning is a positive training technique used by many professional trainers to help change a dog's aggressive behavior towards other dogs.

A typical example would be a dog which snarls, barks and lunges at other dogs while on the leash. It is the presence of other dogs which is triggering the dog to act in a fearful or anxious manner.

Every time the dog sees another dog, he or she is given a delicious treat to counter the aggression.

With enough steady repetition, the dog starts to associate the presence of other dogs with a tasty treat. Properly and patiently done (it won't happen overnight); the final result is a dog which calmly looks to the owner for the treat whenever he or she sees another dog while on the leash.

Whenever you encounter a potentially aggressive situation, divert your dog's attention by turning his head away from the other dog and towards you, so that he cannot make eye contact with the other dog.

Aggression Towards People

In evolutionary terms, it is not that long ago that dogs were wild creatures, living in packs, hunting for food and defending themselves and their territory against potential enemies.

For today's dog, aggression toward people is born out of fear and surfaces as a result of a real or perceived threat. The classic example is of a person who walks straight up to a dog, stares him in the eyes and pats him on top of his head. To the dog, each one of those actions suggests confrontation.

The person might be communicating: "Hey, fellah, how are you?" But the dog may read the human behavior as dangerous and an attempt to dominate.

It is not the dog's fault, he is reacting instinctively to a given situation. However, it is not acceptable in today's society for a dog to attack people, so he must learn to stop this behavior.

If your dog doesn't like people or is afraid of them, you need to find a way to instill confidence. When somebody comes to your house or into the garden, the dog needs to feel that this is a friend, not an enemy.

If your dog exhibits persistent aggressive behavior towards people, this must be dealt with and we recommend calling in a professional dog trainer or behaviorist.

Techniques

Desensitization is the most common method of treating aggression. It starts by breaking down the triggers for the behavior one small step at a time. The aim is to get the dog to associate pleasant things with the trigger, i.e. people or a specific person which he previously feared or regarded as a threat.

This is done through using positive reinforcement, such as praise or treats. Successful desensitization takes time, patience and knowledge. Again, a professional behaviorist will give you detailed instructions at the outset.

If your dog is starting to growl or snarl at people, there are a couple of techniques you can try to break him of this bad habit before it develops into full-blown biting.

One method is to arrange for some friends to come round, one at a time. When they arrive at your house, get them to scatter kibble on the floor in front of them so that your dog associates the arrival of people with tasty treats. As they move into the house, and your dog eats the kibble, praise your canine for being a good boy – or girl.

Manage your dog's environment. Don't over-face him. If he's at all anxious around children, manage him carefully around kids or avoid them altogether. Children typically react to dogs enthusiastically and some dogs may regard this as an invasion of their space.

Some canines are aggressive towards the partner of a dog owner. Many people have written to our website about this and it usually involves a male partner or husband and a Miniature Schnauzer.

Often the Mini is jealous of the attention his owner is giving to the man, or it could be that the dog feels threatened by the man.

The nature of the breed is that Minis are not as laid back as, say, a Labrador, and have a tendency to be more anxious about changes, such as a new person, dog or cat on the scene.

They key here is for the partner to gradually gain the trust of the dog. (S)he should show that (s)he is not a threat by speaking gently to the dog and giving treats when the dog is well behaved. Avoid eye contact, as the dog may perceive this as a challenge.

If the subject of the dog's aggression lives in the house, then try letting this person give the dog his daily feeds. The way to a dog's heart is often through his stomach.

Excessive barking

Some puppies start off by being noisy from the outset while others hardly bark at all until they reach adolescence or adulthood.

On our website we get emails from Schnauzer owners worried that their young pets are not barking enough. However, we get many more from owners whose dogs are barking too much!

Although not naturally noisy dogs, Schnauzers are generally good watchdogs, especially Giants and Standards, and barking is their way of alerting their owners of the arrival of other people or animals - whether friend or foe.

As humans, we use can use our voice in many different ways: to express happiness or anger, to scold, to shout a warning, and so on. Dogs are the same; different barks give out different messages.

To start out with, when your dog barks at an arrival at your house, gently praise your dog after the first few barks. If he persists, gently tell him that that is enough. Like humans, some dogs can get carried away with the sound of their own voice, so try and discourage too much barking from the outset.

Excessive, habitual barking is a problem which should be corrected early on before it gets out of hand and drives you and your neighbors nuts. The problem often develops during adolescence or early adulthood as the dog becomes more confident.

Listen to your dog and try and distinguish the different meanings. A dog does not have different words to express himself, he has to rely on the tone of his bark. Learn to recognize the difference between an alert bark, an excited bark, an aggressive bark or a plain "I'm barking coz I can" bark.

Your behavior can also encourage a dog to bark excessively. If your dog barks non-stop for several minutes and then you give him a treat to quieten him, he will associate his barking with getting a nice treat and keep doing it.

A better way to deal with it is to say in a firm voice "Quiet" after he has made a few barks. When he stops, praise him and he will get the idea that what you want him to do is stop. The trick is to nip the bad behavior in the bud before it becomes an ingrained habit.

Speak and Shush!

One technique is the Speak and Shush technique where you teach your dog or puppy to bark and be quiet on command. Get a friend to stand outside your front door and say "Speak" (or "Woof" or "Alert"). This is the cue for your accomplice to knock or ring the bell.

When your dog barks, praise him profusely. You can even bark yourself to encourage the dog! After a few good barks, say "Shush" and then dangle a

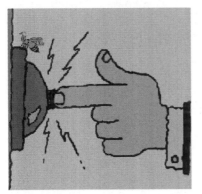 tasty treat in front of his nose. He will stop barking as soon as he sniffs the treat, because it is impossible to sniff and woof at the same time.

Praise your dog again as he sniffs quietly and then give him the treat.

Repeat this routine a few times a day and your dog will learn to bark whenever the doorbell rings and you ask him to speak.

Eventually your dog will bark after your request but BEFORE the doorbell rings, meaning he has learned to bark on command. Even better, he will learn to anticipate the likelihood of getting a treat following your "Shush" request and will also be quiet on command.

With "Speak and Shush" training, progressively increase the length of required shush time before offering a treat - at first just a couple of seconds, then three, five, ten, twenty and so on.

By alternating instructions to speak and shush, the dog is praised and rewarded for barking on request and also for stopping barking on request.

Always use your favorite teacher voice when training, speak softly when instructing your dog to shush, and reinforce the shush with whisper-praise. The more softly you speak, the more your dog will be likely to pay attention.

Coprophagia (Eating Feces)

It is hard for us to understand why a dog would want to eat his or any other animal's feces, but it does happen. Nobody fully understands why dogs do this, it may simply be an unpleasant behavior trait or there could be an underlying reason.

If your dog eats feces from the cat litter tray (a problem several owners have contacted us about), the first thing to do is to place the litter tray somewhere where the dog can't get to it – but the cat can.

 Perhaps on a shelf or put a guard around it, small enough for the cat to get through but not your Schnauzer.

Our Schnauzer Max eats cow manure or horse muck sometimes when we take him out into the countryside. I don't know why he does it, but he usually stops when we tell him to and he hasn't suffered any after effects – so far!

Vets have found that canine diets with low levels of fiber and high levels of starch increase the likelihood of coprophagia. If your dog is exhibiting this behavior, first check that the diet you are feeding is nutritionally complete.

Look at the first ingredient on the dog food packet or tin – is it corn or meat? Does he look skinny? Check that you are feeding him enough, but don't overfeed.

If there is no underlying medical reason, then you will have to modify your dog's behavior. Remove cat litter trays, clean up after your dog and do not allow him to eat his own feces. If it's not there, he can't eat it.

Don't reprimand the dog for this behavior. A better technique is to distract him while he is in the act and then remove the offending material.

Coprophagia is usually seen in pups aged between six months to a year and often disappears after this age.

Separation Anxiety

It's not just Schnauzers that experience separation anxiety - people do too. About 7% of adults and 4% of children suffer from this disorder. Typical symptoms for humans are:

* distress at being separated from a loved one

* fear of being left alone

Our canine companions aren't much different to us. When a dog leaves the litter, his owners become his new family or pack.

It's estimated that as many as 10% to 15% of dogs suffer from separation anxiety. All three types of Schnauzer are susceptible because they thrive on interaction with people and generally do not do well if left alone for long periods.

Separation anxiety is on the increase and recognized by behaviorists as the most common form of stress for dogs.

Distressing

It can be equally distressing for the owner - I know because Max suffers from this. He howls whenever we leave home without him. Fortunately his problem is only a mild one. If we return after only a short while, he's usually quiet.

Although, if we silently sneak back home and peek in through the letterbox, he's never asleep. Instead he's waiting by the door looking and listening for our return.

It can be embarrassing. Whenever I go to the Post Office, I tie him up outside and even though he can see me through the glass door, he still barks his head off.

Luckily the lady behind the counter is a dog lover and, despite the large **GUIDE DOGS ONLY** sign outside, she lets Max in. He promptly dashes through the door, sits down beside me and stays quiet as a mouse!

Tell-Tale Signs

Does your Schnauzer do any of the following -

- Dig, chew, or scratch at doors and windows trying to join you?
- Howl, bark or cry in an attempt to get you to return? (This is what Max does.)
- Foul inside the house, even though he is housetrained? (This **only** occurs when left alone).

- Follow you from room to room whenever you're home?
- Restlessness - such as licking his coat excessively, pacing or circling?
- Greet you ecstatically every time you come home – even if you've only been out to empty the garbage?
- Get anxious or stressed when you're getting ready to leave the house?
- Dislike spending time outdoors alone?

If so, he or she may suffer from separation anxiety. Fortunately, in many cases, this can be cured.

Canine Separation Anxiety in Puppies

Canine separation anxiety in puppies is fairly common, especially in those adopted from animal shelters. They may have been abandoned once already and fear it happening again.

A puppy will emotionally latch on to his new owner who has taken the place of his mother and siblings. Although you want to shower your new puppy with love, it's important to leave him alone for short periods to avoid him becoming totally dependent on you.

I was working from home when we got Max. With hindsight, it would have been better if we'd regularly left him alone for a couple of hours more often in the few weeks after we brought him home.

Symptoms are not commonly seen in middle-aged dogs, although dogs that develop symptoms when young may be at risk later on.

Separation Anxiety is also common in older dogs. Pets, age and - like humans - their senses, such as hearing and sight, deteriorate. They become more dependent on their owners and may then become more anxious when they are separated from them - or even out of view.

So what can you do if your dog is showing signs of canine separation anxiety? Every dog is different, but here are some tried and tested techniques which have proved effective for some dogs.

Techniques

* Keep arrivals and departures low key. For example when I return home, I make Max sit and stay and then let him out into the garden without patting or acknowledging him. I pat him several minutes later.

* Leave your dog a "security blanket" such as an old piece of clothing you have recently worn which still has your scent on it.

* Leave a radio on - but not too loud - in the room with the dog so he doesn't feel so alone. Try and avoid a heavy rock station!

* Associate your departure with something good. As you leave, give your dog a rubber toy like a Kong filled with a tasty treat. This may take his mind off of you leaving. We've tried this with Max, but he "punishes" us by refusing to touch the treat until we return home.

* Tire your dog out before you leave him alone in the house. Take him for a long walk or play fetch until he runs out of steam. When you leave the house he'll be too tired to make a big fuss.

* If your dog is used to a crate, then try crating him when you go out. Many dogs feel safe in a crate, and being in a crate can also help to reduce their destructiveness. Pretend to leave the house, but listen for a few minutes. A word of warning – if your dog starts to show major signs of distress, remove him from the crate immediately as he may injure himself.

* Begin with very short departures to see how long you can leave your dog before he or she gets anxious. It may only be a few seconds, so start there. Leave for anything from a few seconds up to a minute, return, and if your dog has remained calm, give him a reward.

* Always return before your dog becomes anxious, and reward him for staying calm. Gradually increase the time you are gone to several hours. This may take weeks to months, so be patient.

*In severe cases, the dog may require medication from a qualified vet. Before this happens, the dog needs a thorough history and medical examination to rule out any other behavioral problems or illnesses.

Sit-Stay-Down

Another technique for reducing separation anxiety in dogs is to practice the common "sit-stay" or "down-stay" training exercises using positive reinforcement.

The goal is to be able to move briefly out of your dog's sight while he is in the "stay" position. Your dog then learns that he can remain calmly and happily in one place while you go to another.

To do this, gradually increase the distance you move away from your dog. As you progress, you can do this during normal daily life.

For example, if you're watching TV with the dog by your side and you get up for a snack, tell him to stay and leave the room. When you come back, give him a treat or praise him quietly.

What You Must Never Do

Canine Separation Anxiety is NOT the result of disobedience or lack of training. It's a psychological condition, your dog feels anxious and insecure.

- NEVER punish your dog for showing signs of separation anxiety. This will only make him worse.
- NEVER leave your dog in a crate if he is frantic to get out. It may cause him physical or mental harm.

Important: This chapter provides only a general overview of dog behavior. If your dog does have behavior problems, particularly if he or she is aggressive towards people or other dogs, you should seek help from a reputable canine behaviorist.

Chapter 12. Exercise

Regular Exercise

One thing all dogs – including all Schnauzers - have in common is that they do need daily exercise, preferably regular walks.

Regular exercise keeps your dog's heart pumping, blood flowing, muscles working and joints functioning.

Exercise helps to keep your dog healthy, happy and free from disease and illness.

Whether you live in an apartment or on a farm, it's a good idea to start regular exercise patterns early so the dog gets used to his daily routine and adapts to a constant amount of exercise.

Miniature Schnauzers

The subject of Miniature Schnauzer exercise provokes a wide response. Speak to 10 different owners and you'll get 10 different answers as to how much exercise their Mini needs.

One reason for the growing popularity of the breed is indeed their versatility. As far as exercise goes, these small dogs can adapt to living in a small home in the suburbs, an apartment in the city or a log cabin in the middle of nowhere.

This dog breed is suitable for older people, single people living alone or as a pet for the whole family. They make very adaptable companions. However, being an excellent companion dog to people doesn't mean that the Mini Schnauzer has no needs of his own - he DOES!

Before we got our puppy Max, we read that as far as Miniature Schnauzer exercise goes, these dogs are easy to please They are as happy running round the garden as going for a five-mile hike.

That is largely - although not entirely - true. Max is definitely happier going for a five or even 10-mile hike than staying in the garden. This is partly because he has been used to a lot of daily exercise since being a pup.

Around the time of his two daytime walks, (we also take him out for five or 10 minutes last thing at night), he starts pacing around the house. He has got used to daily exercise routine and is now happiest when he gets his two walks a day. He is an active dog and needs that exercise. To suddenly stop it would not be fair.

Establishing regular exercise routines early on for your Mini is the key. We have people who contact us to ask if the Miniature Schnauzer can go on a day-long hike or if they make suitable running partners. We have others who keep Miniature Schnauzers as companions and they are happy living in the home and garden with the occasional walk.

The trick is to get your Schnauzer into an exercise routine early on which fits into your lifestyle and which keeps your dog content. If you start out by taking your Mini out three times a day and then suddenly stop, he will become restless and demand your attention because he has been used to having a lot of exercise.

Schnauzers can and do go on all-day hikes. But they are small dogs and need to build up to this. Start off with a couple of hours or a half day and gradually increase the amount of exercise.

Generally, Miniature Schnauzers are not ideal running partners. Firstly, they are small dogs with no great speed and secondly, they are ratters by nature with a keen sense of smell and are easily distracted by scents and small furry animals. A Standard or even a Giant might be a better choice.

If you have a busy life and can only take your Miniature out once a day, get into the routine early on. This will help your dog's body and mind to adjust to your lifestyle.

How Much Exercise?

Veterinarians advise that you take your Mini out for at least one decent walk every day - and two or three times daily is even better. At least 30 minutes a day is the **minimum** recommended exercise for a Miniature Schnauzer.

You shouldn't think about getting one if you cannot commit to at least one daily walk with your dog.

Like humans, dogs' energy levels do vary and a dog with lots of energy will need longer than half an hour. Mini Schnauzers are not slothful by nature, they are similar to terriers and enjoy running around given half a chance.

Our Mini Max gets about 90 minutes a day spread over three walks. We've taken him on six-hour hikes in the hills and he's still running energetically at the end of the day. Although once back home he sleeps and snores all night. I think this is where the expression "dog tired" comes from!

The Mini Schnauzer loves playing games. Their compact bodies lend themselves to a short stride and small turning circle. This is helping the breed gain success in agility classes in both the USA and UK.

Throwing a ball or a toy is a good way of burning off your dog's excess energy. Although if he's anything like Max, you'll get more exercise than him. If you throw the ball, do not expect your Mini to fetch it back. It's quite likely will go off and sniff something more interesting on the way back and you'll have to retrieve the ball yourself.

Minis have many qualities, but attention span and fetching balls are not two of them. If you want a dog to bring the ball back, we suggest you consider a Retriever! (Having said that, there are some Minis who actually love to return the ball to you).

In a dog's mind, nothing can beat going for a walk. Whether to a new place with new scents or revisiting regular haunts - just see how excited he gets when you get the leash out.

Look on the bright side, a brisk walk is a great way of keeping both you and your dog fit – even when it's raining or snowing. In fact, most Schnauzers love snow.

The Miniature Schnauzer's ancestors were bred for ratting and this instinct is still alive and kicking in many Minis today. Many of them love to chase cats, birds and small rodents.

If you take your Mini out for a walk where there are likely to be these small creatures around, bear in mind he might high tail it after them.

If you walk him near busy roads, it is highly recommended to keep them on a leash until you reach a safe traffic-free area. Most Minis have no or very little road sense.

Standard Schnauzers

The Standard Schnauzer – known simply as the Schnauzer in the UK - is a robust dog with high energy levels. He is agile and active and not recommended for owners who aren't prepared to take him out for regular daily walks.

Standards need sufficient exercise for physical well-being – heart, muscles and joints – but also for mental well-being. They are intelligent dogs and without sufficient exercise can become bored and restless, which can result in poor or destructive behavior.

On the other hand, a Standard at the heart of the family getting plenty of daily exercise is a happy Schnauzer and a wonderful, loyal companion.

How Much Exercise?

The amount of exercise a Standard needs will vary from one dog to the next, but generally the breed is considered one which needs moderate exercise. The minimum amount an adult should get is the equivalent of a brisk one to two-mile walk at least three times a day, or a longer walk twice a day. A rough guideline is an hour or more. You should let him trot or run around for part of that time to keep him in good physical condition.

Get into a pattern of exercise so he gets used to the same routine. Play sessions or letting him run free in a well-fenced garden all adds to the exercise, but it should not replace daily walks. This bright, attractive dog likes to be challenged physically and mentally.

This is a dog which would really enjoy all-day hikes and would potentially make a good running partner. Again, the amount of exercise should be built up gradually.

The Standard Schnauzer puppy is constantly exploring, learning and testing his limits. As an adult, he is always ready for a walk in the woods, a ride in the car, a training session or any other activity which allows him to be engaged with his owner.

Bear in mind that the Standard was bred as a rat catcher and this breed's instinct to chase small furry or feathered creatures is still quite strong. Keep him on a leash near traffic or where he might run off after a rodent and into danger.

They were also bred as working dogs and this need to work – or burn off energy - is still part of their DNA. Standards are always on the alert, even when they seem to be relaxing by your feet.

As an all-around performance event dog, it is hard to beat the Standard Schnauzer. Agility is one of the newest AKC events, it's open to all breeds and Standard Schnauzers excel in this sport due to their enthusiasm, athletic ability, and intelligence. Many are also very good at tracking, rallying and herding.

Giant Schnauzers

The Giant Schnauzer is a very athletic and muscular dog. They are also energetic and intelligent. They love to be with their owners and can be territorial. These factors mean that Giants are both extremely rewarding dogs as well as high maintenance.

Do NOT get a Giant Schnauzer unless you can devote the time each day that he or she needs. You should be prepared to give up a couple of hours a day to exercise, train and groom him.

Giants need a lot of daily exercise and will enjoy a good run around with other dogs. Quite a percentage of owners have more than one Giant, but you need quite a lot of outside space for this to work well. They are quick learners and love to have a job to do or a game to play. A Giant is a dog that is not going to be happy left on his or her own all day without company and without much exercise.

They become very attached to their owners. Their natural tendency to guard and protect makes the Giant a valuable asset as a watch dog for its family - as long as he or she is part of the family, and not left outside on his own.

If Giants do not get enough attention and exercise, they will get bored and may become badly behaved and difficult to control. If, on the other hand, your Giant is involved in family life and getting plenty of regular daily exercise, then owners will tell you that you'll have a friend for life second to none.

How Much Exercise?

As a minimum, a Giant Schnauzer needs at least an hour to an hour and a half of exercise out of the home or yard every day – two hours is better.

Ideally his should be split over at least two daily exercise sessions.

If you are a keen runner or jogger looking for a running mate, this could be a breed to consider.

If you get a Giant, be prepared to spend the time to properly train them when young and give them plenty of daily exercise. They also enjoy a challenge and need to be stimulated mentally.

Some people get a Giant Schnauzer because they are so handsome; they turn heads when you walk along the street with them. However, the rescue centers have many Giants who have become too much of a handful for inexperienced owners who were not able or prepared to give their dog the time he or she needed.

If you can give a Giant a couple of hours of your time every day and involve him in your daily life, then you will have a friend for ever.

Regularly exercised, these dogs are very agile for their size. This, combined with their intelligence and willingness to learn quickly, has brought them success in agility and obedience events.

Many Giant Schnauzers love water...and snow.

Schnauzer Exercise Tips

1. A Schnauzer is not like a sheepdog or a German Shepherd. If you are hoping that you can throw a ball and your dog will retrieve it to his heart's content and get lots of exercise, you might be disappointed! Schnauzers are easily distracted …..by interesting smells….other people…..other dogs……

   You may well find that while your Schnauzer will happily head off after the ball, getting him to bring it back is another matter.

   If you start going and fetching the ball yourself, he will never fetch it back. Try and train him while he is a puppy to fetch the ball back.

   The best way to do this is to give him praise or a treat when he does bring the ball or toy back to your feet.

2. Most Schnauzers love snow. If you live in an area with a lot of the white stuff, you may want to invest in a set of doggie boots for the winter. Schnauzers have the type of fur on their legs which attracts sticky snow.

   This results in their paws and legs becoming covered in snowballs, which can actually be quite painful for your dog. Some owners bathe their Schnauzer's legs in lukewarm water when they come home covered in snowballs. You must **never** bathe them in hot water.

3. Many Schnauzers have a stubborn streak. If yours stares at you and tries to pull you in another direction when on the leash, ignore him.

   Do not return his stare, he is challenging you. Simply continue along the way YOU want to go, not him!

Exercising Puppies

We are often asked how much exercise a puppy needs. This will vary depending on whether you have a Miniature, Standard or Giant Schnauzer. It will also depend on the energy level of your dog.

Schnauzers, like humans, have their own characters and some will be livelier and need more exercise than others.

Puppies need much less exercise than fully-grown dogs. If you over-exercise a growing puppy you can overtire him and damage his developing joints, especially with Giants, causing early arthritis or other problems.

The golden rule is to start slowly and build it up. Once your puppy has completed his inoculations, start with short walks once or twice a day.

A good guideline is **five minutes exercise per month of age** (up to twice a day) until the puppy is fully grown. That means 15 minutes when he is three months old, 20 minutes when four months old, and so on.

Gradually increase the time as he gets used to being exercised and this will build up his muscles and stamina. Once he is fully grown, he can go out for much longer.

It is important that puppies go out for exercise every day in a safe and secure area or they may become frustrated.

Time spent in the garden or yard, however big, is no substitute for exploring new environments and socializing with other dogs and people. Get them used to being outside the home environment and experiencing new situations as soon as they are clear after vaccinations.

Start to train your puppy to come back to you so that you are soon confident enough to let him roam free off the leash.

You can start training – in small doses – right from the beginning.

Things To Avoid

* You should never exercise your dog on a full stomach as this can cause bloat. Your dog should not be given rigorous exercise within an hour before or after eating.

Canine bloat happens when something goes wrong during food digestion.

It causes gases to build up quickly in the stomach, blowing up the stomach like a balloon. This cuts off normal blood circulation to and from the heart.

The dog can go into shock and then cardiac arrest within hours of the start of bloat. If you suspect this is happening, get him to a vet immediately.

Larger breeds like the Giant Schnauzer are more susceptible than smaller breeds. See Chapter 13. **Health** for more information.

* Do not throw a ball or toy repeatedly for a puppy, as he may run and run to fetch it in order to please you - or because he thinks it is a great game.

He may become over-tired, or pull a muscle, strain his heart or otherwise damage himself.

* Similarly with swimming. This is a very exhausting exercise for a dog, so do not repeatedly throw toys or sticks into the sea or lakes for him to fetch – no matter how much he begs you. He may overstretch himself and get into difficulties.

When a dog is over-exercised, it can place a strain on his heart – just like with humans.

Try and vary your exercise route – it will be more interesting for you and the dog.

Make sure your Schnauzer has constant access to fresh water. Dogs can't sweat and Schnauzers don't shed hair either. They need to drink water to cool down.

Socializing

It's a good idea to get your Schnauzer used to other dogs at an early age. That helps him from becoming over-protective or too territorial. Aggression towards other dogs is often grounded in fear. A dog which mixes easily with others is less likely to be aggressive or have other bad habits.

As soon as your puppy has had all his jabs and got the all-clear to go out, start introducing him to other dogs in the neighborhood.

Introduce your dog on neutral territory, so that neither dog feels he has to protect "his patch." Puppy classes are a great way of getting him used to other dogs while learning discipline.

Although Miniature Schnauzers do not need as much exercise as their larger cousins, it is still good practice to take them on a walk out every day.

If a dog is at home or in the garden/yard all day, he can become bored, too territorial or over-protective with you and your family. These can lead to bad behavior such as excessive barking, destructive behavior or aggression.

As with humans, getting out to different places and mixing is both sociable and healthy. Dogs are pack animals. If properly socialized, they enjoy meeting or playing with other canines.

Some Schnauzer owners have more than one, as they tend to do well with other Schnauzers. Only do this is you have time to look after both or all of the dogs. Getting a canine companion for your Schnauzer should not be a substitute for your time and attention. Walking along the street, in the park, or hiking with your Schnauzer is great activity for both you and your dog.

Schnauzer Circles

Several readers of our website have asked why their Schnauzer runs round and round in circles at full speed. Is something wrong with the dog?

The answer is that these are what are known as 'Schnauzer circles'. It is just a way of your dog letting off some steam. He may do it outdoors or even in the house when he is feeling full of energy.

Our Mini loves going on long walks and when he gets on top of the open moorland, he is so excited that he starts running in Schnauzer circles. Round and round as fast as his legs will carry him. He usually tries to grab chunks of grass in his teeth as he goes.

The game of Schnauzer circles is even more fun for the dog if you pretend to chase him! Here is Max running Schnauzer circles:

You can't catch me!

Chapter 13. Schnauzer Health

The no. 1 piece of advice for anybody looking to get a healthy Schnauzer - whether it's a Giant, Standard or Miniature - is to buy a well-bred puppy.

Scientists have come to realize the important role that genetics have to play in determining a person's long-term health. Well, the same is true of dogs. This means getting your Schnauzer puppy from a reputable breeder who selects the parent dogs based on a number of factors, including:

- **body shape**
- **conformation**
- **temperament**
- **lineage**
- **health history**

Far better to spend time choosing a dog which has been properly bred from good stock than to expend a lot of time and money later on at the vet's when the dog develops hereditary problems caused by poor breeding.

As the English upper classes say (in a very posh accent): *"There is no substitute for good breeding, darling!"*

Robust Schnauzers
Fortunately, Giant, Standard and Miniature Schnauzers are by and large regarded as healthy and robust dog breeds.
They are relatively free of many genetic problems that affect some other purebreds (or pedigree, as they are known in the UK). They also remain active until quite late in life, particularly Minis and Standards.

As with any pet, you will probably encounter some health issues during the (hopefully) many years of your dog's life. Your pet's health is of interest to all owners, so we have listed some of the main health topics relevant to Schnauzers.

Disclaimer: *We are not canine health experts. If you are worried about your Schnauzer's health, our advice is always the same: consult a veterinarian.*

Firstly, how can you tell if your dog is in good health? Well, our Top Ten Signs are a good start. Here are some positive things to look out for which show you have a healthy Schnauzer.

Top Ten Signs of a Healthy Dog

1. **Eyes** - a healthy dog's eyes are shiny and bright. The area around the eyeball (known as the conjunctiva) should be a healthy pink.

Paleness could be a sign of underlying problems. There should be no thick, green or yellow discharge from the eyes. A cloudy eye may be a sign of cataracts.

2. **Coats** - these are easy-to-monitor indicators of a healthy dog. They should be full and soft to the touch. Wiry coats like the Schnauzer's should be springy and full of life. A dull, lifeless coat could be a sign that something is amiss.

3. **Skin** - This should be smooth without redness. (Normal skin pigment can vary from pink to black or brown according to the color of the Schnauzer.) Open sores, scales, scabs or growths can be a sign of a problem. Signs of fleas, ticks and other external parasites should be treated immediately.

4. **Ears** - need to be clean with no dark or bloody discharge. Redness or swelling can be a sign of problems. Miniature Schnauzers' ears should be checked regularly. They are prone to ear problems as they have narrow, ear canals full of fur which does not shed.

This warm place is an ideal breeding ground for mites and infections. The ears should smell normal and not be hot. A bad smell, a hot ear or one full of brown wax is often a sign of infection, so get him to the vet's as soon as you can or it could lead to a burst ear drum or even deafness.

5. **Mouth** – Gums should be pink or pigmented with black. Paleness can be a sign of anemia. Red, inflamed gums can be a sign of gingivitis or other tooth disease. Again, your Schnauzer's breath should smell OK.

Young dogs will have sparkling white teeth whereas older dogs will have darker teeth, but they should not have any hard white, yellow, green or brown bits.

6. **Nose** - a dog's nose is often an indicator of health symptoms. The nose should normally be moist and cold to the touch. The moistness should be from clear, watery secretions. Any yellow, green or foul smelling discharge is not normal. In younger dogs this can be a sign of canine distemper.

7. **Weight** – your Schnauzer should be the correct weight according to breed standards. He should also have a healthy appetite. The rib, back and hip bones should not show, but you should be able to feel them under the skin. Dogs may have weight problems due to factors such as diet, allergies, diabetes, thyroid or other problems. A general rule of thumb is that your Schnauzer's stomach should be in a line or above his rib cage when standing. If his stomach hangs below, he is overweight.

8. **Energy** - Your Schnauzer should have good energy levels with fluid and pain-free movements. Lethargy or lack of energy - if it is not the dog's normal character - could be a sign of an underlying problem.

9. **Temperature** - The normal temperature of a dog is 101°F. Excited or exercising dogs may run a slightly higher temperature.
 Anything above 103 degrees or below 100 degrees should be checked out.
The exceptions are female dogs that are about to give birth. They will often have a temperature of 99 degrees.

10. **Attitude** - a generally positive attitude and personality is the sign of good dog health. Symptoms of illness may be lethargy, sleeping a lot, not eating his food or a general lack of interest in his surroundings.

So now you know some of the signs of a healthy dog – what are the signs of an unhealthy dog? There are many different symptoms that can indicate your beloved canine companion isn't feeling great.

You may think your Schnauzer can't talk, but he can! If you really know your dog, his character and habits, then he CAN tell you when he's not well. He does this by changing his patterns.

Some symptoms are physical, some emotional and others are behavioral. It's important for you to be able to recognize these changes as soon as possible. Early treatment can be the key to keeping a simple problem from snowballing into a serious illness.

If you think your Schnauzer is unwell, it is useful to keep an accurate and detailed account of his symptoms to give to the veterinarian. This will help him or her correctly diagnose and effectively treat your dog.

Most canine illnesses are detected through a combination of signs and symptoms. Here are some signs that your dog may be unwell.

Four Vital Signs of Illness

1. Temperature

A newborn puppy will have a temperature of 94-97º F. This will reach the normal adult body temperature of 101ºF at about 4 weeks old. Anything between 100ºF and 102ºF is normal.

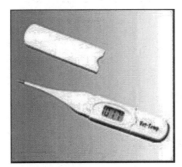

Like all dogs, a Schnauzer's temperature has to be taken via his rectum. Be very careful when doing this. It's easier when you get someone to your dog still while you do this. Digital thermometers are a good choice, but **only use one specifically made for rectal use** as a normal glass thermometer can easily break off in the rectum.

Remember - exercise or excitement can cause the temperature to rise by 2 or 3º when the dog is actually in good health. If your dog's temperature is above or below these norms, get him to the vet.

---

2. Respiratory Rate

Another symptom of canine illness is a change in breathing patterns. This varies a lot depending on the size and weight of the dog. An adult dog will have a respiratory rate of 15-25 breaths per minute when resting. You can easily check this by counting your dog's breaths for a minute with a stopwatch handy. Don't do this if the dog is panting - it doesn't count.

3. Heart Rate

You can feel for your dog's heartbeat by placing your hand on his lower ribcage - just behind the elbow. Don't be alarmed if the heartbeat seems irregular compared to a human. It IS irregular in many dogs.

Have your vet show you how and get used to your dog's normal heartbeat.

* Big dogs like Giant Schnauzers have a normal rate of 70 to 120 beats per minute.

* Medium dogs like Standard Schnauzers have a normal rate of 80 to 120 beats per minute.

* Small dogs like Miniature Schnauzers have a normal rate of 90 to 140 beats per minute.

---

4. Behavior Changes

Classic symptoms of illness are any inexplicable behavior changes.

If there's NOT been a change in the household atmosphere, such as another new pet, a new baby, moving home or the absence of a family member, then the following symptoms may well be a sign that all is not well with your Schnauzer:

- Depression
- Anxiety
- Tiredness
- Trembling
- Falling or stumbling
- Loss of appetite
- Walking in circles

If your dog shows any of these signs, he needs to be kept under close watch for a few hours or even days. Quite often he will return to normal of his own accord. Like humans, dogs have off-days too!

If he is showing any of the above symptoms, then don't over-exercise him and try to avoid stressful situations for him. Make sure he has access to clean water. There are many other signals of ill health, but these are four of the most important.

If your dog does need professional medical attention, Most veterinarians will want to know -
WHEN the symptoms first appeared
WHETHER they are getting better or worse, and
HOW FREQUENT the symptoms are. Are they intermittent, continuous or increasing in frequency?

Remember - keep a record for your vet.

Here are some canine maladies and the signs to look out for. It is by no means a complete list and if you are at all worried about your Schnauzer, make an appointment to see a vet.

By the way, we have a completely separate section on skin problems. See Chapter 14 on **Schnauzer Skin.**

Canine Cataracts

These are one of the most common forms of eye problems affecting dogs. They can affect all ages and breeds, but certain types of cataract show up more commonly in certain breeds.

Unfortunately Schnauzers, especially Miniatures, may be more likely to suffer from canine cataracts than many other dog breeds. Other susceptible breeds include Spaniels, Poodles, Retrievers, German Shepherds and several types of terrier.

Symptoms

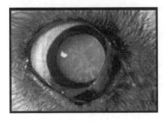

The symptoms of canine cataracts are fairly straightforward. Cataracts cause the dog's eye to become white or cloudy.

Sometimes this is described as the lens having a white or crushed ice appearance. Our image shows a dog with a moderate cataract.

Note that it is not unusual for older dogs' eyes to become slightly blue-gray. Called nuclear sclerosis, this usually occurs in dogs over six years old and doesn't usually affect their vision, so treatment is not normally necessary.

Causes

The normal, transparent lens in the eye focuses beams of light onto the retina at the back of the eye. This enables your dog to see clearly.

The word **cataract** literally means 'to break down.' It is a disruption of the normal arrangement of the lens fibers.

In simple terms, a complex biological pump keeps the lens covered in a special water/protein solution. When this is damaged, extra water is pumped into the lens which in turn damages the lens fibers and causes calcium and sodium to be retained.

This interferes with the dog's sight by partially or completely blocking the clarity of the lens, resulting in a reduction of the dog's vision.

Canine cataracts may be quite small and not significantly affect the dog's sight. However, if the condition is left untreated and the cataract becomes dense enough, the dog may eventually go blind.

Congenital Canine Cataracts

Healthy Canine Eye

These are hereditary and are one of the most common forms of cataracts. This type of cataract is also the most common one suffered by Miniature Schnauzers and often affects both eyes. It is also known as CJC or Congenital Juvenile Cataracts.

Another cause of cataracts is **diabetes mellitus**. With diabetes, the cataracts are always in both eyes and grow rapidly. In these cases, treatment of the diabetes can often reduce the cataracts.

With hereditary or **congenital cataracts**, symptoms can appear in puppies as young as five weeks old.

With Schnauzers this is far less of a problem than it was 20 years ago. Responsible breeders have taken dogs testing positive for congenital cataracts out of their breeding stock.

(Of course that is not the case with puppy farms or mills, which is a reason why the problem, although it has been reduced, still exists.)

Good breeders have their sire's and dam's eyes annually tested by a veterinarian as well as testing all puppies before they leave with the new owners. In the UK, puppies can be tested from five weeks of age by a specialist BVA vet. The current cost is £35 per litter for up to 5 puppies, then £5 per additional puppy.

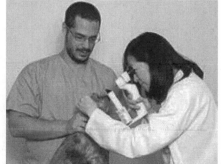

For this reason, many UK Miniature Schnauzer breeders believe that all Schnauzer puppies should be tested and they would welcome compulsory eye testing for puppies before they leave for a new home and are registered with the Kennel Club.

This is what the American Miniature Schnauzer Club has to say: "*The AMSC recommends having breeding stock tested by a Certified Veterinary Ophthalmologist once a year.*

It also recommends having the pups checked as some eye problems can be seen by a Veterinary Ophthalmologist as early as eight weeks of age.

"Eye problems cannot be detected by your regular veterinarian until full fruition of the condition. A VO can see the condition before it becomes apparent to the owner and thus maybe before it is bred. The AMSC has sponsored research into some of the more common hereditary eye diseases seen in the breed.

"A test breeding program was developed to help eradicate congenital cataracts, a very common problem a few years ago. This condition has been virtually wiped out and eye checks are recommended to make sure the progress made by dedicated breeders is not reversed."

Standard Schnauzers are generally an extremely healthy breed, but hereditary eye disease is one ailment which they can suffer from, along with hip dysplasia.

Both problems can be tested for breeding dogs before they pass the trait onto the next generation The Standard Schnauzer Club of America recommends that every breeder tests their stock for hip and eye problems and to breed from only healthy animals.

TIP: If you are buying a Schnauzer puppy, select a reputable breeder and check if their breeding stock has certificates to say their dogs are free from hip dysplasia (Giants and Standards) or eye problems. See Chapter 7 on **Puppies** and how to select a reputable breeder.

Treatment

If you think your Schnauzer may have cataracts, it is important to get him to a vet as **soon as possible.**

Early removal of cataracts can restore vision and provide a dramatic improvement in the quality of your Schnauzer's life. Our photo below shows an eye with cataracts on the left. The photo on the right is the same eye after surgery with an artificial lens:

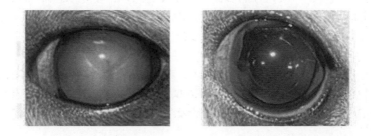

The only treatment for canine cataracts is surgery (unless the cataracts are caused by another condition like canine diabetes). Despite what you may have heard, laser surgery does not exist for canine cataracts, neither is there any proven medical treatment other than surgery.

The good news is that surgery is almost always (85-90%) successful. The dog has to have a general anesthesia but the operation is often performed on an outpatient basis.

The procedure is similar to small incision cataract surgery in people. An artificial lens is often implanted in the dog's eye to replace the cataract lens. Dogs can see without an artificial lens, but the image will not be in focus. You'll have to discuss with the ophthalmologist whether your dog would benefit from an artificial lens.

Even better news is that once the cataract is removed, it does not recur.

However, before your dog can undergo this procedure, he has to be fit and healthy and a suitable candidate for surgery.

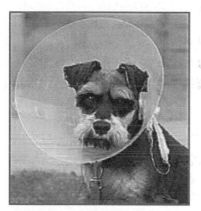

After the operation, he will probably have to stay at the surgery overnight so that the professionals can keep an eye on him. Once back home, he will have to wear a protective Elizabethan collar, or E collar, for about one to two weeks while his eye is healing.

You will also have to keep him quiet and calm (not always easy with Schnauzers!) You'll also have to give him eye drops, perhaps four times a day for the first week and then less frequently after that.

The success of cataract surgery depends heavily on the owner doing all the right things. But all the effort will be worth it when your Schnauzer regains his sight.

Bladder Stones

Miniature Schnauzers are one of the breeds considered to be more at risk than other breeds of bladder stones.

The stones are produced when excess minerals and other waste products solidify or crystallize in the dog's bladder area.

Symptoms

These may vary, but they are generally painful for all dogs. Early recognition and treatment is recommended.

Female dogs are more prone to bladder stones than male dogs and they are more common in smaller breeds than larger breeds.

More often than not, bladder stones only become a problem once one blocks the flow of urine. At this point, your dog won't be able to urinate properly.

If not attended to right away, serious complications can arise, especially if the stone is too big for him or her to pass.

Signs of bladder stones:

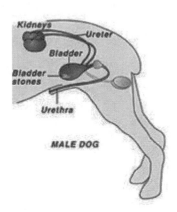

1. Blood in the urine
2. Increased frequency of urination
3. The dog is straining to urinate
4. The urine may be cloudy or have an unpleasant odor
5. Loss of appetite
6. Lack of energy

Prevention

Bladder stones are caused by too many minerals in the blood. **It is important not to overfeed your Schnauzer.** A healthy, balanced diet is what he or she needs. Feed the right amount and at the right times.

Stick to mealtimes – usually twice a day for an adult Mini Schnauzer – and try to avoid feeding tidbits throughout the day.

Calcium and magnesium can actually prevent bladder stones. Consider giving your Schnauzer a daily half cup of milk with one of her meals.

Apple cider vinegar is a recommended remedy for dogs that suffer from recurring bladder stones as they regulate the acidity levels in the stomach.

Make sure your Schnauzer has access to water 100% of the time. This will help to naturally flush out excess minerals and unwanted waste products before they start to solidify.

NOTE: Bladder and kidney stones are similar, as are the symptoms. They are both urinary stones.

Treatment

Your vet may take a urine sample from your dog or use Ultrasound to diagnose bladder stones (see photo, right). If caught early enough, they can often be treated by a course of antibiotics.

In an emergency when a bladder stone has caused a blockage, a catheter (long tube) may be inserted into the dog's urinary tract and bladder to try and remove both the urine and the stone in one go.

As a last resort, if the bladder stones are large and it is impossible to take them out with the use of a catheter, surgery may be the answer.

If your dog has suffered from bladder stones, your vet will probably prescribe a special diet for her.

Hip Dysplasia

Canine Hip Dysplasia (CHD) is the most common cause of hind leg lameness in dogs. It is a hereditary condition which occurs mainly in large, fast-growing breeds such as the Giant Schnauzer.

Smaller breeds may also suffer, but the effects are not as obvious.

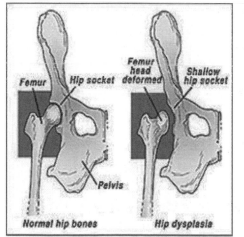

The hip is a ball and socket joint. Hip dysplasia is caused when the head of the femur (leg) fits loosely into a shallow and poorly-developed socket in the pelvis. The right of our picture shows a shallow hip socket and a deformed femur head, causing hip dysplasia. The healthy joint is on the left.

The joint carries the weight of the dog and becomes loose and unstable. Muscle growth lags behind normal development. Early diagnosis gives your vet the best chance to tackle the problem as soon as possible, minimizing the chance of arthritis developing.

Symptoms

1. Lameness in hind legs, particularly after exercise
2. Difficulty or stiffness when getting up or climbing uphill
3. A "bunny hop" gait

181

4. Dragging the rear end when getting up
5. Waddling rear leg gait
6. A painful reaction to stretching the hind legs, resulting in a short stride
7. A side-to-side sway of the croup (area above the tail) with a tendency to tilt the hips down if you push down on the croup
8. A reluctance to jump, exercise or climb stairs

Symptoms range from mild discomfort to extreme pain.

 A puppy with canine hip dysplasia usually starts to show signs between five and 13 months old.

Causes and Triggers

Canine hip dysplasia is an inherited condition. There are, however, factors which can trigger or exacerbate the condition. These include:

1. Overfeeding your Giant, especially on a diet high in protein and calories
2. Excess calcium, also usually due to overfeeding
3. Extended periods without exercise – or too much vigorous exercise, especially when your dog's bones are growing
4. Obesity

Feeding a high-calorie diet to growing dogs can trigger a predisposition to hip dysplasia as the rapid weight gain places increased stress on the hips. Make sure your young Giant is on the right diet for a growing dog.

Treatment

As with most conditions, early detection leads to a better outcome. Your vet will need to take an X-ray to diagnose hip dysplasia. Treatment is geared towards preventing the hip joint getting worse and decreasing pain.

Various medical and surgical treatments are now available to ease the dog's discomfort and restore some of his or her mobility.

Treatment depends upon several factors, such as the dog's age, how bad the problem is and, sadly, how much money you can afford to spend on treatment.

Management of the condition usually consists of restricting exercise, keeping body weight down and then managing pain with analgesics and anti-inflammatory drugs.

As with humans, cortisone injections may sometimes be used to reduce inflammation and swelling. Cortisone can be injected directly into the affected hip to provide almost immediate relief for a tender, swollen joint.

In extreme cases, surgery may also be an option, especially with older dogs.

Regarding Standard Schnauzers – these are generally a very healthy breed with few inherent problems, but hip dysplasia is one ailment which can affect some.

TIP: If you are getting a Giant or Standard Schnauzer puppy, pick a reputable breeder and check if there is any history of CHD in either of the parents or grandparents of your puppy.

Cushing's Disease

This is a complex ailment best described as a set of symptoms caused by the dog producing too much of a hormone called Cortisol.

It is a condition that usually develops over a period of time, which is why it is more often seen in older dogs. It affects some Miniature Schnauzers.

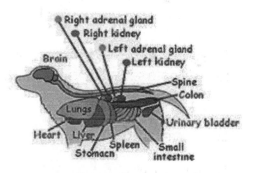

Cortisol is released by the adrenal gland located near the kidneys. Normally it is produced during times of stress to prepare the body for strenuous activity.

It alters the metabolism, allowing the body to draw energy from stored fats and sugars while retaining sodium and water. Think of an adrenaline rush.

The problem occurs when the body is constantly being exposed to Cortisol and in effect is in a persistent state of breakdown.

Symptoms

It can be very difficult to diagnose. The most common signs of Cushing's are similar to those for old age, making it hard to diagnose and then monitor.

If you can, it is a good idea to keep a note of any changes you notice in your dog's habits, behavior and appearance and take these notes with you to the vet.

The most noticeable signs of Cushing's Disease include:

1. Drinking excessive amounts of water
2. Urinating frequently and possible urinary incontinence
3. A ravenous appetite
4. Hair loss or recurring skin problems
5. Pot belly
6. Thin skin
7. Muscle wastage
8. Lack of energy, general lethargy
9. Panting a lot

Causes and Diagnosis

There are three types of Cushing's, but 80-85% of cases are caused by a tumor on the pituitary gland. Usually benign and often very small, this tumor will put pressure on the gland, causing an increase in the pituitary secretion. This then causes the adrenal gland to release additional Cortisol.

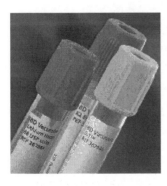

In some cases, the over-use of steroids (artificial hormones), such as Cortisone, Prednisone and others can lead to Cushing's Disease. There are two blood tests for Cushing's Disease. Your vet may carry out one or both of these.

You may have to leave your Schnauzer at the surgery for a few hours to have her tested, as levels of Cortisol naturally rise and fall throughout the day.

Treatment

Cushing's Disease cannot be cured, but it can be managed and controlled with medication, usually giving your dog a longer, happier life. Lysodren (Mitotane) is the drug of choice for treating the most common pituitary-dependent Cushing's Disease. The medication has to be given for the remainder of the dog's life.

If you suspect your Schnauzer does have Cushing's Disease, you should contact your vet immediately.

Epilepsy

Thanks to www.canineepilepsy.co.uk for the information for this article. If your Schnauzer has epilepsy, we recommend reading this excellent website to gain a greater understanding of the illness.

If you have witnessed your dog having a seizure (convulsion), you will know how frightening it can be. Seizures are not uncommon in dogs, but many dogs have only a single seizure.

If your dog has had more than one seizure it may be that he or she is epileptic. Just as in people, there are medications for dogs to control seizures, allowing your dog to live a more normal life.

Epilepsy is an ailment which can affect some Giants and Miniatures.

"Epilepsy" means repeated seizures due to abnormal activity in the brain and is caused by an abnormality in the brain itself. If seizures happen because of a problem somewhere else in the body, such as heart disease (which stops oxygen reaching the brain), this is not epilepsy.

Your vet may do tests to try to find the reason for the epilepsy but in many cases no cause can be identified. Epilepsy affects around four in every 100 dogs. In some breeds it can be hereditary.

Symptoms

Some dogs seem to know when they are about to have a seizure and may behave in a certain way. You will come to recognize these signs as meaning that a seizure is likely. Often dogs just seek out their owner's company and come to sit beside them when a seizure is about to start.

Once the seizure starts, the dog is unconscious - they cannot hear or respond to you. Most dogs become stiff, fall onto their side and make running movements with their legs. Sometimes they will cry out and may lose control of their bowels or bladder.

Most seizures last between one and three minutes - it is worth making a note of the time the seizure starts and ends because it often seems that a seizure goes on for a lot longer than it actually does.

After a seizure, dogs behave in different ways. Some dogs just get up and carry on with what they were doing, while others appear dazed and confused for up to 24 hours afterwards.

Most commonly, dogs will be disoriented for only 10 to 15 minutes before returning to their old self. They often have a set pattern of behavior that they follow - for example going for a drink of water or asking to go outside to the toilet.

If your dog has had more than one seizure, you may well start to notice a pattern of behavior which is typically repeated.

Most seizures occur while the dog is relaxed and resting quietly. It is very rare for a seizure to occur while exercising. Often seizures occur in the evening or at night. In a few dogs, seizures seem to be triggered by particular events or stress. It is common for a pattern to develop and, should you dog suffer from epilepsy, you will gradually recognize this as specific to your dog.

What Should I Do?

The most important thing is to **stay calm**. Remember that your dog is unconscious during the seizure and is not in pain or distressed. It is likely to be more distressing for you than for him

Make sure that he is not in a position to injure himself, for example by falling down the stairs, but otherwise do not try to interfere with him. Never try to put your hand inside his mouth during a seizure or you are very likely to get bitten.

Seizures can cause damage to the brain and if your dog has repeated occurrences, it is likely that further seizures will occur in the future. The damage caused is cumulative and after a lot of seizures there may be enough brain damage to cause early senility (with loss of learned behavior and house-training or behavioral changes).

It is very rare for dogs to injure themselves during a seizure. Occasionally they may bite their tongue and there may appear to be a lot of blood, but is unlikely to be serious; your dog will not swallow his tongue.

If a seizure goes on for a very long time (more than 10 minutes), his body temperature will rise and this can cause damage to other organs such as the liver and kidneys as well as the brain. In very extreme cases, some dogs may be left in a coma after severe seizures.

When Should I Contact the Vet?

Generally, if your dog has a seizure lasting more than five minutes, or is having more than three a day, you should contact your vet.

When your dog starts a seizure, make a note of the time. If he comes out of it within five minutes, then allow him time to recover quietly before contacting your vet. It is far better for your dog to recover quietly at home rather than be bundled into the car and carted off to the vet right away.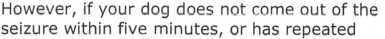

However, if your dog does not come out of the seizure within five minutes, or has repeated seizures close together, contact your vet immediately, as he or she will want to see your dog as soon as possible. If this is his first seizure, your vet may ask you to bring him in for a check and some routine blood tests.

Always call your vet's practice before setting off to be sure that there is someone there who can help your dog. There are many things other than epilepsy which cause seizures in dogs. When your vet first examines your dog, he or she will not know whether your dog has epilepsy or another illness.

It's unlikely that the vet will see your dog during a seizure, so it is vital that you're able to describe in some detail just what happens. You might want to make notes or take a video. These days you can take a video with most mobile phones.

Epilepsy usually starts when the dog is aged between one and five. So if your dog is older or younger, it is more likely he has a different problem.

Your vet may need to run a range of tests to ensure that there is no other cause of the seizures. These may include blood tests, possibly X-rays, and maybe even a scan (MRI) of your dog's brain. If no other cause can be found, then a diagnosis of epilepsy may be made.

If your Schnauzer already has epilepsy, remember these key points:

- Don't change or stop any medication without consulting your vet.
- See your vet at least once a year for follow-up visits.
- Be sceptical of "magic cure" treatments.

Remember, live *with* epilepsy not *for* epilepsy. With the proper medical treatment, most epileptic dogs have far more good days than bad ones. Enjoy all those good days.

Treatment

It is not usually possible to remove the cause of the seizures, so your vet will use medication to control them.

This treatment will not cure the disease, but merely manage the signs – even a well-controlled epileptic will have occasional seizures. Sadly, as yet there is no miracle cure for epilepsy.

There are many drugs used in the control of epilepsy in people, but very few of these are suitable for long-term use in the dog. Many epileptic dogs require a combination of one or more types of drug to achieve the most effective control of their seizures.

Treatment for epilepsy is decided on an individual basis and it may take some time to find the best combination and dose of drugs for your pet. You must have patience when managing an epileptic pet.

It is important that medication is given at the same time each day. Once your dog has been on treatment for a while, he will become dependent on the levels of drug in his blood at all times to control seizures.

If you miss a dose of treatment, blood levels can drop and this may be enough to trigger a seizure. Never adjust the dose or stop treatment without asking your vet.

Each epileptic dog is an individual and a treatment plan will be designed specifically for him. It will be based on the severity and frequency of the seizures and how they respond to different medications.

Keep a record of events in your dog's life, note down dates and times of seizures and record when you have given medication. Each time you visit your vet, take this diary along with you so he or she can see how your pet has been since their last check-up.

If seizures are becoming more frequent, it may be necessary to change the medication.

It is rare for epileptic dogs to stop having seizures altogether. However, provided your dog is checked regularly by your vet to make sure that the drugs are not causing any side-effects, there is a good chance that he will live a full and happy life.

Visit the website at **www.canineepilepsy.co.uk** for more information

---

Diabetes

There are two types of diabetes in dogs: **diabetes mellitus** and **diabetes insipidus.** Diabetes mellitus is the most common form and affects one in 500 dogs.

Schnauzers, particularly Miniatures, are regarded as having a moderate risk of contracting diabetes.

Thanks to modern veterinary medicine, the condition is now treatable and need not shorten your Schnauzer's lifespan or interfere with his quality of life.

Diabetic dogs undergoing treatment now have the same life expectancy as non-diabetic dogs of the same age and gender. However, if left untreated, the disease can lead to cataracts, increasing weakness in the legs (neuropathy), other ailments and even death.

In dogs, diabetes is typically seen between the ages of four to 14 years, with a peak incidence at seven to nine years. Both males and females can develop diabetes; unspayed females have a slightly higher risk.

Diabetes usually affects middle-aged and older dogs, but there are also juvenile cases. The typical canine diabetes sufferer is middle-aged, female and overweight.

Diabetes insipidus is caused by a lack of vasopressin, a hormone which controls the kidneys' absorption of water.

Diabetes mellitus occurs when the dog's body does not produce enough insulin and cannot successfully process sugars.

What is Diabetes?

Dogs, like us, get their energy by converting the food they eat into sugars, mainly glucose. This glucose travels in the dog's bloodstream and individual cells then remove some of that glucose from the blood to use for energy.

The substance that allows the cells to take glucose from the blood is a protein called *insulin.*

Insulin is created by beta cells that are located in the pancreas, which is next to the stomach. Almost all diabetic dogs have type 1 diabetes: their pancreas does not produce any insulin.

Without it, the cells have no way to use the glucose that is in the bloodstream, so the cells 'starve' while the glucose level in the blood rises.

Your vet will use blood samples and urine samples to check glucose concentrations in order to diagnose diabetes. Early treatment helps to prevent further complications developing.

Symptoms

The most common symptoms of diabetes in dogs include:

- Extreme thirst
- Excessive urination
- Weight loss
- Increased appetite
- Coat in poor condition
- Lethargy
- Vision problems due to cataracts

Cataracts and Diabetes

Some diabetic dogs go blind. Cataracts may develop due to high blood glucose levels which cause water to build up in the lens of the eye. This leads to swelling, rupture of the lens fibers and the development of cataracts.

In many cases, the cataracts can be surgically removed to bring sight back to the dog. Vision is restored in 75% to 80% of diabetic dogs that undergo cataract removal.

However, some dogs may stay blind even after the cataracts are gone, and some cataracts simply cannot be removed. Blind dogs are often able to get around surprisingly well, particularly in a familiar home.

Treatment

Treatment starts with the right diet. Your vet will prescribe meals low in fat and sugars. He will also recommend medication. Many cases of canine diabetes can be successfully treated with diet and medication. More severe cases may require insulin injections.

In the newly-diagnosed dog, insulin therapy begins at home. Normally, after a week of treatment, you will take him back to the vet who will do a series of blood sugar tests over 12 to 14 hours to see when the blood glucose peaks and hits its lows.

Adjustments are then made to the dosage and timing of the injections. Your vet will explain how to prepare and inject the insulin. You may be asked to collect urine samples using a test strip (a small piece of paper that indicates the glucose levels in urine).

If your dog is already having insulin injections, beware of a "miracle cure" for diabetes offered on some internet sites. It does not exist. There is no diet or vitamin supplement which can reduce your dog's dependence on insulin injections. This is because vitamins and minerals cannot do what insulin does in the dog's body.

If you think that your dog needs a vitamin or mineral supplement, discuss it with your vet first to make sure that it does not interfere with your dog's other medications.

Exercise

Managing your dog's diabetes also means managing his activity level. Exercise 'burns up' blood glucose the same way that insulin does. If your dog is on insulin, any active exercise on top of the insulin might cause him to have a severe low blood glucose episode, called hypoglycemia.

Keep your dog on a reasonably consistent exercise routine. Your usual insulin dose will take that amount of exercise into account.

If you plan to take your dog out for some extra demanding exercise, such as swimming at the lake or playing in the snow, give the dog only half of its usual insulin dose.

Tips

- You can usually buy specially formulated diabetes dog food from your veterinarian

- You should feed the same type and amount of food at the same time every day

- Most veterinarians recommend twice a day feeding for diabetic pets. It is OK if your dog prefers to eat more often

- If you have other pets in the home, they should also be placed on a twice-a-day feeding schedule, so that the diabetic dog cannot eat from their bowls

- Help your dog to achieve the best possible blood glucose control by not feeding him table scraps or treats between meals

- Watch for signs that your dog is starting to drink more water than usual. Call the vet if you see this happening, as it may mean that the insulin dose needs adjusting.

Food raises blood glucose
Insulin and exercise lower blood glucose
Keep them in balance

"I DON'T SEE TABLE SCRAPS."

Pancreatitis

The pancreas is a V-shaped organ located behind the stomach and the first section of the small intestine, the duodenum. It has two main functions:

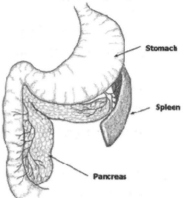

1. It aids in metabolism of sugar in the body through the production of insulin
2. It is necessary for the digestion of nutrients by producing pancreatic enzymes. These enzymes help the body digest and absorb nutrients from food.

Acute pancreatitis is a sudden onset of pancreatic inflammation. Chronic pancreatitis can also occur. The Miniature Schnauzer is a breed which may have a moderate risk of developing pancreatitis.

Causes

This is a complicated illness. There are many factors which can contribute to the development of pancreatitis in dogs, such as:

* Certain medications, especially potassium bromide, as well as some anti-cancer drugs and some antibiotics

*Metabolic disorders including hyperlipidemia (high amounts of lipid in the blood) and hypercalcemia (high amounts of calcium in the blood)

*Hormonal diseases such as Cushing's Disease, hypothyroidism and diabetes mellitus

*Obesity. Overweight dogs appear to be more at risk

*Genetics may play a role, with Schnauzers and Yorkshire Terriers appearing to be more prone to the disease

*Nutrition: dogs with high-fat diets, dogs who have recently eaten trash or have been fed table scraps and dogs who 'steal' or are fed greasy 'people food' seem to have a higher incidence of the disease

*Abdominal surgery, trauma to the abdomen (e.g. being hit by a car), shock or other conditions that could affect blood flow to the pancreas

*Previous pancreatitis

Symptoms

Symptoms of acute pancreatitis may range from mild to very severe. The symptoms are similar to those of other diseases and may include:

* a very painful abdomen
* abdominal distention
* lack of appetite
* depression
* dehydration
* a 'hunched up' posture
* vomiting
* perhaps diarrhea.

Fever often accompanies these symptoms.

Animals with more severe disease can develop heart arrhythmias (irregular heartbeat), sepsis (body-wide infection), difficulty breathing and a life-threatening condition called disseminated intravascular coagulation (DIC), which results in multiple hemorrhages.

If the inflammation is severe, organs surrounding the pancreas could be 'autodigested' by pancreatic enzymes released from the damaged pancreas and become permanently damaged. Dogs with chronic pancreatitis may show signs similar to those in acute pancreatitis, but they are often milder & severe complications are less likely.

Diagnosis and Treatment

To diagnose pancreatitis, other causes of the symptoms must be ruled out. A complete history is taken and a thorough physical exam, a complete blood count, chemistry panel and urinalysis are performed.

Blood levels of two pancreatic enzymes, amylase and lipase may be obtained. The cPLI (canine pancreatic lipase immunoreactivity) test is another diagnostic tool.

 In addition, radiography (X-rays) and ultrasound can also help in making the diagnosis. A biopsy can result in a conclusive diagnosis, but is not common. The goals of treatment are to:

* Correct dehydration
* Provide pain relief
* Control vomiting
* Provide nutritional support
* Prevent complications

Dehydration and electrolyte imbalances are common in dogs with acute pancreatitis, so supplemental fluids are given either by the subcutaneous or intravenous route, depending upon the severity of the condition.

Dogs that are experiencing pain can be treated with pain relievers such as meperidine or butorphanol. Medication is often given to decrease the amount of vomiting. If vomiting is severe, food, water and oral medications are withheld for at least 24 hours.

Depending upon the dog's response, food intake can be started again after a day or more. The dog is generally fed small meals of a bland, easily digestible, high-carbohydrate and low-fat food. In some cases it may be necessary to use tube feeding to provide proper nutrition.

If the pancreatitis was caused by a medication, this should be stopped. If it was caused by a toxin, infection or other condition, the vet should start the appropriate treatment for the underlying condition.

In rare instances where there are intestinal complications or the development of a pancreatic abscess, surgery may be necessary.

Prognosis (Outlook)

Pancreatitis can be a very unpredictable disease. In most cases, if the pancreatitis was mild and the dog only had one episode, chances of recovery are good. Keeping the dog on a low-fat diet may be all that is necessary to prevent recurrence or complications.

In other cases, what appears to be a mild case may progress, or may be treated successfully only to have recurrences, sometimes severe.

Some animals develop chronic pancreatitis, which can lead to diabetes mellitus and/or pancreatic insufficiency, also called 'maldigestion syndrome.'

In pancreatic insufficiency, the nutrients in food are passed out in the feces undigested. A dog with this disease often has a ravenous appetite, diarrhea, and weight loss. Even though he is eating, he could literally starve to death.

Treatment for pancreatic insufficiency is lifelong and expensive, but is possible. The dog's digestive enzymes are replaced through a product processed from pancreases of hogs and cattle which contain large quantities of the digestive enzymes.

A change in diet with added nutritional supplements may also be necessary.

Summary

Acute pancreatitis can be a life-threatening condition and early recognition and treatment can improve chances of recovery. Fever, lack of appetite, depression and vomiting are the most common signs.

Treatment is based on correcting the dehydration and maintaining proper fluid and electrolyte balances, controlling other symptoms and providing nutritional support.

Tips

Good habits can go a long way in preventing pancreatitis, as well as many other health conditions.

Pancreatitis is most commonly present in dogs that have eaten foods with a high fat content. The best way to ensure that your dog is a lower risk is to feed him a healthy, **low fat diet**. Since obese dogs are commonly afflicted with pancreatitis, a **regular exercise** routine is important as well.

Pancreatitis is a degenerative, self-fuelling illness that can eventually cause irreversible damage to your dog's system. Since the symptoms of pancreatitis will usually begin long before serious damage, **it is important to identify the condition and begin treatment as soon as possible.**

Hypothyroidism

Hypothyroidism is a common hormonal disorder in dogs and is due to under-active thyroid gland.

The gland (located on either side of the windpipe in the dog's throat) does not produce enough of the hormone thyroid, which controls the speed of the metabolism. Dogs with very low thyroid levels have a slow metabolic rate.

It occurs mainly in dogs over the age of five. Although Giant Schnauzers are not listed in the ten breeds most likely to contract the disease, they are more prone to hypothyroidism than some other breeds.

Congenital or *juvenile onset hypothyroidism* is an inherited condition that can sometimes be seen in Giant Schnauzers and German Shepherds.

Generally, hypothyroidism occurs most frequently in large, middle-aged dogs of either gender. The symptoms are often non-specific and quite gradual in onset, and they may vary depending on breed and age. Most forms of hypothyroidism are diagnosed with a blood test.

Common Symptoms

The following symptoms have been listed in order, with the most common ones being at the top of the list:

- High blood cholesterol
- Lethargy
- Hair Loss
- Weight gain or obesity
- Dry coat or excessive shedding
- Hyperpigmentation – or darkening of the skin (seen in 25% of cases)
- Intolerance to cold (seen in 15% of dogs with the condition)

Treatment

Although hypothyroidism is a type of auto-Immune disease and cannot be prevented, the good news is that symptoms can usually be easily diagnosed and treated. Most dogs suffering from hypothyroidism can be well-managed on oral thyroid hormone replacement therapy (tablets).

The dog is normally placed on a daily dose of a synthetic thyroid hormone

called thyroxine (levothyroxine). The dose and frequency of administration of the drug varies depending on the severity of the disease and the response of the individual dog to the drug.

A dog is usually given a standard dose for his weight and then blood samples are taken periodically to check his response and the dose is adjusted accordingly.

Depending upon your dog's preferences and needs, the medication can be given in different forms, such as a solid tablet, in liquid form, or a gel that can be rubbed into the your Schnauzer's ears. Once started, the dog will have to be on treatment for the rest of his life.

In some less common situations, surgery may be required to remove part or all of the thyroid gland. Another treatment is radioiodine, where radioactive iodine is used to kill the overactive cells of the thyroid.

While this is considered one of the most effective treatments, not all animals are suitable for the procedure and a lengthy hospitalization is often required.

Happily, once the diagnosis has been made and treatment has started, whichever treatment your dog undergoes, the majority of symptoms disappear.

NOTE: **Hyper**thyroidism (as opposed to **hypo**thyroidism) is caused by the thyroid gland producing too much thyroid hormone. It is quite rare in dogs, being more commonly seen in cats. A common symptom is the dog being ravenously hungry all the time, but actually losing weight.

Bloat

Canine bloat is a serious medical condition which requires urgent medical attention. Without it, the dog can die.

Bloat – or Gastric Dilitation-Volvulus (GDV) to give the ailment its correct term – occurs when the dog's body becomes overstretched with too much gas.

Bloat usually affects large, deep-chested dogs such as Giant Schnauzers, Great Danes and Dobermans. It occurs when gas is taken in as the dog eats or drinks. It is thought that stress can also act as a trigger.

Bloat can occur with or without the stomach twisting (volvulus). As the stomach swells with gas, it can rotate 90° to 360°. The twisting stomach traps air, food, and water inside and the bloated organ stops blood flowing properly to veins in the abdomen, leading to low blood pressure, shock and even damage to internal organs.

Bloat can kill a dog in less than one hour. If you suspect your Giant Schnauzer has bloat, get him in the car and to the veterinarian **IMMEDIATELY.** Even with treatment, mortality rates range from 10% to 60%. With surgery, this drops to 15% to 33%.

Causes

The causes are not completely clear, despite research being carried out into the condition.

However, the following conditions are generally thought to be contributory factors:

* Air is gulped down as the dog eats or drinks.
This is thought more likely to cause a problem when the dog 's bowls are on the floor.

To avoid bloat, some Giant Schnauzer owners buy or construct a frame for the bowls so they are at chest height. However, some experts believe that this may actually increase the risk of bloat. Discuss the situation with your veterinarian before deciding what to do.

* A large meal eaten once a day. For this reason, many owners of Giants feed their dog two smaller feeds every day.

* Diet may be a factor: avoid dog food with high fats or which use citric acid as a preservative, also avoid food with tiny pieces of kibble. Don't overfeed your dog and try and prevent him or her from eating too fast.

* Drinking too much water just before, during or after eating. Remove the water bowl just before mealtimes, but be sure to return it soon after.

* Vigorous exercise before or after eating. Allow one hour either side of mealtimes before allowing your dog strenuous exercise.

* Age, temperament and breeds: older dogs are more susceptible than younger ones and more males suffer than females. Deep-chested dogs are most at risk and some dogs have a hereditary disposition for bloat.

Stress can possibly be a trigger, with nervous and aggressive dogs being more prone to the illness. Try and maintain a peaceful environment for your dog.

Symptoms

Bloat is extremely painful and the dog will show signs of distress, although it may be difficult to distinguish them from other types of stress.

He may stand uncomfortably or seem to be anxious for no apparent reason. Dry retching. A dog with bloat will often attempt to vomit every five to 30 minutes, but nothing is fetched up, except perhaps foam.

Other signs include swelling of the abdomen – this will usually feel firm like a drum – general weakness, difficulty breathing or rapid panting, drooling or excessive drinking.

His behavior will change and he may do some of the following: whine, pace up and down, look for a hiding place or lick the air.

Treatment

Bloat is an emergency condition. Get your dog the a veterinary surgery **immediately.**

Canine Cancer

This is the biggest single killer of dogs and will claim the lives of one in four dogs. It is the cause of nearly half the deaths of all dogs aged ten years and older, according to the American Veterinary Medical Association.

Symptoms

Early detection is critical. Some things to look out for are:

- Swellings anywhere on the body
- Lumps in a dog's armpit or under his jaw
- Sores that don't heal
- Bad breath
- Weight loss
- Poor appetite, difficulty swallowing or excessive drooling
- Changes in exercise or stamina level
- Labored breathing
- Change in bowel or bladder habits

If your dog has been spayed or neutered, the risk of certain cancers decreases. These cancers include uterine and breast/mammary cancer in females, and testicular cancer in males (if the dog was neutered before he was six months old).

Along with controlling the pet population, spaying is especially important because mammary cancer in female dogs is fatal in about 50% of all cases.

Diagnosis

Just because your dog has a skin growth doesn't mean that it's cancerous. As with humans, tumors may be benign (harmless) or malignant (harmful).

Your vet will probably confirm the tumor using X-rays, blood tests and possibly ultrasounds. He or she will then decide whether it is benign or malignant via a biopsy in which a tissue sample is taken from your dog and examined under a microscope.

If your dog is diagnosed with cancer, there is hope. Advances in veterinary medicine and technology offer various treatment options, including chemotherapy, radiation and surgery. Unlike with humans, a dog's hair will not fall out with chemotherapy.

Treatment

Canine cancer is growing at an ever-increasing rate. One of the difficulties is that your pet cannot tell you when a cancer is developing, but if cancers can be detected early enough, they often respond well to treatment.

Over recent years, we have all become more aware of the risk factors for human cancer. Responding to these by changing our habits is having a significant impact on our health. For example, stopping smoking, protection

from over-exposure to strong sunlight and eating a healthy, balanced diet all help to reduce cancer rates.

We should keep a close eye on ourselves, go for regular health checks and report any lumps and bumps to our doctors as soon as they appear. Increased cancer awareness is certainly improving human health.

The same is true with your dog. While it is impossible to completely prevent cancer from occurring, a healthy lifestyle with a balanced diet and plenty of exercise can help to reduce the risk. Also be aware of any new lumps and bumps on your dog's body and any changes in his or her behavior.

The success of treatment will depend on the type of cancer, the treatment used and on how early the tumor is found. The sooner treatment begins, the greater the chances of success.

One of the best things you can do for your dog is to keep a close eye on him for any tell-tale signs. This shouldn't be too difficult and can be done as part of your regular handling and grooming.

The Future

Research into earlier diagnosis and improved treatments is being conducted at veterinary schools and companies all over the world. Advances in biology are producing a steady flow of new tests and treatments which are now becoming available to improve survival rates and canine cancer care.

If your dog is diagnosed with cancer. Do not despair, there are many options and new, improved treatments are constantly being introduced.

Our Happy Ending

We know from experience that canine cancer can be successfully treated if it is diagnosed early enough.

Max, our Miniature Schnauzer, was diagnosed with T-cell lymphoma when he was four years old. We had noticed a black lump on his anus which grew to the size of a small grape within a few days.

We took him to the vet within the first few days of seeing the lump and, after a test, he was diagnosed with the dreaded T-cell lymphoma. This is a particularly nasty and aggressive form of cancer which can spread to the lymph system and is often fatal for dogs.

As soon as the diagnosis was confirmed our vet Graham operated on Max and removed the lump. He also had to remove one of his anal glands, but as dogs have two, this was not a serious worry. Afterwards, we were on tenterhooks, not knowing if another lump would grow or if the cancer had already spread to his lymph system.

After a few months, Max had another blood test and was finally given the all-clear. Max is now a happy, healthy eight-year-old. We were very lucky. I would strongly advise anyone who suspects that their dog has cancer to get him or her to your local vet as soon as possible.

Chapter 14. Schnauzer Skin

Schnauzer skin conditions are not uncommon. In fact, we could write a whole book on this subject alone. The topic generates a lot of questions, particularly from Miniature Schnauzer owners, on our website at:
  www.max-the-schnauzer.com/schnauzer-faq.html
If you visit this section, you'll find some useful suggestions of tried and tested remedies from our readers.

 While most Schnauzers have no problems at all, some do suffer from sensitive skin, allergies or skin disorders, causing them to scratch, bite or lick themselves excessively. Symptoms may vary from mild itchiness to a chronic reaction.

Canine skin disorders are a complex topic. Some dogs can spend hours running through fields, digging holes and rolling around in the grass with no after-effects at all. Others may spend most of their time indoors and have an excellent diet, but still experience severe itching.

Skin problems may be the result of one or more of a wide range of causes - and the list of potential remedies and treatments is even longer.

It's by no means possible to cover all of them in this chapter. What we hope to do is give you a broad outline of some of the most common ailments which we and our readers have come across. We have also included some of the symptoms and remedies tried by ourselves and other Schnauzer owners.

 This information is not intended to take the place of professional help. We are not animal health experts and **you should always contact your veterinarian when your dog appears physically unwell or uncomfortable.**

This is particularly true with skin disorders. A vet may well be able to find the source of the problem and treat it before it develops into anything more serious for your Schnauzer.

Before a vet can diagnose the problem, you'll have to be prepared to tell him or her all about your dog's diet, exercise regime, habits, medical history and local environment. The vet will then carry out a thorough physical examination, possibly followed by further tests, before he or she can prescribe the correct treatment.

Types of Allergies

"Canine dermatitis" means inflammation of the dog's skin and it can be triggered by a whole range of things. These causes can be divided into several categories. They are:

Environmental or Contact Irritations

These are often considered to be allergies. But they aren't really. They are a direct reaction to something the dog physically comes into

contact with. It could be as simple as grass, specific plants or other animals.

If the trigger is grass or other outdoor materials, these allergies are often seasonal. The dog may require treatment (often tablets, shampoo or localized cortisone spray) for spring and summer, but be perfectly fine with no medication for the other half of the year. Our Mini Schnauzer is like this.

Other possible triggers include dry carpet shampoos, caustic irritants, new carpets, cement dust, washing powders or fabric conditioners. If you wash your dog's bedding, or if he or she sleeps on your bed, you should use a gentle, fragrance-free laundry detergent and fabric conditioner.

The irritation may be restricted to the part of the dog - such as the underneath of the paws or belly - which has touched the offending object. Symptoms are skin irritation - either a general problem or specific hotspots - itching (your vet may call this "pruritis") and sometimes hair loss. Readers sometimes report to us that their Mini Schnauzer will incessantly lick one part of the body – often the paws, butt, belly or back.

Diet and Food Allergies

Without proper food a dog's whole body - not just his skin and coat - will continuously be under stress. Cheap dog foods bulked up with grains and other ingredients can cause problems. If you do feed your dog a dry commercial dog food (like we do) then make sure that the first ingredient listed on the sack is meat or poultry and not grain.

There is also considerable anecdotal evidence that dogs with nutritional skin problems can do well on a purely vegetarian diet. Another option is to put your Schnauzer on a high protein pure meat diet. Both of these options are expensive and time-consuming for the owner, but can have impressive results in some cases. See Chapter 9 **Feeding** for more information.

Allergies are one of the most common causes of skin conditions affecting Schnauzers. This is a BIG subject, whole books have been written on it. Here are some of the main ones in a nutshell:

Inhalant Allergies

Substances which can cause an allergic reaction in dogs are similar to those causing allergies in humans and include pollens, trees, other animals, dust mites and mold.

A clue to diagnosing these allergies is to look at the timing of the reaction. Does it happen all year round? If so, this may be mold or dust. If the reaction is seasonal, then pollens may well be the culprit.

Symptoms of inhalant allergies include scratching, biting, chewing at paws and constant licking.

The itching may be most severe on feet, flanks, groin and armpits. Schnauzers may also rub their beard on the carpet.

Flea Bite Allergies

This type of reaction is not to the flea itself, but to proteins in flea saliva, which are deposited under the dog's skin when the flea feeds.

Just one fleabite in an allergic Schnauzer will cause intense and long-lasting itching. Most of the damage is done by the dog scratching, rather than the flea bite. This can result in the dog's hair dropping out or skin abrasions.

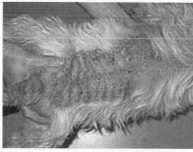

Some dogs will develop round, red, painful sores called hot spots. These can occur anywhere, but are often along the back and base of the tail.

Flea bite allergy is the most common form of canine skin allergy (see picture, left, for a severe example) and can only be totally prevented by removing all fleas from the dog's environment. If you suspect your dog may be allergic to fleas, consult your veterinarian for the proper diagnosis and medication.

NOTE: There is considerable anecdotal evidence that flea and worm tablet **Trifexis** may cause severe side effects in some dogs. Read owners' experiences here:
http://www.max-the-schnauzer.com/trifexis-side-effects-in-schnauzers.html

Some Allergy Treatments

Treatments and success rates vary tremendously from dog to dog and from one allergy to another, which is why it is so important to consult a vet at the outset.

Our Personal Experience

Our Miniature Schnauzer was perfectly fine until he was about two years old when he began to scratch a lot (he is eight now).
He seemed to scratch more in spring and summer, which meant that his allergies were almost certainly inhalant or contact-based and related to pollens, grasses or other outdoor triggers.

One option is to have a barrage of tests on the dog to discover exactly what he is allergic to.

This can also be expensive. We decided not to do this, not because of the cost, but because it is highly likely Max is allergic to pollens and he is an active dog getting three walks a day, mostly in the countryside where we live.

Max, our Mini

If we had confirmed that he is allergic to pollens, we were not going to stop taking him outside for walks. Our vet treated him on the basis that he thought he had had seasonal allergies probably related to pollen.

At first he was put on to a tiny dose of Piriton, an antihistamine for hay fever sufferers (human and canine) and for the first spring and summer, this worked well.

One of the problems with allergies is that they can change and the dog can build up a tolerance to a treatment – this was the case with Max. We know that his allergies are definitely related to pollen as they are seasonal. Every spring he starts scratching again and we visit the vet for treatment and every October we stop the treatment and he is fine for six months.

The symptoms have varied over the years. One year he bit his butt a lot and a couple of years ago he started biting his paws, which he had never done before. We have tried a number of treatments, all of which have worked for a while – and we bring him off the medication in autumn for about five or six months when plants and grasses stop growing outdoors. He manages perfectly fine the rest of the year without any medication.

One year he was on a short, but effective course of **steroids.** These worked very well for a season, and then he came off them. Steroids are not a long-term solution, as prolonged usage can cause organ damage.

 Another spring he went on to a non-steroid treatment, which in the UK is sold only through vets, called **Atopica.** This was expensive, but very effective for a couple of years, after which he started scratching again.

When he was scratching and biting his butt for a while, we also had an antiseptic wash to dab on, plus a cortisone spray from the vet. These seemed to work and he doesn't do it any more - thankfully!

Last went back on the **Piriton,** a slightly higher dose than when he was two years old, and this worked very well again. One advantage of this drug is that is it manufactured by the million for dogs and is therefore very inexpensive. Our vet says that canine allergies seem to be on the increase, as every spring his waiting room is full of dogs of all breeds with allergies.

Next spring when Max starts scratching again, we will visit the vet and discuss what treatment will be best. (We'll try and combine it with his annual vaccinations to keep the cost down). All dogs scratch and lick, it's natural. It only becomes a problem if the dog does it incessantly or if it causes sores, redness or other problems.

Many vets recommend adding fish oils to a daily feed to keep your dog's skin and coat healthy all year round – whether or not he has problems. So these days we also add a liquid supplement called Yumega Plus, which contains **Omega 3 and 6**, to one of his two daily feeds all year round and this

 definitely seems to help. Although his coat is wavy – due to the fact that we have him machine-clipped rather than hand stripped - it shines.

The main point is that Max's condition is manageable. He still scratches, but not so much now.

He may have allergies, but he wouldn't miss his walks for anything and all in all, he is one happy Schnauzer.

Other Skin Problems

Parasites

When you see your dog scratching and biting, your first thought is probably: "He's got fleas!" and you may well be right. Fleas don't fly, but they do have very strong back legs and they will take any opportunity to jump from the ground or another animal into your Schnauzer's lovely warm coat.

You can sometimes see the fleas if you part your dog's fur. The first things to eliminate would be parasites.

There are plenty of commercial solutions such as Frontline and Advantix for fleas, ticks and other parasites. By the way, flea bites are different from flea bite allergies. (See our note on page 205 about people's experiences with Trifexis).

If you do find a tick on your Schnauzer's coat (like the one on our photo, left) it is recommended that you see a vet to have it removed. Pulling it out yourself and leaving a bit of the tick behind can be detrimental to your dog's health.

It really is worth spending the money on a good flea treatment, such as the two mentioned above, as cheaper brands may not rid your Schnauzer of 100% of pests. It is recommended that dogs are given flea medication every eight weeks. This may vary slightly depending on how hot or cold the weather is (fleas do not breed as quickly in the cold) and how much time your dog spends outdoors.

Other parasites include mange, ear mites, lice and ticks. The narrow, furry ear canals of Mini Schnauzers are a fertile breeding ground for ear mites. They are also prone to infections.

If your dog is scratching his ears a lot, have him checked out, as untreated conditions can result in a lot of pain for your dog, deafness or even surgery. Every time you take your Schnauzer to the groomer's, be sure to ask for the hairs **inside** his ears to be plucked out by hand. This will help to keep them free from mites and infection.

If your Schnauzer has particularly sensitive skin, you might want to try a natural flea or tick remedy.

Ringworm

This is not actually a worm, but a fungus and is most commonly seen in puppies and young dogs. It is highly infectious and often found on the face, ears, paws or tail. (See photo, right, for a typical sign of ringworm).

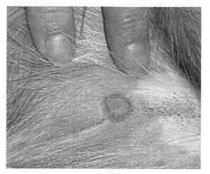

Ringworm is transmitted by spores in the soil and by contact with the infected hair of dogs and cats, which can be typically found on carpets, brushes, combs, toys, and furniture.

Humans can catch ringworm from pets, and vice versa. Children are especially susceptible, so hygiene is extremely important. If a member of your family catches ringworm, make sure they use separate towels from everyone else, or the fungus may spread.

The fungi live in dead skin, hairs and nails and the head and legs are the most common areas affected. Tell-tale signs are bald patches with a roughly circular shape. Ringworm is usually treated with fungicidal shampoos or antibiotics from your vet.

Bacterial infection (Pyoderma)

Pyoderma literally means "pus in the skin," and fortunately this condition is not contagious. Early signs of this bacterial infection are itchy yellow or red spots filled with pus. This can possibly later develop into red ulcerated skin with dry, crusty patches.

If you notice symptoms, get your dog to the vet quickly before the condition develops from superficial pyoderma into severe pyoderma, which is much more unpleasant for the dog and takes a lot longer to treat.

Dogs have a higher risk of developing an infection when they have a fungal infection or an endocrine disease such as hyperthyroidism, or have allergies to fleas, food ingredients or parasites. Mini Schnauzers have narrow, hairy ear canals and some are prone to fungal infections inside their ears.

Bacterial infection, no matter how bad it may look, usually responds well to medical treatment, which is generally done on an outpatient basis. Superficial pyoderma will often be treated with a three or four-week course of antibiotic tablets or ointment. Severe or recurring pyoderma looks awful, causes your dog some distress and can take two or three months' of treatment to completely cure. Medicated shampoos and regular bathing, as instructed by your vet, also form part of the treatment.

Hormonal Imbalances.

These are often difficult to diagnose and occur when the dog is producing either too much (hyper) or too little (hypo) of a particular hormone. One visual sign is often hair loss on both sides of the dog's body. The condition is not usually itchy.

Hormone imbalances can be serious as they are often indicators that glands which affect the dog internally are not working properly. However, some types can be diagnosed by special blood tests and treated effectively.

Schnauzer Bumps

Their official name is Schnauzer Comedone Syndrome - sometimes Comedo Syndrome – and they are thought to be a genetic condition which the dog inherits from one or other of his parents.

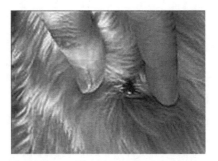

Symptoms are bumps, sometimes filled with pus, are usually found on the dog's back (see photo, right). They are often described as canine acne. And, like human acne, are actually blocked sebaceous glands – or blackheads. They affect some Miniature Schnauzers, but not Standards or Giants.

Quite often, having Schnauzer Bumps doesn't seem to bother the dog or affect his or her health, unless they become infected. Once infected, they can become itchy and may even develop into small pus-filled abscesses or bumps, which is not very nice for your Mini.

Some Miniature Schnauzers have them all the time, while others have an occasional flare-up. Unfortunately, there is no cure for them and if your dog is unlucky enough to have inherited them, they will probably stay for life. The good news, however, is that they can be treated.

There are a number of actions and medications which can help Schnauzer Bumps, but the first stop is a visit to the vet so that he can make a proper assessment of the severity of the condition and prescribe the correct treatment.

Treatments

Miniature Schnauzer owners have found that there are a number of things to help either reduce the symptoms or get rid of them completely. These include:

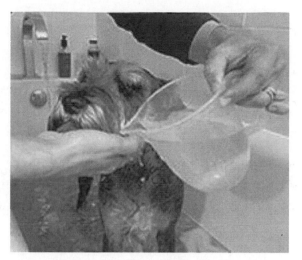

Bathing - Regularly bathing your dog – anything from twice a week to once every two weeks - using shampoos that break down the oils which plug the hair follicles.

These shampoos contain antiseborrheic ingredients such as benzoyl peroxide, salicylic acid, sulfur or tar. One example is Sulfoxydex shampoo, which can be followed by a cream rinse such as Episoothe Rinse afterwards to prevent the skin from drying out.

Dabbing – Using an astringent such as witch hazel or alcohop, to dry up the bumps.

Grooming – Keeping your Schnauzer's coat short.

Sunshine - Some owners have found that Schnauzer Bumps are not as bad during summer. Try and get your dog regularly out into the sunshine.

Fleas– Sometimes Minis with flea allergies also have Schnauzer Bumps. So use a flea treatment every eight weeks.

Food - Try changing food and avoid foods containing corn or grain. Try a holistic food containing only natural products or feed your Schnauzer a home-made recipe.

Daily supplements - Vitamin E, vitamin A, zinc and omega oils all help to make a dog's skin healthy. Feed a daily supplement which contains some of these, such as fish oil, which provides omega.

Medication – According to the Encyclopedia of Veterinary Medical Information, some Miniature Schnauzers respond well to isotretinoin (Accutane Rx) but this is an expensive treatment and only works in a small percentage of dogs. Consult your vet for details.

Owners' Suggestions for Treating Skin Conditions

Schnauzer skin conditions are topics which create a lot of interest among Schnauzer lovers. Many different remedies have been tried in an effort to alleviate scratching and irritable skin.

Here are some of the ones owners have tried with, they claim, some success. We are not saying whether they work or not, we're just passing on the information. **Check with your vet before trying any new remedies.**

Owners have recommended: a medicated shampoo with natural tea tree oil or dabbing antiseptic mouthwash over the affected area.

For irritable skin, here is what one Schnauzer owner told us: *"My poor schnauzer was biting and itching constantly. My vet said that he may be allergic to grasses and pollens because it seems to only happen in the warmer months.*

"Anyway, she told me to wipe an astringent on his back because he had little bumps all over it. I bought the Stridex Naturals pads that teenagers use for acne. I started wiping his back every day for the last week and he's not scratching anymore.....amazing. Make sure you get the formula with no alcohol so it doesn't dry his skin"

Some owners have reported that switching their dog to a fish-based diet has helped lessen scratching. Others have suggested that home-cooked food is best, if you have the time to prepare the food. Generally, a small supplement of fish oil in the meal once a day also helps skin to stay healthy.

Here is a comment from Ann G. on Schnauzer allergies: *"Try Natural Balance Sweet Potato and Fish formula. My schnauzer Charlie has skin issues and this food has helped him tremendously! Plus he LOVES it!"*

Several readers have said that they have taken their pets to the vet with Schnauzer Bumps. If the bumps stay small, they are not a problem, but if they become larger and fill with mud or pus, the vet can drain them with a syringe – usually the dogs do not seem to mind this. The bumps may come back and you might need to return to the vet periodically, but they are not life threatening.

This is what a reader had to say about contact skin dermatitis: *"My 8-month-old mini schnauzer also had a contact dermatitis around his neck and chest. I was surprised how extensive it was when I clipped his hair. The vet recommended twice-a-week baths with an oatmeal shampoo. I also applied organic coconut oil daily for a few weeks.*

"This completely cured the dermatitis. I also put a capsule of fish oil with his food once a day and continue to give him twice-weekly baths. His skin is great now."

And from another reader: *"I have been putting a teaspoon of Canola Oil in my Schnauzer's food every other day and it has helped with the itching.*

"I have shampooed the "new" carpet in hopes of removing any of the chemicals that could be irritating her and I have changed laundry detergent. After several loads of laundry everything has been washed."

Another reader wrote that her dog is being treated for seasonal allergies with half a pill of Claratin a day.

Reader Cindi says that local health food stores may be able to offer advice on suitable ingredients for a diet - for dogs and humans. She also suggests rubbing pure Emu Oil into affected areas.

This chapter has only just touched on the complex subject of skin disorders. As you have read, the causes and treatments are many and varied.

One thing is true, whatever the condition:

Good quality diet and attention to cleanliness and grooming go a long way in preventing and managing Schnauzer skin problems.

If your Schnauzer is experiencing a problem with his or her skin, our advice is to get a professional diagnosis from your veterinarian before attempting to treat the condition. Early professional diagnosis and treatment can sometimes alleviate the problem before it develops into anything more serious.

Some skin conditions cannot be treated, but they can be successfully managed, allowing your Schnauzer to live a happy, pain-free life.

Chapter 15. Grooming

Advantages of a Schnauzer

The great news about Schnauzers is that none of them – not the Mini, the Standard nor the Giant - shed hair. And neither should the Schnoodle – at least the first-generation crosses between a Schnauzer and a Poodle should not, as both parents are non-shedding.

The reason for them being non-shedding breeds – and also why most allergy sufferers are NOT allergic to Schnauzers - is that the Schnauzer's coat is made up of two layers. It is the dander (like dandruff) which most allergy sufferers react to and in the case of the Schnauzer, this is trapped between the layers.

We should just add here that NO dog is 100% non-shedding, but the Schnauzer's double coat sheds so little that it is all but unnoticeable.

In the eight years of owning Max, we may have found a very occasional fur ball when he was due for a trim, but we virtually never find any hairs. It is not a myth, other Schnauzer owners agree – Schnauzers don't shed.

Another great advantage of getting a Schnauzer is that they usually do not generally have a doggy odor. In fact, if regularly bathed and groomed, they smell rather nice.

The outer coat of all Schnauzers is hard and wiry, while the undercoat is soft. In the case of salt and pepper Schnauzers, the brown pepper color on top of the gray is contained in the outer wiry coat.

If your salt and pepper schnauzer is regularly machine-clipped, the pepper color will gradually disappear and your Schnauzer will just be gray. Our Schnauzer Max is like this. If you are not planning on showing your dog or unless you particularly like the pepper color, electric clippers are fine.

The coat also generally becomes softer with electric hand clippers, which may cause some black Schnauzers to lose a bit of shine to their coat, while others may develop a slight brownish tinge.

Disadvantages

The downside of having a non-shedder is that the Schnauzer coat is relatively high maintenance, compared with breeds with hair that falls out naturally.

Because Schnauzers do not molt like most other dogs, they need regular grooming at home and a trip to the grooming parlor every few weeks – unless you learn to machine clip or hand strip your own dog.

If you want to show your Schnauzer in Kennel Club events, your dog should be hand stripped. Trimming with clippers destroys the wiriness and color bands of the outer coat. Clipper trimming can also cause the coat to go wavy. This is does not harm the dog at all, but will prevent you from showing him or her under Kennel Club rules.

It also does not matter at all if you clipper-trim your dog and are planning on entering him for your local community dog show in the park. Schnauzers are extremely handsome dogs and your pet may well come away with the prize for "Judge's Favorite" or "Cutest Dog," even if he has been trimmed with machine clippers.

Dog Groomers

Unless your dog is a show dog, which will need regular hand stripping (plucking out the hairs by hand), a trip to the groomers every few weeks is normal for a Schnauzer. Here in Yorkshire, in the North of England, we pay between £20 to £25 (US$30 to $48) a visit for a full wash and clipper trim at the dog groomers, but this will vary depending on where you live.

You can pay a lot more. We take our dog every eight weeks, some groomers may recommend more, but coming from Yorkshire, we are cost-conscious!

It is advisable not to leave your dog too long between visits or other problems may occur. During the summer, you may find that your Schnauzer starts to scratch more.

215

Schnauzers are prone to skin complaints (see Chapter 14 **Schnauzer Skin**). A thick, wiry coat, which they are unable to shed when it gets hot, can become uncomfortable and itchy for your dog.

A good dog groomer will do more than just wash and trim your Schnauzer. They will also clip his or her nails and squeeze the anal glands, which prevents blockages.

Many Schnauzers – particularly Miniatures – have narrow ear canals with very furry ears. These conditions can lead to the ears becoming an ideal breeding ground for infection-causing bacteria.

You should regularly check your Schnauzer's ears, particularly if he is scratching them a lot. A hot or smelly ear may well be a sign of infection. When you take your Schnauzer to the groomers, ask for the anal glands to be squeezed and the hairs inside the ears to be plucked out.

This should be done carefully by hand, as the loud noise of the clippers inside the ear is distressing for the dog. It is also impossible for the clippers to get right down to the hairs inside the narrow ear channel.

When you are choosing a groomer, don't just go for the cheapest; ask around other dog owners to see who is recommended. Some groomers will come to the house with mobile dog grooming parlors.

A trip to the grooming parlor can be distressing for a young dog, so don't pick one like a production line where the dogs are all stacked up in crates waiting to be clipped. This only adds to the stress. It would be a bit like us waiting nervously in a big room with lots of other people where a dentist is drilling teeth while we watch on!

Take your time to find a good groomer. If your dog is the only one in there, he or she will be dealt with quicker and more relaxed.

First Trim

We get many people writing to us to ask at what age a young Schnauzer should have his or her first trim. This is surprisingly quite a controversial subject. If you want the Schnauzer coat to fully develop naturally, then don't have your dog machine-clipped for the first few months.

This does not mean that he or she should not be groomed or trimmed. Your dog can also be gently hand stripped from a few months' old.

It is a good idea to get him or her used to a little gently grooming early on – both at home and at the grooming parlor.

It's also advisable to make your first visit to the groomer's a quick trip to get him used to the experience and groomer, rather than waiting until your dog requires a major trim on his or her first visit, which could be very traumatic for him.

Trimming is especially important in a hot climate or warm weather, as your dog cannot cool down by shedding hair (or sweating).

Hand-stripping is the removal of dead hair from the hair shaft. This method keeps the natural hard, wiry texture of the outer "jacket" of the Schnauzer's distinctive coat. This can be done from as little as four months old on a puppy, but only a very small amount at a time should be carried out at first – and gently, by someone who knows what they are doing.

If you are not intending to show or breed your puppy, and if you don't mind if his or her coat is a little softer and wavier, then you can have your puppy clippered at a few months of age.

Many groomers do a "puppy clip," which is a small-scale trim. It is often a good idea to book one to get your puppy used to the whole experience. When taking your pet to a groomer for the first time, be very specific about whether you want to have your dog **hand stripped** or **clippered** (machine-trimmed).

To sum up:

- A Schnauzer puppy can be trimmed or from any age after she has had all of her vaccinations.
- We would recommend having her gently hand-stripped until her full adult coat has grown naturally. Then you can decide how you want him trimmed as an adult.

- If you are not showing your Schnauzer, there is no reason (other than aesthetics) why you should not have your dog trimmed with electric clippers. The changes in the Schnauzer coat do not affect the dog's health. The wiry topcoat will disappear, but electric clippers an easy way to maintain a neat-looking Schnauzer, unless you know how to hand strip.

Home Maintenance

Your Schnauzer does not shed hair like most other breeds of dogs. This is a big advantage with the breed, but it means that the Schnauzer coat does require regular maintenance. (Our picture, left, shows a well-groomed Standard).

You should brush your dog a couple of times a week and book him in for regular trips to the groomer's for a trim. Failure to do so will result in a scruffy, dog with matted fur which will be uncomfortably hot in summer and very likely cause him or her to scratch a lot.

He may also smell if his beard or teeth are dirty, or if the ears have picked up an infection due to the hairs in the narrow ear canal not being plucked. Normally, Schnauzers do not have a particularly 'doggie' smell unless they need a bath.

Bathing

Some owners like to bath their Schnauzer often, maybe every couple of weeks, but this is not necessary. (Schnauzers with allergies may require regular bathing in a medicated shampoo if your vet advises it.)

Unless the dog has rolled in something unmentionable, your Schnauzer's regular bath at the grooming parlor should be sufficient. Over-use of shampoo can change the balance of the skin and dry out the coat, causing skin problems.

We bathe our Schnauzer when he has rolled in something horrible (usually cow dung, which is a particular favorite) or when he is itching a lot, particularly in summer. We use a medicated shampoo supplied by our veterinarian; it is expensive but lasts a long time.

As many Schnauzers have sensitive skin, it is recommended that if you bathe your dog, you use a specialist dog shampoo, or better still, a medicated shampoo from your vet. And when you do, have plenty of dry towels on the floor ready to dry your dog before he runs off!

Regular bathing with a medicated shampoo can also help with certain Schnauzer skin conditions – but only do it after consulting your vet. Some owners prefer to use a pet shampoo made only from natural and organic ingredients.

Do not use shampoos made for humans, as these can upset the PH balance of a Schnauzer's skin. You must avoid getting any shampoo in the eyes or water in the ears, as this can cause problems later. You also need a non-slip surface, such as a rubber mat, for your dog to stand on in the bath.

Only use tepid water. Massage the soap into the skin, working your way from tail to head, as you do not want any shampoo to get into their eyes while you are washing the rest of the body. Shield the eyes with your hand while you are rinsing the head.

Make doubly sure that you rinse all the shampoo off. Traces of soap left behind can cause dry skin, flaky dandruff and other skin irritations. Then STAND BACK unless you want a bath yourself. He can't wait to get out and shake all over.

 (Our picture, above right, shows our Max, our Miniature Schnauzer, in the bath at home after a long hike in the hills where he encountered some smelly organic substances deposited by cows!)

Day-to-Day Grooming

Grooming is one of your Schnauzer's basic needs and an important responsibility of a dog owner. It is a good idea to start with gentle brushing while your puppy is still young to get them used to being groomed.

 Most dogs enjoy the attention, but some are more difficult to groom as they are either too lively or don't enjoy being brushed. If your dog shies away and doesn't want you to touch him or her at all, this could be a sign that something is wrong – either physically or emotionally.

How often you groom your dog depends on when they were last at the grooming salon, how long the coat has grown and whether they are outside getting dirty on walks in the countryside or park. You should aim to brush your dog at least once or twice a week.

As well as brushing, there's a few other things you should be doing.

Matter can gather at the corner of the eyes and it is important to clean this out with a clean, damp tissue to keep the tear ducts free.

Most Schnauzer beards – particularly white ones – are prone to getting dirty and should be wiped with a damp tissue or cloth regularly. This will prevent them becoming smelly and remove any trapped food particles.

Owners of white Schnauzers are particularly busy keeping their pet's face nice and white. Tear stains may cause their Schnauzer's face to get a browny-red tinge. There are several products on the market, such as Angels' Eyes, which can help to keep their fur a bright white.

Your dog may also need his or her nails trimming regularly, particularly if they do not do a lot of walking on hard surfaces, such as the sidewalk. Nail trimming should be done as part of the normal visit to the grooming parlor.

Grooming Kit

If you do decide to clip or strip your Schnauzer yourself, this is a list of some of the things you might need:

- Pin Brushes and a Bristle Brush
- Slicker Brushes
- Metal Comb with fine and medium teeth
- Good Quality Scissors
- Dog Shampoo and Conditioner/Cream Rinse
- Ear Cleaner and Powder
- Cotton Wipes
- Nail Clippers
- EITHER electric clippers or a stripping knife
- A Grooming Table or Rubber Mat

If the dog visits the grooming salon every couple of months, then you should only need a brush, a comb, cotton wipes, shampoo and conditioner, a dog toothbrush and toothpaste.

You can also buy treats, such as Greenies, Vetradent and Dentastix, which improve your dog's dental health and reduce bad breath.

The Schnauzer Look

There's no denying it, Schnauzers are strikingly handsome dogs! Their square, boxy shape with its clean, angular lines and the bearded face attract attention wherever they go.

The Schnauzer trim or Schnauzer clip is a very specific look which enhances the appearance of these attractive animals. The exact details of the trim vary from country to country, but generally, the look is the same.

Here is a broad outline of a typical trim:

The fur on the back and sides of the body is kept fairly short, usually clipped with a #10 blade – or #15 for a shorter clip. The beard is left long while the rest of the head is trimmed, with the area between the eyes being trimmed to a diamond shape. The fur on the legs is left longer.

The fur on the lower sides of the Miniature may be kept longer – this is referred to as the "skirt."

Standard Schnauzers

Two healthy looking Standard Schnauzers with different trims. The one on the left with the cropped ears is in the USA, the right hand one is from the UK and simply called a Schnauzer.

Giant Schnauzers

Two fine specimens of the Giant Schnauzer. The Giant on the left is Jafrak Philippe Olivier, the British Crufts champion. The one on the right is an American Giant with cropped ears.

Miniature Schnauzers

Above are two different looks for the Miniature Schnauzer. The one on the left is more typical of an American show dog. Show dogs are generally not machine clipped, but stripped by hand. The Schnauzer on the right is from Britain, the dog is older, as tail docking has been illegal since April 2007 in the UK. This dog also has a "skirt" under the belly.

Chapter 16. The Birds and the Bees

Many owners contact us with a variety of questions regarding the breeding of Schnauzers and topics surrounding this subject.

The want to know whether they should breed from their Schnauzer or if and at what age they should have their dog spayed (females) or neutered (males).

If they have females they often ask when she will come on heat, how long this will last and how often it will occur. Sometimes they want to know how you can tell if a female Schnauzer is pregnant or how long a pregnancy lasts.

So here, in a nutshell, is a short chapter on the facts of life as far as Schnauzers are concerned.

Breeding From Your Dog

The breed societies discourage regular pet owners from breeding from their dogs, as breeding to produce healthy purebred pups with good temperaments is a specialized business.

The proper breeding of dogs has become a complex, expensive and demanding practice. It should be backed up by genetic information and screening as well as a thorough knowledge of the desired traits of the breed.

Casual breeding performed by friends or neighbors who happen to own Schnauzers (or other dogs) seldom produces anything but mediocre Schnauzers. It is not just about the look of the dogs, health and temperament are important factors too.

Top breeders have many years' experience in selecting the right pair for mating after they have looked at the history, lineage, health and temperaments of the two dogs involved.

If you want to breed from your dog, consider these questions:

* Are you 100% sure that your dog has no health or character problems which may be inherited by his or her puppies?

* Have you researched his or her ancestry to make sure there are no problems lurking in the background? Puppies inherit traits from their grandparents and great-grandparents as well as from the dam (female) and sire (male).

* Are you positive that the same can be said for the dog you are planning on breeding yours with?

Females and Heat

Just like all other animal and human females, a female Schnauzer also has a menstrual cycle - or to be more accurate, an estrus cycle. This is the period when she is ready (and willing!) for mating and is more commonly called **heat** or being **on heat**, **in heat** or **in season**.

A female has her first cycle from about six months to one year of age. Small breeds like the Miniature Schnauzer tend to start early, but a large dog like a Giant Schnauzer may not begin her heat cycles until she is over one year old.

She will come on heat every six to eight months, though the timescale becomes more erratic with old age and can also be irregular with young dogs when cycles first begin.

This will last on average from 12 to 21 days, although it can be anything from just a few days up to four weeks.

Within that time there will be several days which will be the optimum time for her to get pregnant. This middle phase of the cycle is called the *estrus.*

The third phase, called *diestrus*, then begins. During this time, her body will produce hormones, whether or not she is pregnant. Her body thinks and acts like she is pregnant. All the hormones are present; only the puppies are missing. This can sometimes lead to what is known as a **false pregnancy**.

While a female dog is on heat, she produces hormones which attract male dogs. The first sign which you may notice of her being on heat is when she begins to lick her butt – or vulva to be more precise.

She will then bleed, this is sometimes called spotting. It will be a dark red at the beginning of the heat cycle, but the blood will become less and a lighter color as the cycle evolves.

With a small dog like a Miniature Schnauzer, there is not much blood. Obviously, there is more with larger dogs like Giant Schnauzers.

As she is approaches perfect time for mating, your Schnauzer may bend her tail to one side. She will also start to urinate more frequently. This is her signal to all those virile male dogs out there that she is ready for mating.

Because dogs have a sense of smell hundreds of times stronger than ours, when your female is on heat, she is a magnet for all the males in the neighborhood.

They may congregate around your house or follow you around the park, waiting for their chance to prove their manhood – or mutthood in their case.

Don't expect your precious Schnauzer princess to be fussy. Her hormones are raging when she is on heat and during her most fertile days, she is usually ready, willing and able...!

Allowing your female to become pregnant during the first heat cycle is not recommended, as she is not yet mature and complications for the mother and puppies are more likely.

Unlike women, female dogs do not go through the menopause and can have puppies even when they are quite elderly. A first litter for an elderly female can result in complications.

 If you definitely don't want your female Schnauzer to get pregnant, you should have her spayed.

In the United States and Europe, humane societies, animal shelters and rescue groups urge dog owners to have their pets spayed or neutered to prevent unwanted litters which contribute to too many animals in the rescue system.

Generally, all dogs coming from rescue centers and shelters will have been spayed or neutered.

Spaying

Spaying is the term used to describe the removal of the ovaries and uterus (womb) of a female dog so that she cannot become pregnant. Although this is a routine operation, it is major abdominal surgery and she has to be anesthetized.

A popular myth is that a female dog should have her first heat cycle before she is spayed, but this is not the case. Even puppies can be spayed. You should consult your vet for the optimum time for spaying, should you decide to have your dog done.

One of the advantages of spaying is that, if done before the first heat cycle, she will have an almost zero risk of mammary cancer (the equivalent of breast cancer in women). Even after the first heat, spaying reduces the risk of this cancer by 92%.

Some vets claim that the risk of mammary cancer in unspayed female dogs can be as high as one in four. Some females may put weight on easier after spaying and will require slightly less food afterwards.

As with any major procedure, there are pros and cons. Spaying is a much more serious operation for a female than neutering is for a male. This is because spaying involves an internal abdominal operation for the female, whereas the neutering operation is carried out on the male's testicles, which are located outside of his abdomen.

For:
1. Spaying can reduce behavior problems, such as roaming, aggression to other dogs, anxiety or fear.
2. Infections, cancer, and other diseases of the uterus and ovaries are prevented.
3. Your dog will have a greatly reduced risk of mammary cancer.
4. Spaying reduces hormonal changes which can interfere with the treatment of diseases such as diabetes or epilepsy.
5. A spayed dog does not contribute to the pet overpopulation problem.

Against:
1. Complications can occur, including an abnormal reaction to the anesthetic, bleeding, stitches breaking and infections.
2. Occasional long-term effects connected to hormonal changes. These may include weight gain, urinary incontinence or less stamina and these problems may occur years after a female has been spayed.

3. Older females may suffer some urinary incontinence. Some Giant Schnauzers may experience this, but it only affects about one in six or seven spayed females. Discuss it with your vet.

If you talk to a vet or a volunteer at a rescue shelter, they will say that the advantages of spaying usually far outweigh any disadvantages.

If you have a female puppy, you can discuss with your vet whether, and at what age, spaying would be a good idea for your Schnauzer when you take her in for injections.

False Pregnancies

As many as 50% or more of unspayed female dogs may display signs of a false pregnancy. Symptoms become noticeable six to 12 weeks after estrus.

In the wild, it was common for female dogs to have false pregnancies and to lactate (produce milk). This female would then nourish puppies if their own mother died.

Typical symptoms may include:

- Mothering or adopting toys & other objects
- Making a nest
- Producing milk (lactating)
- Appetite fluctuations
- Barking or whining a lot
- Restlessness, depression or anxiety
- Swollen abdomen
- She might even appear to go into labor

 If symptoms are mild, no treatment is needed, as this behavior will usually stop within three weeks. Try not to touch any your dog's nipples, as touch will stimulate further milk production.

If she is licking herself repeatedly, she may need an Elizabethan collar (a large plastic collar from the vet) to minimize stimulation.

If the false pregnancy persists, a trip to the vet would be advised where diuretics or hormonal medications can be prescribed.

 Under no circumstances should you restrict her water supply to try and prevent her from producing milk. This is dangerous, as she can become dehydrated.

Spaying during a false pregnancy may actually prolong the condition. Better to wait until the false pregnancy is over and then have her spayed to prevent it happening again.

False pregnancy is not a disease, but an exaggerated response to normal hormonal changes. Owners should be reassured that even if left untreated, the condition almost always will resolve itself.

Neutering

Neutering male dogs involves castration; the removal of the testicles.

This can be a tough decision for an owner, as it causes a drop in the pet's testosterone levels, which some feel affects the quality of their dog's life.

Fortunately, dogs do not think like people and male dogs do not miss their testicles or the loss of sex! Our own experience is that our male Miniature Schnauzer is much happier having been neutered.

We decided to have him done after he went missing three times on walks – he ran off on the scent of a female on heat. Fortunately, he is micro-chipped and has our phone number on a tag on his collar and we were lucky that he was returned to us on all three occasions.

Unless you specifically want to breed from or show your dog, or he has a special job, such as a police dog, neutering is recommended by many vets and most animal rescue staff.

There are countless unwanted puppies, especially in the USA, and many of them have to be destroyed.

Neutering is usually performed around puberty, i.e. about six months old. It can be done at any age over age 8 weeks, provided both testicles have descended and the operation is a relatively straightforward procedure.

Dogs neutered before puberty tend to grow a little larger than dogs done later. This is because testosterone is involved in the causing bones to stop growing, so without testosterone the bones grow for longer.

The neutering operation for a male is less of a major operation than spaying for a female. Complications are less common and less severe than with spaying a female.

Although he will feel tender afterwards, your dog should return to his normal self within a couple of days.

When he comes out of surgery, his scrotum (the sacs which held the testicles) will be swollen and it may look like nothing has been done. But it is normal for these to slowly shrink in the days following surgery.

Many canine experts feel that the advantages outweigh the disadvantages. Here are the main pros and cons:

For:

1. Behavior problems such as roaming and aggression are usually reduced.
2. Unwanted sexual behavior, such as mounting people or objects, is usually reduced or eliminated.
3. They are less, likely to wander off after females on heat.

4. Testicular problems such as infections, cancer and torsion (painful rotation of the testicle) are eradicated.
5. Prostate disease, common in older male dogs, is less likely to occur.
7. A submissive entire male dog (one which has not been castrated) may be targeted by other dogs. After he has been neutered, he will no longer produce testosterone and so will not be regarded as much of a threat by the other males, so he is less likely to be bullied.
6. A neutered dog is not fathering unwanted puppies.

Cons:

1. Bleeding after surgery can occur, so you should keep an eye on him after the operation for any blood loss.
2. Infections can occur - usually on the wound itself. Generally they are caused by the dog licking at the incision during the first week or so after surgery, so try and prevent him doing this. If he persists, use an E collar.
3. Some dogs' coats may be affected, but supplementing their diet with fish oil can compensate for this.

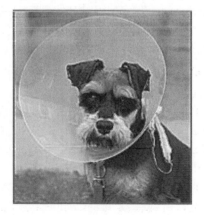

Myths

Here are some common myths about neutering and spaying:

Neutering or spaying will change the dog's character

There is no evidence that any of the positive characteristics of your dog will be altered. He or she will be just as loving, playful and loyal. Neutering may reduce aggression or roaming, especially in male dogs, because they are no longer competing to mate with a female.

A female needs to have at least one litter

There is no proven physical or mental benefit to a female having a litter. Pregnancy and whelping (giving birth to puppies) can be very stressful and can have complications. In a false pregnancy, a female is simply responding to the hormones in her body.

Mating is natural and necessary

Dogs are not humans, they do not think emotionally about sex or having and raising a family. Because Schnauzers like the company of humans so much, we tend to ascribe human emotions to them.

Unlike humans, their desire to mate or breed is entirely physical, triggered by the chemicals called hormones within their body. Without these hormones – i.e. after neutering or spaying – the desire disappears or is greatly reduced.

Male dogs will behave better if they can mate

This is simply not true; sex does not make a dog behave better. In fact, it can have the opposite effect. Having mated once, a male may show an increased interest in females.

He may also consider his status elevated, which may make him harder to control or call back.

Pregnancy

Regardless of whether you have a Miniature, Standard or Giant Schnauzer, a pregnancy will normally last for 61 to 65 days, or two months. Sometimes the pregnancy referred to as the *gestation period.*

So how do you tell if your female is pregnant? Here are some of the signs:

1. She may produce a slight discharge about one month after mating.

2. Her teats (nipples) will become more prominent, pink and erect 25 to 30 days into the pregnancy. Later on, you may notice a fluid coming from them.

 3. After about 35 days, or seven weeks, you will notice her body weight increase.

4. Her abdomen will become noticeably larger from around day 40, although first-time mums and females carrying few puppies may not show as much.

5. Her behavior may change. She may display slight depression and/or a drop in appetite. However, these signs can also mean there are other problems, so you should consult your vet.

6. Many dogs' appetite will increase in the second half of pregnancy.

7. Her nesting instincts will kick in as the delivery date approaches. She may seem restless or scratch her bed or the floor.

During Pregnancy

Females need special attention as well as a suitable diet during pregnancy. Foods which are rich in calcium should not be fed during this time.

She still needs daily exercise, but after the first month of pregnancy, you should restrict vigorous activity and any agility events. You may consider supplementing her food at this stage.

In the sixth week, you should make or buy a whelping box and place it in a quiet area of your house – not the hall or the kitchen where people are in and out all the time. This is a box with newspapers or old towels in the bottom where your dog can give birth and which will be the puppies' first home.

The whelping box should be big enough so that your female can stretch out, leaving plenty room for the puppies.

Ensuring that your pregnant female is properly looked after involves time and knowledge. We recommend that you consult your vet for advice and read as much as possible on the subject.

How Many Puppies?

Depending on which type of Schnauzer you are getting, litter size will vary.

- Miniature Schnauzers generally have a litter of three to five or six puppies, although can have as many as eight.
- Standard Schnauzers have larger litters averaging six to 10 puppies, but can have as many as 13.
- Giant Schnauzers usually have five to eight Schnauzer puppies.

Very young and very old dogs have smaller litters. A female's first litter will also tend to be smaller.

Chapter 17. Schnauzer Rescue

Are you thinking of adopting a dog from a Schnauzer rescue organization?

What could be kinder and more rewarding than adopting a poor, abandoned Schnauzer and giving him or her a happy, loving home for the rest of his life?

Well, not a lot really. Every year many people in North America, the UK and countries all around the world adopt a Schnauzer and the story often has a happy ending.

The Dog's Point of View...

But if you are serious about adopting a Schnauzer, then you should do so with the right motives and with your eyes wide open.

If you're expecting a perfect dog, you could be in for a shock. Rescue Schnauzers can and do become wonderful companions, but much of it depends on you.

Schnauzers are people-loving dogs. Many of them in rescue centers are extremely traumatized by the loss of their beloved owners.

They don't understand why they have been abandoned and in the beginning they may arrive with problems of their own until they adjust to being part of a loving family home again. Ask yourself a few questions before you take the plunge:

- Are you prepared to accept and deal with any problems - such as bad behavior, shyness, aggression or making a mess in the house - which the dog may display when he initially arrives in your home?
- How much time are you willing to spend with your new pet to help him integrate back into normal family life?
- Can you take time off work to be at home and help the dog settle in at the beginning?

- Are you prepared to take on a new addition to your family that may live for another 10 years or so?

Think about the implications before taking on a rescue dog - try and look at it from the dog's point of view.

What could be worse for the unlucky Schnauzer than to be abandoned again if things don't work out between you?

Have You Thought About This...?

It IS a big commitment for all involved. Here are some more points to consider before embarking on a Schnauzer rescue:

- Schnauzer adoption is NOT a cheap way of getting a purebred or pedigree dog and shouldn't be viewed as such. It could cost you several hundred dollars - or pounds. You'll have adoption fees to pay and often vaccination and veterinary bills as well as worm and flea medication and spaying or neutering. Make sure you're aware of the full cost before committing.

- Schnauzer rescue dogs may not be suitable for families with young children. The dog may be jealous of the attention given to the children or may not like being handled or teased a lot - especially at first.

- Many have had difficult lives. You need plenty of TIME to help them to rehabilitate.

- Some rescue Schnauzers have initial problems with housebreaking. Others may need socialization training with people as well as other dogs.

- If you are serious, you may have to wait a while until a suitable dog comes up.

- It is not just the dogs that are screened. You'll probably have to undergo a screening by your chosen Schnauzer rescue organization to make sure you can provide a suitable home. You might have to provide references too.

With any luck, you may not have to leap over all of the above hurdles, but it's best to be aware of possible drawbacks at the outset.

Still Interested?

If we haven't managed to put you off with all of the above.....
Congratulations, you may be just the family or person that poor abandoned
Schnauzer is looking for!

 If you can't spare the time to adopt - and
remember - **adoption means forever**, you might
want to help rescue dogs in other ways.

Many rescue groups foster out the Schnauzers
until a suitable home can be found. This is a
shorter term arrangement than adopting for life -
but still needs your commitment and patience.

Or you could be a fundraiser and help to generate cash to keep these very
worthy rescue groups providing such a wonderful service.

However you decide to get involved, Good Luck!

Stitch, rescued in Arizona

Lucy, a rescued Giant

**Saving one dog will not change the world,
But it will change the world for one dog**

List of USA Schnauzer Rescue Groups

There are quite a large number of rescue groups in the USA and these are usually manned by volunteers and members who help to re-home mostly Miniature and Giant Schnauzers.

There are less Standard Schnauzers in rescue shelters, mainly because the Standards are fewer in numbers than the other two breeds.

Rescuing an abandoned Schnauzer can be an incredibly rewarding experience. But it's a good idea to be aware that some of them have been hurt- usually only emotionally, thank goodness.

This means that these dogs often need extra care and TLC from you. Be sure you've got the time and energy to give before making the commitment.

We've done a lot of research and contacted many USA Schnauzer Rescue groups and are now able to provide the most comprehensive up-to-date list of Schnauzer rescue organizations in the USA. All of those listed have websites with contact details. The list is accurate as of early 2013:

ALABAMA
Schnauzer love Rescue Inc –
http://www.schnauzerloverescue.org/

ARIZONA
Valley of the Sun Giant Schnauzer Rescue -
http://www.vsgiantschnauzerrescue.org
Arizona Schnauzer Rescue –
http://www.azschnauzer.org/

CALIFORNIA
Southern California Giant Schnauzer Rescue -
http://www.socalgiantschnauzerrescue.org/

COLORADO
Vintage Dog Rescue
http://www.cominischnauzerrescue.com/

DELAWARE
Schnauzer Rescue Cincinnati
http://www.schnauzerrescuecincinnati.org/
Schnauzer Rescue of the Mid Atlantic
http://www.schnauzerrescue.net/

FLORIDA
Schnauzer love Rescue Inc –
http://www.schnauzerloverescue.org/
Schnauzer Rescue Cincinnati and Florida
http://www.schnauzerrescuecincinnati.org/

GEORGIA
Schnauzer love Rescue Inc –
http://www.schnauzerloverescue.org/

IDAHO
Maple Creek Miniature Schnauzer Rescue
http://www.maplecreekmsr.org/

ILLINOIS
Chicago Miniature Schnauzer Club Rescue –
http://www.chicagominiatureschnauzerclub.org/Rescue.html

INDIANA
Schnauzer Friends for Rescue and Adoption –
http://www.sfra.net/
Schnauzer Rescue Cincinnati
http://www.schnauzerrescuecincinnati.org/

KANSAS
Kansas Furever
http://www.petfinder.com/shelters/KS133.html

KENTUCKY
Schnauzer Friends for Rescue and Adoption –
http://www.sfra.net/
Schnauzer Rescue Cincinnati
http://www.schnauzerrescuecincinnati.org/

LOUISIANA
Schnauzer Rescue of Louisiana -
http://www.louisianaschnauzerrescue.com/

MASSACHUSETS and NEW ENGLAND
Schnauzer Paws Rescue –
http://schnauzerpawsrescue.com/

MARYLAND
Schnauzer Rescue of the Mid Atlantic
http://www.schnauzerrescue.net/

MICHIGAN
Schnauzer Friends for Rescue and Adoption –
http://www.sfra.net/

MINNEAPOLIS
Minneapolis/St Paul Miniature Schnauzer Rescue
http://www.mspmsr.org/

MISSISSIPPI
Schnauzer love Rescue Inc –
http://www.schnauzerloverescue.org/

MISSOURI
Boxer-Schnauzer Rescue of the Ozarks
http://www.bsro.org/

MONTANA
Montana Schnauzer Rescue –
http://schnauzer.rescueme.org/Montana

NEBRASKA
Nebraska Schnauzer Network
www.petfinder.com/shelters/NE74.html

NEVADA
Southern Nevada Schnauzer Rescue
http://www.petfinder.com/shelters/NV87.html

NEW JERSEY – also covers parts of NJ/PA/NY/CT/DE/MD/WV/VA
New Jersey Schnauzer Rescue Network Inc
http://www.njsrn.org/

NORTH CAROLINA
North Carolina Schnauzer Rescue Inc
http://www.ncschnauzers.org/
Schnauzer Rescue of the Carolinas
www.schnauzerrescueofthecarolinas.org

OHIO
Schnauzer Friends for Rescue and Adoption –
http://www.sfra.net/
Schnauzer Rescue Cincinnati
http://www.schnauzerrescuecincinnati.org/

OREGON
Maple Creek Miniature Schnauzer Rescue
http://www.maplecreekmsr.org/
Miniature Schnauzer Rescue Inc (also serves Pacific North West)
http://www.msrnorthwest.org/

PENNYSYLVANIA
Schnauzer Rescue Cincinnati
http://www.schnauzerrescuecincinnati.org/
Schnauzer Rescue of the Mid Atlantic
http://www.schnauzerrescue.net/

SOUTH CAROLINA
Schnauzer love Rescue Inc –
http://www.schnauzerloverescue.org/
Schnauzer Rescue of the Carolinas
www.schnauzerrescueofthecarolinas.org

TENNESSEE
Schnauzer love Rescue Inc –
http://www.schnauzerloverescue.org/
Schnauzer Rescue Cincinnati
http://www.schnauzerrescuecincinnati.org/

TEXAS
Miniature Schnauzer Rescue of Houston
http://www.msrh.org/

Miniature Schnauzer Rescue of North Texas
http://www.msrnt.com/

VIRGINIA
Schnauzer Rescue of the Mid Atlantic
http://www.schnauzerrescue.net/

WASHINGTON
Maple Creek Miniature Schnauzer Rescue
http://www.maplecreekmsr.org/
Schnauzer Rescue of the Mid Atlantic
http://www.schnauzerrescue.net/

If none of these organizations are in your area and you want to adopt a **Miniature Schnauzer,** then email the American Miniature Schnauzer Club at:
 rescue@amsc.us

For **Standard Schnauzers** - although there are usually not many Standards which need rescuing – contact National Rescue Coordinator Diane Mitchell at the Standard Schnauzer Club of America by emailing: dinamyt@zoominternet.net

For **Giant Schnauzers** email the Giant Schnauzer Club of America at: board@giantschnauzerclubofamerica.com

TIP: New organizations are springing up all the time. So to find if there's a rescue group in your area, go to Google and type the name of your state followed by "schnauzer rescue" in the search box.

Minneapolis/St Paul Miniature Schnauzer Rescue

UK Schnauzer Rescue Contacts

There are a number of groups in the UK who help to re-home Miniatures, Giants and Schnauzers (or Standard Schnauzers as they are called in many other countries).

Rescuing an abandoned Schnauzer can be an incredibly rewarding experience. But prospective owners should be aware that some of them have been neglected or damaged, either emotionally or physically, and will need extra care and attention from you.

Be sure you've got the time and energy to devote to a rescue Schnauzer before you make the commitment.

There follows a list of contacts and websites of organizations and individuals involved in UK Schnauzer rescue. If you are unable to find a Schnauzer, you might want to check out this page on our website –

http://www.max-the-schnauzer.com/uk-schnauzer-rescue.html

People who are looking to re-home a Schnauzer occasionally get in touch with us for help from time to time. Good luck with your search:

Miniature Schnauzers

Miniature Schnauzer Club Re-Home and Rescue Trust

http://www.the-miniature-schnauzer-club.co.uk/

Try Janet Callow on 0161 439 3233 or Kevin Durso on 01376 563072. Or email Secretary Mrs Pat Kidd at PatKidd@thekidds.demon.co.uk

Miniature Schnauzer Rescue
Mr & Mrs A Leadbetter, Dyfed, Wales. Tel: 01646 692943.

(Standard) Schnauzers

The Schnauzer Club of Great Britain –
http://www.schnauzerclub.co.uk/rescue.shtml

"Schnauzer Rescue is an informal arrangement where some members of SCGB act as co-ordinators to put dogs looking for new homes in touch with people looking to give a new home.

 "The prospective owners must reassure themselves that they are aware of the rescue dog's history and will be able to cope."

Giant Schnauzers

Giant Schnauzer Club
http://www.giantschnauzerclub.co.uk/

Mr K Carroll 01524 411220

All three types of Schnauzer

The Northern Schnauzer Club
http://www.northernschnauzerclub.co.uk/

Co-ordinator, Ann McElroy Tel: 01706 831847

There is also the non-commercial website Dog Pages at
http://www.dogpages.org.uk/ which is run by volunteers and re-homes all
breeds of dogs.

The RSPCA re-homes many types of dogs and other animals. They have a
website at http://www.rspca.org.uk/home

Chapter 18. Schnauzer Quiz

Questions

So, you think you know your Schnauzers? Well, here are ten brainteasers to test the old gray matter. Answers are at the end of the quiz.

1. What were Giant Schnauzers once known as? Was it:

   a) Berliners
   b) Muncheners
   c) Frankfurters
   d) Badeners
   e) Hamburgers

.

_____

2. According to Stanley Coren, PhD, Professor of Psychology at the University of British Columbia, what is the world's most popular name for a male dog in English-speaking countries? Is it:

   a) Harley
   b) Sammy
   c) Buster
   d) Max
   e) Charlie

_____

3. Which of these breeds of dog has webbed feet? Is it:

   a) Newfoundland
   b) Standard Schnauzer
   c) English Foxhound
   d) Duckhound
   e) Chihuahua

   _____

4. According to the American Kennel Club, how tall should a fully-grown male Giant Schnauzer be at the withers (top of the shoulders)?

   a) $18\frac{1}{2}$ to $20\frac{1}{2}$ inches
   b) $20\frac{1}{2}$ to $22\frac{1}{2}$ inches
   c) $22\frac{1}{2}$ to $24\frac{1}{2}$ inches
   d) $23\frac{1}{2}$ to $25\frac{1}{2}$ inches
   e) $25\frac{1}{2}$ to $27\frac{1}{2}$ inches

   _____

5. What country did Schnauzers originate in? Was it:

   a) Germany
   b) Sweden
   c) England
   d) USA
   e) South Africa

   _____

6. Humans have about 9,000 taste buds. How many do Schnauzers have?

a) 1,700
b) 7,700
c) 70,700
d) 700,000
e) 7 million

7. What is the gestation period for Giant, Standard and Miniature Schnauzers? Or in other words, how long does a pregnancy last?

a) One month
b) Two months
c) Three months
d) Four months
e) Five months

Ever since I've started showing, my husband has affectionately called me "Three Humps"...

8. Schnauzers are hypoallergenic. What does this mean?

    a) They are more likely to have lots of allergies

    b) They have low blood sugars

    c) They are less likely to cause an allergic
reaction in others

    d) They are allergic to hypodermic needles and
syringes

    e) They are super alert watchdogs.

_____

**9. If allowed to get away with things, some Miniature
Schnauzers can develop   "Little Emperor" tendencies.**

 Does this mean?

a) They like dressing up in fancy clothes

b) They start ordering other
Schnauzers around

c) They try to take over other
Schnauzers' beds and toys

d) They will only eat very expensive
food

e) They become cocksure and behave
badly

_____

10. **What is a parti Schnauzer? Is it:**

a) One which loves to go wild and drink cocktails with other Schnauzers, especially at night
b) One which has been crossed with another breed of dog, usually a Poodle
c) A Giant Schnauzer crossed with a Standard Schnauzer
d) A colored Schnauzer, usually with some white in the coat
e) One which shares a similar temperament to his or her mother

———————————

Answers

1. **b) Munchener** In German this means "from Munich". Schnauzers are thought to have originated from Southern Germany – where Munich is the major city – as early as 600 years ago.

2. **d) Max** Second most popular is Jake. The most popular name for a female is Molly, followed by Bella. The names Rover, Fido, Bowser and Lassie do not make the top 50.

3. **a) Newoundland** Many of the dogs with webbed feet were bred by hunters to swim and retrieve ducks and other waterfowl.

Other dogs which have webbed feet include the Akita, Brussels Griffon, Chesapeake Bay Retriever, Chinook, Field Spaniel, German Short Haired Pointer, German Wire Haired Pointer, Irish Water Spaniel, Labrador Retriever, Leonberger, Newfoundland, Nova Scotia Duck Tolling Retriever, Otterhound, Plott Hound, Portuguese Water Dog, Redbone Coonhound, Spanish Water Dog, Weimaraner and Wire Haired Pointing Griffon.

There is no such dog as a Duckhound.

4. **e) $25\frac{1}{2}$ to $27\frac{1}{2}$ inches** Anything shorter than this is considered "undesirable" in the AKC and UK Kennel Club Breed Standards. Male Giant Schnauzers can weigh anything from 60 to 105 pounds (27 to 48 kg) and females from 55 to 75 pounds (25 to 34 kg).

5. **a) Germany** It is thought that the Schnauzer originated in Southern Germany in the 14th or 15th century. Tradesmen and farmers travelled around the countryside with heavily laden carts and needed a medium -sized, versatile dog to guard the cart and keep down the rats at home. The original ones were Standard Schnauzers.

6. **a) 1,700** which is the same as all other dogs. Cats only have about 470. However, if you often wondered why your Schnauzer enjoys drinking from muddy puddles instead of his metal bowl, it is because he enjoys the flavor, as he has taste buds for water, something we do not have.

7. **b) Two months** or 61 to 65 days, regardless of whether the Schnauzer is a Mini, Standard or a Giant.

8. **c) They are less likely to cause an allergic reaction in others.** All Schnauzers have a double coat and are non-shedding. The dander is trapped in their coat and therefore they do not usually cause people with allergies to have a reaction. (No dog is guaranteed 100% not to cause a reaction as allergies vary from person to person).

9. **e) They become cocksure and behave badly.** As a result of being pampered or spoilt, they think that they rule the roost and begin to behave badly. When this happens, a firm hand is needed along with some training sessions.

10. **d) A colored Schnauzer.** These days, partis come in a range of different colors, but one of the colors is always white. "Parti" comes from the French word for *divided* and means two colors. Colors include black parti, salt and pepper parti, liver parti, liver tan parti, liver pepper parti, black and silver parti.

———————

The End – how many did you get right?

Chapter 19. True Schnauzer Stories

Here is a selection of nine of the best stories sent to our website at www.max.the.schnauzer.com from Schnauzer owners who live all over the world.

All of the stories are genuine and some of them are addressed to Max, our Mini Schnauzer. They show what incredible bonds can develop between Schnauzers and humans and just what fantastic and unique dogs they are.

---

1. Skippy's Story

Did you know that Schnauzers are particularly suitably as therapy dogs?

Therapy dogs are dogs which provide affection and comfort to people in environments such as hospitals, retirement homes, nursing homes and schools. They can also help people with learning difficulties, terminal illnesses or those in stressful situations, such as disaster zones.

Therapy dogs come in all shapes, sizes and breeds. The most important characteristic is temperament.

As Schnauzers love being with people, they are particularly suitable for this kind of work. Therapy dogs must be friendly, patient, confident, at ease in all situations and gentle with people. They must enjoy human contact and be content to be petted and handled, even clumsily sometimes.

Schnauzers Love Humans
Schnauzers are very human-oriented dogs. Put simply, they LOVE being with people. They enjoy the companionship of their owners and family and thrive on being the centre of attention.

Most of them are happy to sit and be patted all day long! And it is this characteristic and their sociability which makes Schnauzers so suitable as therapy dogs.

Testament to the Schnauzer as a therapy dog comes from a story sent to us by one of our readers, Rae from Texas, who had a wonderful Miniature Schnauzer named Skippy.

She sent us this heartwarming - if sad - story of the bond which can develop between a dog and human.

Here is Rae and Skippy's story, as told by Rae:

"Hi, I have a story for you.

I am 39-years-old, and disabled. I cannot drive or work, so my days become pretty lonely when our 10-year-old son is at school and my husband is at work for over 12 hours a day.

Our lives were blessed with Skippy, a Miniature Schnauzer, because he came into my life at a hard time. Skippy was not only my companion, he was my best friend and a member of our family.

I bought him Christmas presents, Valentine's presents and often presents just for being Skippy! He was faithfully always by my side, through sickness and health. I cannot describe to you just how much happiness and love that he brought into our lives, into my life.

I have a terminal illness and he helped me more than once to remain positive and happy. I can only pray that he knew how much he was and is loved.

On the morning of March 2, 2009, he had gone outside to potty, as usual. He had never suffered with any health problems. When he came into the house, he fell to the floor and I knew something was wrong.

He was not normal all day and evening. I phoned every Vet that I could and they all told me the same advice: "You need to get him in now".

My husband was working and I have no family. I could do nothing for him but pray. When my husband came home we decided that we were taking him to our vet to be seen first thing.

 But at around 4:30am we could not find him. He always sleeps on one of his two beds in our room, never far from me.

We searched the house over and then my husband found him. Skippy had gone into another room and quietly passed away.

I cannot explain my feelings. I have been very sad, but I know that I have to stay healthy for myself and for my family because they need me.

Skippy was buried in our front yard, underneath our big cedar tree. He never wandered out of our yard and was afraid of the dark, so I wanted him close. I take flowers from the yard to him daily.

I miss him terribly, but I feel like I may be ready for a new companion now. I would like another Miniature Schnauzer because Skippy was the best dog that I have ever owned.

He was also a "therapeutic" dog and it always seemed that he and I were very much in tune with each other. I really am partial to Schnauzers after having had nine beautiful years with Skippy.

I enjoy coming to your website and looking at the pictures as well. It gives me so much hope that I will love again.
Thank you and God bless you."   Rae.

---

2. Philip's Story

Here is a very different story from husband and wife team Kevin and Sandie Cullen in Sussex, England.

Kevin and Philip at Crufts

The couple has been involved with dogs for most of their lives and began showing Giant Schnauzers in 1995.

2008 was a marvelous year for them; their Giant Schnauzer Philip beat the other dogs from all the other breeds to become the Supreme Champion of Crufts, England, the oldest dog show in the world.

"Hello, we are Kevin and Sandie Cullen who own Crufts 2008 Best in Show Champion Jafrak Philippe Olivier - better known as Philip. Our introduction to Giants was through Floyd, a dog we bought when we were first married 25 years ago. He was a Giant Schnauzer-German Shepherd cross.

Floyd was the most fantastic dog - so intelligent -and actually looked more like a Giant than a German Shepherd.   We liked him so much that we said we would have the real thing next time - a pedigree (purebred) Giant.

We bought Jake our first purebred Giant Schnauzer when he was six months old. At that time we only wanted a pet - we were not thinking about showing. We did, however, think we should take Jake to obedience classes because he was a real live wire.

When we arrived at the class we knew we had mistakenly gone to the wrong place! It was in fact a training class for Show Dogs and people were standing and moving their dogs around like they would at a proper dog show. But when we were there, people began saying to us that we should show Jake. They thought he was beautiful.

Philip the Supreme Champion of Crufts enjoying a swim

So, we took their advice..... We went to a couple of shows, we were hooked and the rest - as they say - is history! Giant Schnauzers are addictive. You start with one and end up with two or more - like us.

It's true, though, that Giant Schnauzers are not for everyone. They want your time and attention and **loads and loads** of exercise. They know every move you make and everything you say. They are creatures of habit and know what time of day it is and what gets done at that time - and you had better be there to do it!

In return you get the most loyal companion you could ever wish to own. He will guard you and your home with his life. There is no other breed for us. Nothing comes close to a Giant.

We own the top dog, the top bitch in the breed, Grace - in partnership with Rita Thomas - and now the Crufts Supreme Champion."

It's our dream come true."

3. Caesar's Story

Here is another Giant Schnauzer story. This one comes from Julie in Phoenix, Arizona.

It's such an amazing coincidence and shaggy dog tale that you almost wouldn't believe it could happen – but it did!

Julie already has her hands pretty full with a family along with four Giants and a Mini Schnauzer. But she somehow also manages to find the time to help with Valley of the Sun Giant Schnauzer Rescue.

Here is her amazing story -

"A few weeks ago a male Giant Schnauzer was scheduled to be euthanized through no fault of his own. He had been dumped in the nearest pound in northwest Indiana and had been there for some time.

Being an older big black dog, no one had offered him a new chance at life. Through the efforts of many people, Valley of the Sun Giant Schnauzer Rescue was able to get him sprung. A volunteer drove from the Chicago area to the shelter and got him out on his 8th birthday. What a gift that was!

She drove him to the near north side of Chicago to his foster home. His fosterers frequently took him and his foster four-legged Giant Schnauzer sister to the park for walks.

My youngest brother lives in Chicago, which is the third largest city in the US and has 9.5 million people. I add that to emphasize how small this world of ours really is.

My brother runs on the weekends to keep in training for marathons that he sometimes runs. He was on a five-mile run a few weekends ago and as he neared the half-way point in his run, a large black dog barked at him.

He wondered if it might be a Giant Schnauzer but didn't check to find out. He turned to head back home and by now the big black dog and his human were directly in his path.

So he stopped to chat and ask if this dog was indeed a Giant Schnauzer. The human replied that it was. My brother told the human that his sister does Giant Schnauzer rescue in Phoenix, Arizona. The human of the big black dog asked if her name was Julie.

A slightly stunned brother replied that it was!!

He then learned that the big black dog that had barked at him was Caesar that he already knew about from my emails. He met Caesar and then proceeded on his way home. But he did stop to send an email that said, "I just met Caesar!"

Caesar will shortly travel across the country to his new home with another Giant and a loving family.

It is indeed a very small world!

The photo *on the previous page) shows Caesar after his grooming today.

He is gorgeous!"

---

4. Goldie's Story

It is not only in the USA and Europe that Schnauzers are loved. Here is a short, funny story from Mimi in Marikina City, Philippines:

"My husband and I adopted a cute white Schnauzer early this year. She was given to us by our daughters who are based in Singapore to ease our pain for the lost of our seven dogs (Shitzu, Poodle and Maltese) to a killer flood here in the Philippines.

Two Labradors survived the flood, but we still missed our small "play dogs". We didn't know anything about Schnauzers because this breed is not common here in this part of the world.

Goldie had had a interesting past... she was originally owned by a senior citizen couple in Singapore. They were forced to give her up when they couldn't care for Goldie and her mother, Clover, who was salt and pepper.

Clover was left in Singapore and is being cared by my daughters. Goldie is a very obedient dog and easily trained.

My husband fell in love with Goldie, who now sleeps in our bedroom. She can recognize my husband's car many meters away.

One night I heard my husband uttering the words "I love you" and I was going to say "I love you too," but turned to find out…….. he was talking to Goldie!!

---

5. Coco's Story

Schnauzers get very attached to their owners. But it is not just adults that bond with their pets. Schnauzers are usually good with children. Here is a super story from a little girl called Sibel in Scotland who has completely fallen in love with a Miniature Schnauzer:

"Coco is the best schnauzer puppy that I have ever seen. She sleeps nearly all day if we don't play with her. If you blow into her face she starts licking you all over. Her sister Purdey is her best friend. If I tell her that Purdey is outside she runs outside and comes back in!

When she sleeps she is usually sleeping on or beside my Dad. I am a bit unlucky because I only get to see her on weekends but I know I will love her for always. She is also a VERY good watchdog.

Every time someone passes our street she starts barking like mad. I think she is getting smarter because before she took one bit of dog food and then she started taking two, then three, now as many as she can carry in her mouth!

My dad says that she is half sheep - because of her woolly tummy - and half Schnauzer, because she is one. When Coco was a baby, her moustache was like a toilet brush! Every day that I am with Coco I say that we have to clean her moustache because it is tangled and there are lots of things stuck in it.

Her brother Casper is a white Schnauzer and a bit bigger than Coco. When Casper comes to our garden to play with Coco, he his completely terrified of Coco the Conqueror, which is what we sometimes call Coco.

If giant dogs pass our street Coco barks even more loudly. Once a girl on a horse passed our street Coco barked even MORE loudly than when a giant dog passes.
The horse was scared and cantered away. It might be strange that such a small dog like Coco could scare a such a GIANT horse.

I hope that I have given enough information about...COCO THE CONQUEROR!!!

P.S Everything is true.
P.P.S She is the best creature EVER!"   Sibel.

6. Koty's Story

Here is a story from Mary in Fenton, Missouri. She and her husband thought they had got out of buying their granddaughter a dog by saying they would only get a non-shedding dog, never believing that such an animal existed!

"Our granddaughter starting asking us for a puppy at about age four. She asked constantly and finally when she was about eight years old. My husband said: "OK. If Grandma can find a dog that doesn't shed and stays little, I'll get you one."

Since my husband and I were not animal people, neither of us thought there was such a thing as a dog that didn't shed, so my husband thought he had a sure-fire way of getting out of getting her a dog!

We had just purchased our first computer and neither of us had any idea how to work it, but I decided to try and find out if there was such a dog as a non-shedding one. It took a little while to figure out how to work the computer and then I was shocked at how many dogs don't shed. After looking up all of the descriptions of different dogs, I decided on a Mini Schnauzer.

That weekend the newspaper had two breeders with puppies for sale. I called one of them and she was so informative and helpful, plus only 100 miles away, so we decided to go and see the puppies.

However, they were only three days old and sure didn't look like much - actually they were kind of ugly. No hair yet and eyes all swollen and closed. But we put a deposit down and anxiously waited for 8 weeks to pass. I had told my granddaughter several times that I would not complete the sale if the puppy wasn't cute.

I had never seen a Schnauzer, not even a picture of one, so I had no idea what they looked like. The day of pick-up finally arrived and we anxiously went to go get her.

The breeder had already given the puppy her first grooming, so she already had the traditional Schnauzer cut, beard and all. As the breeder handed my granddaughter the puppy, she smiled from ear to ear and said: "Is she cute enough Grandma?"

Then this little gray and white Schnauzer, with a beard so perfect it would make a grown man envious, actually turned to look at me as if to say, "Well, am I ??"

Her big, solid black eyes just stared at me and I fell in love immediately. We named her Princess Koty Grace. That little dog quickly moved into our hearts. Koty is now 9 years old & the apple of our eye, she goes everywhere with us and means everything to us. She has enriched our lives completely. She protects us, loves us and makes us laugh constantly.

I have thanked God many, many times for this little angel, that is definitely 'Cute enough! ' "

---

7. Zippy's story

Here's a lovely story about three-legged Zippy, a Schnauzer-Chinese Crested cross rescued by Schnauzer Rescue Cincinnati. Zippy's story is told by his owner, Amy from Aurora, USA:

"My husband and I are both huge dog lovers, in particular we love Mini Schnauzers. But we are also big advocates of rescue and knew that we would someday adopt a rescued Schnauzer.

After a tragic house fire in '07 in which we lost two pet cats and one dog, we decided, upon moving back home, that our elderly Mini Nikki, who was 15 at the time, could use a companion.

A search on Petfinder.com led us to Ringo. He had been rescued from a shelter by a rescue group the day before he was to be put down because the neighbors complained. He's some kind of Schnauzer mix, maybe a little cattle dog thrown in. A cutie and a sweetheart!

This summer, we lost our old girl, Nikki. At almost 17, her little body just couldn't take it anymore and we had to help her cross the Rainbow Bridge. We knew we had to have another dog so back to Petfinder we went and found Zippy.

Zippy's story is something else. He's a Mini Schnauzer/Chinese Crested mix who looks 90% Schnauzer (see photo above of Zippy sunbathing). He was pulled from a shelter in West Virginia by Schnauzer Rescue Cincinnati. His chances of getting adopted from the shelter were not good as he was lame. His right front leg had been caught in a steel trap and never healed correctly, leaving his paw at a 90 degree angle and him walking sideways on his foot.

After the kind folks at Schnauzer Rescue Cincinnati got him, his leg was amputated to give him a better quality of life and lessen his chances of bigger joint problems as he ages. We adopted Zippy in June. He is absolutely amazing!

The fact that he is missing a front leg does not slow him down at all. He can jump a baby gate, run up and down the stairs, jump on and off the furniture and never have I seen such a little guy run so fast!

My shoulder has come close to being yanked out of the socket when he decides to take off running on the leash! He and Ringo were immediate friends and have bonded to become true brothers. And Zippy's outlook on life is unbelievable. He is always happy, that nub of a tail always wagging, always hoping to play a game of tug-o-war or tennis ball chase.

The rescue member that pulled him from the shelter said he was just as happy then - despite being way underweight, dull coated and stuck in a cold, strange place. He is already teaching us how to stay positive and have fun in life.

Both Zippy and Ringo are great examples of how wonderful rescue dogs can be. Despite rough starts in life, both of them are so sweet and loving and have given us no issues, settling down into their forever homes almost immediately.

I truly believe they are grateful for being rescued - rescue dogs just seem to know they've been saved and try all their lives to pay you back tenfold.

It doesn't get any better than that!"

---

8. Zara's Story.

This is a true story about Zara, a Miniature Schnauzer from England, UK, as told to us by her owner. It is written from Zara's point of view:

"Hi Max, I just wanted to tell you about me and my adventures. I'm a Mini Schnauzer and was born as Sara's Girl to a family of breeders who made me have lots of litters of pups.

I lived in a piggery and had other Mini Schnauzers for company as well as Kelpies, Pekes, Poodles etc. (Our photo shows a sad and thin Zara photographed during the first week at her new home)

On October 24th, a family from Dorset came to get me. It was the week of my 7th birthday. I was tired and still full of milk, plus my teeth were falling out. I found it hard at first as I never even had a collar on, but I really loved the beach where my new family took me for walks and I especially liked sleeping in their bed!

And so I became 'Zara.'

I did hate it when my new family went out, though, and I really missed my pups. So what a surprise last Spring to find a new pup arriving in our household.

Kasha is my lovely girl and now a naughty teenager.
I feel very lucky to be warm and have lots of food - but I could do without be groomed every six weeks!

I hear my daughter Poppy is looking for a new home and may come to stay.

How differently things turn out!"

(Our picture shows Zara now looking happy and healthy on her morning beach walk).

---

9. Chloe's Story

For those of you who were saddened to read Rae's letter about Skippy. Here is her story eight months later – and this tale DOES have a happy ending. This is Chloe's story as told by Rae:

"Hi Max Once Again,
This is Rae from Jacksonville (Texas). I read my letter to you that was placed under "Therapy Dogs" and I could never thank you enough.

It was almost as if I could give Skippy's beautiful memory to whoever cared to receive it through your kindness. Although it has been 8 months since his passing, his memory is so much a part of our lives even today and will remain with us until we are reunited once again with our Lord and Savior.

I continue to visit with him through prayer and although he remains with me in spirit, the pain has only been relieved through God's good graces and in time. Time is the only thing that can heal.

I cannot wait to tell you that on October 7, we officially adopted our very own Chloe, a robust, active 2½-year-old Salt/Pepper registered Schnauzer who has already brought many smiles and so much joy into our lives (funny how quickly they can help put pieces of your life back together once again).

She will play fetch with her Elmo stuffed toy and "Bear" for as long as you will throw it and she faithfully brings the toys right back to your feet. She is devoted, protective and extremely intelligent. It is funny sometimes how life works.

I adopted her from a very nice man and woman here in Texas because his wife has terminal cancer and "Chloe", being 2½-years-old and full of life, was just simply too playful for her due to her illness.

We met the gentleman who owned Chloe and what a special soul. I can only imagine how difficult the parting was because I too have a terminal illness and don't know how I could've parted with Skippy if life would have been different.

I wish I could describe Chloe to you, words won't do her justice. She is the perfect specimen of a Miniature Schnauzer in every way!

I can't explain life, the why's or how's and maybe that old saying is true that it's best we don't know what lies ahead for us in the future. You know, to be honest, I was scared to love Chloe. Loving and having to eventually let go is hard, but I believe Skippy would want me to share my own special kind of love with another Schnauzer.

I have so much love to give that maybe it'd be unfair to not share that love with yet another Schnauzer. Myself, my husband and our son are very happy with Chloe and look forward to her being in our life and teaching us from day to day how to slow down and remember to cherish the simpler things God has given to us.

Again, thank you Max for presenting my letter to the world and will keep you updated on our Chloe.

God Bless you and your family."

Rae.

———————————————

Disclaimer

The information provided in this book is designed to provide helpful information on Schnauzers and Schnoodles. This book is not meant to be used, nor should it be used, to diagnose or treat any medical condition. For diagnosis or treatment of any animal medical problem, consult a qualified veterinarian. The author is not responsible for any specific health or allergy conditions that may require medical supervision and is not liable for any damages or negative consequences from any treatment, action, application or preparation, to any person reading or following the information in this book. References are provided for informational purposes only and do not constitute endorsement of any websites or other sources.

Printed in Great Britain
by Amazon.co.uk, Ltd.,
Marston Gate.